DOCUMENTS IN WORLD HISTORY

Volume I

DOCUMENTS IN WORLD HISTORY

Volume I

The Great Traditions: From Ancient Times to 1500

Peter N. Stearns, SENIOR EDITOR
Carnegie Mellon University

Stephen S. Gosch
University of Wisconsin, Eau Claire

Jay Pascal Anglin
University of Southern Mississippi

Erwin P. Grieshaber
Mankato State University

1817

HARPER & ROW, PUBLISHERS, New York
Cambridge, Philadelphia, San Francisco, Washington,
London, Mexico City, São Paulo, Singapore, Sydney

Sponsoring Editor: Robert Miller
Project Coordination: R. David Newcomer Associates
Cover Design: Bob Bull
Text Art: Fineline Illustrations, Inc.
Photo Research: Mira Schachne
Compositor: Auto-Graphics, Inc.
Printer and Binder: R. R. Donnelley & Sons Company
Cover Printer: NEBC

Documents in World History, Volume I, The Great Traditions:
From Ancient Times to 1500

Library of Congress Cataloging-in-Publication Data

Documents in world history.

  Contents: v. 1. The great traditions, from ancient times to 1500–
v. 2. The modern centuries, from 1500 to the present.
  1. World history—Sources. I. Stearns, Peter N.
D5.D623   1988   909   87-15036
ISBN 0-06-046382-1 (v. 1)
ISBN 0-06-046432-1 (v. 2)

87 88 89 90 9 8 7 6 5 4 3 2 1

Contents

SECTION TWO
The Classical Period, 1000 B.C. to A.D. 500   **33**

China

Classical India

Greece and Rome

Geographic Contents:
The Major Civilizations

Topical Contents

Preface

When most students—and many teachers—think of world history, they think of a textbook. World history does have a survey element that textbooks serve very well. But world history also stems from the lives of many people in a variety of environments. The flavor of the human aspect of world history can in no way be captured solely by a progression of names, dates, and main developments. These subtleties come through in a sampling of the expressions people have produced, in different societies at various periods.

This book offers a range of documents to illustrate characteristic features of key civilizations during major stages of world history since the beginnings of written records to the start of the modern age around A.D. 1500. The documents were not written for posterity; some were not even intended for a wide audience when written. They are collected here to get beneath the survey level and raise issues of understanding and interpretation that can enliven and enrich the world history course.

The book covers facets of the human experience, again at various times and in a variety of places. It deals with the organization and functions of the state. It treats philosophy and religion and at points literature and science. It explores contacts among civilizations, such as the diverse impacts of Islam or early contacts between Europe and Asia. It also deals with families and women and with issues of social structure.

The book's organization facilitates relating it to a core textbook. Major civilizations are represented with several readings—East Asia, the West, India, the Middle East, Eastern Europe, Africa, and Latin America. Thus a course can trace elements of change and continuity within each civilization. The readings are also divided by basic time periods: early civilization, the classical era to about A.D. 500, the spread of civilization and major religions, to roughly A.D. 1500. This chronological coverage focuses on the establishment of the major civilization traditions still present in the world today.

Though comprehensive, the goal is not maximum coverage. All sorts of attractive and significant documents are left out, of necessity. We chose readings that illustrate key facets of an area or period, that raise challenging problems of interpretation, or that—at least in many cases—express some charm and human drama. The readings also invite comparisons across cultures and over time. Headnotes not only identify the readings, but they also raise some issues that can be explored.

This book was prepared by four world history teachers at work in several kinds of institutions. It is meant, correspondingly, to serve the needs of different kinds of students. It is motivated by two common purposes: first, a strong belief that some perspective on the world is both desirable and possible as a key element in contemporary American education; and second, that understanding world history can be greatly enhanced by exposure not just to an overall factual and interpretive framework, but also to the kinds of challenges and insights raised by primary materials, not written by scholars but by people actually living out the diverse and changing patterns we are grappling to understand.

Dealing with primary sources is not an easy task. Precisely because the materials are not written with American college students in mind, they require some thought: They must be related to other elements we know about the particular society; they must be given meaning; they must be evaluated more carefully than a secondary account or textbook designed deliberately to pinpoint what should be learned. By the same token, however, gaining some ease with the meaning of primary sources is a skill that carries well beyond a survey history course into all sorts of research endeavors. Gaining this skill in the context of the diverse civilizations that compose the world goes some distance toward understanding how our world has become what it is—which is, in essence, the central purpose of history.

Peter N. Stearns

DOCUMENTS IN WORLD HISTORY
Volume I

Introduction

The selections in this volume are designed to provide insight into main developments and characteristics in the history of leading civilizations, and to convey some of the major changes and processes in the field of world history. The selections are source materials—written during significant periods in the past, but not as formal histories or studies. As documents rather than research pieces, they convey a direct sense of other times and places. They also demand some analysis and interpretation to relate them to more general themes and issues.

The need to study world history becomes increasingly apparent. Though the twentieth century has been hailed as "the American century," it is obvious that even given the United States' claim to some world leadership, it must interact with various other societies and, in part, on their terms. As a power with worldwide military responsibilities or aspirations, the United States maintains increasingly close diplomatic contacts with all the inhabited continents. Economically, American reliance on exports and imports—once a minor footnote to this nation's industrial vigor—grows greater every year. Cultural influences from abroad are significant. Even though the United States remains a leading exporter of consumer fads and styles, we can see among the American people European cultural standards and popular fashion and musical imports from Britain joined by interest in various schools of Buddhism or a fascination with Japan's gifts at social coordination. Even the composition of the United States population reflects growing worldwide contacts. The United States is now experiencing its highest rates of immigration ever, with new arrivals from Latin America and various parts of Asia joining earlier immigrant groups from Europe and Africa.

Enmeshed in this world, shaping it but also shaped by it, United States citizens need to know something of how that world has been formed and what major historical forces created its diversities and contacts. We need to know, in sum, something about world history. Study of our own past—that is, United States history—or even the larger history of Western civilization from which many American institutions and values spring, risks now being unduly narrow, though worthy and interesting. This explains why the study of world history is receiving renewed attention.

The need to know leading themes in world history thus involves the need to understand why, because of their earlier traditions, Chinese and Japanese governments are today more effective in regulating personal behaviors such as birth rates than governments in other parts of Asia such as India are. East Asian traditions never posited the boundary line between state and society that other cultures (including our own in the United States) take for granted, and the contemporary version of this special tradition has produced fascinating results. Tradition combined with more recent changes, including bitter experience with Western intrusions, helps explain why many countries in the Islamic world are demonstrating strong opposition to lifestyles and economic forms that modern Westerners take for granted. Alliance patterns (the Soviet Union and the smaller nations of eastern Europe) and military policies—including key differences among cultures not only in levels of power but also in characteristic interest in aggression and expansion—are other "in the news" issues of vital importance that we can only grasp through an understanding of earlier trends in world history. Our world, obviously, is shaped by the past; we can best understand changes we are experiencing now when we compare them to past change. And so, on a small interdependent globe, a grasp of world history becomes an intellectual necessity.

A danger exists, however, in stressing the "need" to study world history too piously. True, growing global interdependence and communication make knowledge of past world patterns increasingly useful as the basis for interpreting policy options open to the United States or American business—or simply for grasping the daily headlines in more than a superficial manner. But the mission of a world history course does not rest entirely on the desire to create a more informed and mature citizenry. It can also rest directly on the intrinsic interest and the analytical challenge world history offers.

World history presents the opportunity to examine and evaluate a fascinating range of human experience. For example, it delves into interactions between humanity and nature through study of disease patterns that influenced particular societies or periods in time and through other aspects of the natural environment as well, including animals available for domestication. The Chinese, for example, built a solid civilization using a wide range of beasts of burden but without a particularly useful horse. They encountered the most advanced forms of the horse only during the Han dynasty, when their borders pushed into Central Asia. Then, delighted with the find, they proceeded to make the horse a common figure in their art. Human–nature interaction went beyond the objective natural environment, of course. Some major cultures venerated particular aspects of nature, removing these from daily use. Thus India held the cow in respect, while Westerners and Middle Easterners—unlike East Asians—refused to eat dog meat. Even human emotions varied by culture and over time. India, though in formal respects a highly patriarchal society, modified the impact of male control in daily family life by strong emphasis on affection and sexual passion. West Europeans, long schooled to view husband-wife relations as an economic arrangement to which emotional attachments were secondary, came to see positive virtues in romance, with suggestions of a new esteem for love some 600 years ago.

Variety and change at the more visible levels of high culture and government are equally familiar themes in world history. Indian society, though successful in commerce and technology, developed an otherworldly emphasis—a concern for spiritual explanations and goals—normally foreign to the higher reaches of Chinese society. Japan built an intricate set of feudal relationships among warriors into a durable tradition of group loyalty; whereas a similar set of warrior relations in Western Europe led less to group cohesion than to institutions—parliaments—that would watch and regulate the doings of kings.

Examples are endless. Not only features of key civilizations or periods, but also major events such as Marco Polo's fascinating journey to China and the formation of Islamic governments in Hindu India, compel attention. Historical events worldwide illustrate ways that different societies interacted and the range of evil and good acts of which humans have proved capable as well. World history, in sum, can be interesting, even enjoyable, unless the human panorama offers no appeal. It has grown unfashionable in American education to emphasize joy in learning lest a subject seem frivolous or irrelevant to careers and earning power. But the fact is that world history, like many but not all other academic subjects, offers potential for pleasure as well as support for an informed citizenry.

But if world history is essential, to give an understanding of why our own world is as it is and because of its great intrinsic interest, it is also, without question, challenging. Putting the case mildly, much has happened in the history of the world; and while some developments, particularly in early societies, remain unknown for want of records, the amount that we do know is astounding—and steadily expanding. No person can master the whole, and in presenting a manageable course in world history, selectivity is certainly essential. Fortunately, there is considerable agreement on certain developments that are significant to a world history study. The student must gain, for example, some sense of the special political characteristics of Chinese civilization; or of the New World economy that Western Europe organized, to its benefit, after about 1500; or of the ways major technological changes developed, spread, and impacted leading societies at various points in time, including the Industrial Revolution and even the more recent innovations in information technology. This list of history basics, of course, is not uniform, and it can change with new interests and new data. The conditions of women, for example, as they varied from one civilization to the next and changed over time have become a staple of up-to-date world history teaching in ways that were unimaginable twenty years ago. Despite changes in the list, though, the idea of approaching world history in terms of basics—key civilizations, key points of change, key factors such as technology or family—begins the process of making the vast menu of information digestible.

In practice, however, the teaching of world history has sometimes obscured the focus on basics with a stream-of-narrative textbook approach. The abundance of facts and their importance and/or interest can produce a way of teaching world history so bent on leaving nothing out (though in fact much must be omitted in even the most ponderous tome) that little besides frenzied memorization takes place. Yet world history, while it must convey knowledge, must also stimulate thought—about why different patterns developed in various key civilizations, about what impact new contacts between civilizations had, about how our present world relates to worlds past.

One way to stimulate thought—and to give a dash of the spice particular currents or episodes in world history offer—is to provide access to original sources. This device is often used in American history or the history of Western civilization. It is less common, however, in world history because the textbook approach has so dominated. Readers designed for world history students have existed in the past, but few are currently available. As a result, it has been difficult to provide reading beyond a core text in world history classes, particularly reading that cuts across individual civilizations. This volume, obviously, is intended to provide a solution to the problem and to facilitate world history teaching that includes but transcends a purely textbook-survey approach.

The readings in this volume are designed to illustrate several features of various civilizations during key periods in world history through direct evidence. Thus the readings convey some sense of what Buddhism is all about through writings by Buddha's early disciples or of how Confucianism helped shape China's political institutions and underlying stability, again through direct statements. They require, then, some effort of interpretation. The writers, by trying to persuade others of their beliefs or reporting what they saw at the time, did not focus on distilling the essence of a religion, a political movement, or a list of government functions for late-twentieth-century students of world history. The reader must generate this distillation, aided by the brief contexts and questions provided in the selection introductions. Analytical thinking is also encouraged and challenged by recurrent comparisons across space and time. Thus documents dealing with social or family structure in China can be compared to documents on the same subject for the Mediterranean world, while a picture of China's bureaucracy two thousand years ago begs for juxtaposition with descriptions of later Chinese politics to see what changed and what persists.

The documents presented are not randomly chosen; and it will help, in using them, if the principles of organization are clear—for these principles correspond to the selection-for-manageability essential in studying world history. The hope is, of course, that the documents reflect particularly interesting insights; we selected them in part because they are lively as well as significant. They were *not* selected to maximize factual coverage. This is a difficult goal even in a text, and it becomes almost impossible in a collection of readings. We made choices of materials in this book in order to present passages of some substance (rather than snippets) and depth (rather than just a law or two, a real discussion of how a government worked). By the same token, the materials leave out vastly more possibilities than they embrace, even in the realm of "famous" documents such as treaties or constitutions. The book is thus intended to stimulate, but it is decidedly not intended to pepper the carcass of world history with as much buckshot as possible.

Eschewing coverage as a goal, the selections do follow certain general principles around which one can organize an approach to world history. Quite simply, these principles involve place, time, and topic. By choosing readings—which may or may not be important documents in themselves—that illustrate important societies in distinctive periods of time and in significant facets of the human experience, the book offers a collection of telling insights that usefully complement and challenge the survey approach. Knowing the principles of selection, in turn, facilitates relating the readings to each other and to a more general understanding of world history.

First is the principle of major civilizations in organizing choice of place. The readings focus on seven parts of the world that have produced durable civilizations that still exist, at least in part. They do not simply focus on the West in a world context. East Asia embraces China and a surrounding zone that came under partial Chinese influence—most notably Japan. Indian civilization, which comprises the second case, had considerable influence in other parts of southern Asia, though we do not offer readings on Southeast Asia directly. The Middle East and North Africa, where civilization was born, forms a third society to be addressed at various points in time, both before and after the advent of its major religion, Islam. Europe, though ultimately sharing some common values through Christianity and a recollection of the glories of Greece and Rome, developed two partially distinct civilizations in the east (centered on Russia) and west. Both East and West European civilizations innovated as new religion, trade, and political organization spread northward. Sub-Saharan Africa, a vast region with great diversity, forms a sixth civilization area. Finally, civilization developed independently in the Americas. Here, as in Africa, signs of civilizations showed early, but a full statement—and elaborate records—developed rather late in time. The seven civilizations represented in the readings are not sacrosanct: They do not embrace all the world's cultures, past or present. They overlap at points, and they contain some marked internal divisions, such as between China and Japan in East Asia. But these civilizations do provide some geographical coherence for the study of world history, and they are all represented repeatedly in the selections that follow.

Time is the second organizing principle. Obviously, some of the civilizations currently important in the world did not exist fifteen hundred years ago, so the factor of chronology is vital just to order the list of civilizations. Further, even ancient civilizations changed over time, and we need a sense of major periods to capture this evolution. Finally, the inhabited world as a whole has gone through various stages of interaction and diversification, and periods in world history reflect these patterns as well.

Because the selections that follow deal with written evidence, no treatment is included of the long, fascinating trajectory of the human species before civilization emerged, around 3500 B.C. Several selections represent the first phase of civilization in Asia and North Africa, when river-valley cultures developed formal political organizations, cities, written laws, and elaborate commerce. River-valley civilizations in the Middle East, Egypt, northwest India, and northern China flourished over a long period of time, gradually giving way to more extensive cultures that built on their technical and cultural achievements. Even during the early civilization period, particularly in the Middle East, civilization began to produce offshoots and variants that would have lasting impact; a crucial example is the monotheistic religion the Jews developed.

Between 1000 B.C. and about A.D. 500, larger civilizations took hold in China, India, and around the Mediterranean. This second, or classical, phase of civilization—though still limited in spatial terms—embraced wider areas than before. These three major classical civilizations also generated value systems (such as the Hindu religion in India and Confucianism in China) that not only described the classical period itself but would also have durable influence lasting into the twentieth century. They produced institutions, such as the Chinese bureaucracy and the Indian caste system, of long-range impact as well. The classical period thus describes the development of elaborate societies in key parts of Eurasia and North Africa that bequeathed core features, not just ruins and scattered traces, for later world history.

Attacked by nomadic invaders and undermined by diverse internal pressures, the classical civilizations declined or collapsed between A.D. 300 and 600. A thousand-year period followed in which a wider array of civilizations developed, some independently and some as offshoots from earlier centers. Christian missionaries from Mediterranean Europe brought cultural and political change to northwestern Europe and Russia—including writing and the other basic trappings of civilization. Civilizations that arose in various parts of sub-Saharan Africa were, in some cases, soon influenced by the Islamic religion and Middle-Eastern commercial and bureaucratic forms. It was during this period that Japan gained civilization by selectively copying China. Finally—but in complete isolation—civilization sprang up in Central America and the Andes. By 1400, some version of the seven civilizations still vigorous in our world had taken shape. In close relationship, major world religions spread or developed during the centuries following the classical age. Islam, the newest of the great faiths, formed around A.D. 600 and anchored Arab dynamism around the Mediterranean and Indian oceans for some centuries thereafter. Christianity took firm hold in Europe, based separately around the Roman papacy and the Eastern Orthodox faith of the Byzantine empire. Buddhism spread from India to southeast Asia and to China and Japan. Thus new religions—or as in the case of Buddhism a new outreach—featuring elaborate doctrines and a new concern for an afterlife helped shape a distinctive period in world history. Even India, already embraced by Hinduism, saw religious change with greater popularization of the Hindu faith and the advent of a new Muslim minority.

Mongol invasions, which swept over much of Asia and Eastern Europe during the thirteenth and fourteenth centuries, helped bring the last traditional period of world civilizations to a close. By the fifteenth century, along with a host of major developments in particular civilizations, the emerging dominant themes of world history were: the spread of more advanced technologies, the rise of a more dynamic Western civilization, and the development of more intricate economic contacts around the world, including the Americas as well as the old continents. Population growth in many societies and heightened levels of commercial exchange were offshoots of these processes. For several centuries, and to an extent into our own day, the West replaced the Islamic Middle East as the world's most dynamic civilization.

Much of the drama of world history, and its relevance in understanding present conditions and even future prospects, lies in playing the traditions of the major civilizations against the trends of more modern times. A second volume of documents, organized on lines similar to the present volume, takes the story of world history into the modern centuries and allows a comparison of recent developments with counterparts in the earlier history of civilizations as a means of measuring change and continuity.

The present volume, however, in covering the many centuries from civilization's first emergence to its spread almost literally worldwide, has its own significant themes, independent of what came later. It allows a grasp of the major features of civilization itself and the kinds of human problems that civilization arose to resolve. Civilizations also brought new problems of their own, particularly in encouraging new inequalities among social groups and, often, between men and women; these too can be evaluated by looking at the way civilization took shape.

Civilizations developed in considerable isolation. There were contacts, particularly for those societies near the Middle East—India and Southeast Asia, parts of Africa, and the two European civilizations as well as the Middle East itself. But political forms, habits of language and thought, and artistic styles in the main sprang up separately in each region. Even basic technologies spread only slowly; for instance, the invention of paper took several centuries to reach the Middle East from its starting point in China, and another four centuries to reach Western Europe. A further way to focus on the materials in this volume, then, involves careful examination of the distinctiveness of each civilization, enhanced by comparison, from one case to the next, of religion, politics, and even daily life.

Although the emphasis of this volume lies in the formation of basic traditions, the theme of change must be traced as well. New religions and the rise and fall of political systems brought important shifts. Contacts among most of the world's civilizations increased, particularly rapidly after about A.D. 800. Tradition itself, as it fed into more modern world history, was the product of evolution; it did not spring full-blown at the outset of a civilization's journey.

In summary, the readings in this book cluster around seven civilizations and three time periods: early civilization, classical, and the centuries of civilization's further spread. Without too much forcing, we can see the three periods as embracing the origin and elaboration of basic traditions in the key civilizations spiced by religious transformations and other innovations; they would be followed by two modern periods that focused on modfications in traditions through Western intrusions, population growth, higher levels of commercial interaction, and industrial technology. Traditional periods were not, of course, static, and the modern periods have hardly displaced all traditions. But world history gains a rough coherence through an understanding that early civilizations built on the basis of agriculture, and that this base was later challenged by new commercial and industrial forms. This central modern drama, in turn, continues to shape primary features of the world today, from China's attempt to develop a political regime suitable for modern economic growth to Islamic or Soviet attempts to build modern societies free from some of the trappings of Western consumerism or family instability.

Finally, in dealing with major periods and civilizations, the readings in this book reflect an attempt to convey four features inherent in human society. Every society (whether part of a civilization or not) must develop some government structure and political values. It must also generate a culture, that is, a system of beliefs and artistic expressions that help explain how the world works. Among these, religion is often a linchpin of a society's culture, but science and art play crucial roles as well. Many civilizations saw tensions pull among these various cultural expressions, which could be a source of creativity. Economic relationships—the nature of agriculture, the level of technology and openness to technological change, the position of merchants—form a third feature of a civilization. And finally, social groupings, hierarchies, and family institutions—including gender relations—organize human relationships and provide for the training of children. Until recently, world history focused primarily on the political and cultural side of the major societies, with some bows to technology and trade. More recently, the explosion of social history—with its inquiry into popular as well as elite culture, families, and social structure—has broadened world history concerns. Readings in this book provide a sense of all four aspects of the leading civilizations—political, economic, cultural, and social—and a feeling for how they changed under the impact of new religions, the rise and fall of empires, or new contacts among civilizations themselves.

The effort to present lively documents that illuminate several time periods, differing cultural traditions, and the variety in features of the way societies function must, again, be evocative. This book is not intended to teach everything one should know about the evolution of Western families, Chinese ideas about nature, or such big processes as the development of the modern world economy. It aims, rather, at providing the flavor of such topics, a sense of how people at the time lived and perceived them, and some understanding of the issues involved in interpreting and comparing diverse documents from the past. The collection is meant to help readers themselves breath life into world history and grasp some of the ways that both great and ordinary people have lived, suffered, and created in various parts of the world at various points in our rich human past.

one

EARLY CIVILIZATIONS

River-valley civilizations developed in several places between 3500 and 500 B.C. They set up more formal governments than had existed before and developed important religious and cultural principles. Both areas of achievement depended on the creation of writing, which in turn left more diverse and explicit records than was possible for preliterate societies.

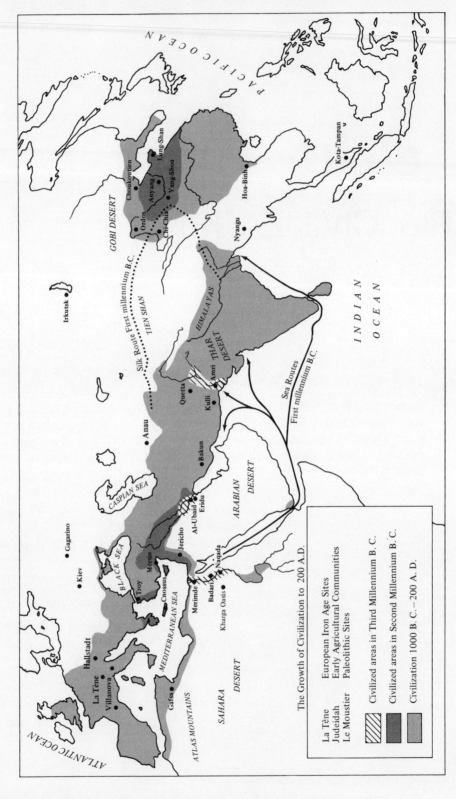

The Growth of Civilization to 200 A.D.

La Tène   European Iron Age Sites
Judeidah   Early Agricultural Communities
Le Moustier   Paleolithic Sites

Civilized areas in Third Millennium B. C.

Civilized areas in Second Millennium B. C.

Civilization 1000 B. C. – 200 A. D.

Eurasia

1

Mesopotamian Values:
A Pessimistic View

Unlike the waters of the beneficent Nile, whose annual floods were predictable and controllable, those of the Tigris and Euphrates rivers proved erratic and often devastating. This factor combined with the harshness of the physical terrain, the absence of protective natural barriers, and the steady intrusion of invaders who used the element of surprise, superb leadership, and technological advantage to gain temporary hegemony over the region, prompted a pessimistic outlook to evolve that found expression in the eclectic civilization that evolved in ancient Mesopotamia. The Sumerians, whose creative genius provided the cultural foundations of the region, perceived humans as lowly mortal servants to a pantheon of immortal gods and goddesses, and they viewed the miserable state of humanity as a consequence of human failure to obey divine commands. These views, frequently reiterated in the literature of the region, are best expressed in the great Babylonian heroic tale, *The Gilgamesh Epic.* This poem was preserved in twelve tablets that were recovered during nineteenth-century excavations of Ashurbanipal's (669–633 B.C.) palace library in Nineveh.

Heavily indebted to a variety of older unrelated sources, the epic describes the vain quest of its hero, Gilgamesh (ca. 2800 B.C.), fifth ruler of the first dynasty of Uruk, to secure immortality. By recounting the perilous ventures and hardships of Gilgamesh, the poem reaffirms that valiant personal efforts cannot prevent one's inevitable death and suggests that energy should instead be directed towards enjoying and making the most of life. During his quest, Gilgamesh sought

From Rossiter Johnson, ed., *Assyrian and Babylonian Literature* (New York: D. Appleton and Company, 1901), pp. 351–357.

and found Per-napishtim, the Babylonian Noah, who had secured immortality because of his piety. Tablet XI focuses on their meeting and provides Per-napishtim's account of the great deluge. A genetic relation between his account and that of the Hebrews in Genesis is obvious, but the historical relation between them is uncertain.

Epic literature developed in many early civilizations—not only that of Mesopotamia, but also in Hebrew, Greek, and Indian cultures. How would tales like *Gilgamesh* help shape and express a civilization's values? What purpose did these stories serve?

[From the shore Per-napishtim, the favourite of the gods, now relates the story of the deluge to the hero, who, sitting in his ship, is listening to him.]

Per-napishtim then said unto Gilgamesh:
"I will reveal unto thee, O Gilgamesh, the mysterious story,
and the mystery of the gods I will tell thee.
The city of Shurippak, a city which, as thou knowest,
is situated on the bank of the river Euphrates.
That city was corrupt, so that the gods within it
decided to bring about a deluge, even the great gods,
as many as there were: their father, Anu;
their counsellor, the warrior Bel;
their leader, Ninib;
their champion, the god En-nu-gi.
But Ea, the lord of unfathomable wisdom, argued with them.
Their plan he told to a reed-hut, (saying):
'Reed-hut, reed-hut, clay-structure, clay-structure!
Reed-hut, hear; clay-structure, pay attention!
Thou man of Shurippak, son of Ubara-Tutu,
Build a house, construct a ship;
Forsake thy possessions, take heed for thy life!
Abandon thy goods, save (thy) life,
and bring living seed of every kind into the ship.
As for the ship, which thou shalt build,
let its proportions be well measured:
Its breadth and its length shall bear proportion each to each,
and into the sea then launch it.'
I took heed, and said to Ea, my lord:
'I will do, my lord, as thou hast commanded;
I will observe and will fulfil the command.
But what shall I answer to (the inquiries of) the city, the
people, and the elders?'
Ea opened his mouth and spoke,
and he said unto me, his servant:
'Man, as an answer say thus unto them:

"I know that Bel hates me.
No longer can I live in your city;
Nor on Bel's territory can I live securely any longer;
I will go down to the 'deep,' I will live with Ea, my lord.
Upon you he will (for a time?) pour down rich blessing.
He will grant you fowl [in plenty] and fish in abundance,
Herds of cattle and an abundant harvest.
Shamash has appointed a time when the rulers of darkness
at eventide will pour down upon you a destructive rain." '

. . .

All that was necessary I collected together.
On the fifth day I drew its design;
In its middle part its sides were ten gar high;
Ten gar also was the extent of its deck;
I added a front-roof to it and closed it in.
I built it in six stories,
thus making seven floors in all;
The interior of each I divided again into nine partitions.
Beaks for water within I cut out.
I selected a pole and added all that was necessary.
Three (variant, five) shar of pitch I smeared on its outside;
three shar of asphalt I used for the inside (so as to make it water-tight).
Three shar of oil the men carried, carrying it in vessels.
One shar of oil I kept out and used it for sacrifices,
while the other two shar the boatman stowed away.
For the temple of the gods (?) I slaughtered oxen;
I killed lambs (?) day by day.
Jugs of cider (?), of oil, and of sweet wine,
Large bowls (filled therewith?), like river water (i.e., freely) I poured out
    as libations.
I made a feast (to the gods) like that of the New-Year's Day.
To god Shamash my hands brought oil.
[* * *] the ship was completed.
[* * *] heavy was the work, and
I added tackling above and below, [and after all was finished,]
The ship sank into water two thirds of its height.
With all that I possessed I filled it;
with all the silver I had I filled it;
with all the gold I had I filled it;
with living creatures of every kind I filled it.
Then I embarked also all my family and my relatives,
cattle of the field, beasts of the field, and the uprighteous people—all them
    I embarked.
A time had Shamash appointed, (namely):

'When the rulers of darkness send at eventide a destructive rain,
then enter into the ship and shut its door.'
This very sign came to pass, and
The rulers of darkness sent a destructive rain at eventide.
I saw the approach of the storm,
and I was afraid to witness the storm;
I entered the ship and shut the door.
I intrusted the guidance of the ship to Purur-bel, the boatman,
the great house, and the contents thereof.
As soon as early dawn appeared,
there rose up from the horizon a black cloud,
within which the weather god (Adad) thundered,
and Nabu and the king of the gods (Marduk) went before.
The destroyers passed across mountain and dale (literally, country).
Dibbara, the great, tore loose the anchor-cable (?).
There went Ninib and he caused the banks to overflow;
the Anunnaki lifted on high (their) torches,
and with the brightness thereof they illuminated the universe.
The storm brought on by Adad swept even up to the heavens,
and all light was turned into darkness.
[   ] overflooded the land like * * *
It blew with violence and in one day (?) it rose above the mountains (??).
Like an onslaught in battle it rushed in on the people.
Not could brother look after brother.
Not were recognised the people from heaven.
The gods even were afraid of the storm;
they retreated and took refuge in the heaven of Anu.
There the gods crouched down like dogs, on the inclosure of heaven they
    sat cowering.
Then Ishtar cried out like a woman in travail,
and the lady of the gods lamented with a loud voice, (saying):
'The world of old has been turned back into clay,
because I assented to this evil in the assembly of the gods.
Alas! that when I assented to this evil in the council of the gods,
I was for the destruction of my own people.
What I have created, where is it?
Like the spawn of fish it fills the sea.'
The gods wailed with her over the Anunnaki.
The gods were bowed down, and sat there weeping.
Their lips were pressed together (in fear and in terror).
Six days and nights
The wind blew, and storm and tempest overwhelmed the country.
When the seventh day drew nigh the tempest, the storm, the battle
which they had waged like a great host began to moderate.

The sea quieted down; hurricane and storm ceased.
I looked out upon the sea and raised loud my voice,
But all mankind had turned back into clay.
Like the surrounding field had become the bed of the rivers.
I opened the air-hole and light fell upon my cheek.
Dumfounded I sank backward, and sat weeping,
while over my cheek flowed the tears.
I looked in every direction, and behold, all was sea.
Now, after twelve (days?) there rose (out of the water) a strip of land.
To Mount Nisir the ship drifted.
On Mount Nisir the boat stuck fast and it did not slip away.
The first day, the second day, Mount Nisir held the ship fast, and did not
let it slip away.
The third day, the fourth day, Mount Nisir held the ship fast, and did not
let it slip away.
The fifth day, the sixth day, Mount Nisir held the ship fast, and did not let
it slip away.
When the seventh day drew nigh
I sent out a dove, and let her go.
The dove flew hither and thither,
but as there was no resting-place for her, she returned.
Then I sent out a swallow, and let her go.
The swallow flew hither and thither,
but as there was no resting-place for her she also returned.
Then I sent out a raven, and let her go.
The raven flew away and saw the abatement of the waters.
She settled down to feed, went away, and returned no more.
Then I let everything go out unto the four winds, and I offered a sacrifice.
I poured out a libation upon the peak of the mountain.
I placed the censers seven and seven,
and poured into them calamus, cedar-wood, and sweet-incense.
The gods smelt the savour;
yea, the gods smelt the sweet savour;
the gods gathered like flies around the sacrificer.

2

Babylonian Law: How a Civilized State Regulated Its Subjects

Once he successfully reunited Mesopotamia by victories over Assyria and the neighboring Sumerian city states, the Babylonian king Hammurabi (ca. 1850–1750 B.C.) played a dominant role in the Near East. In his forty-three-year reign, he earned a reputation for just and efficient administration, secured prosperity within his domain by strict control of western trade routes and judicious regulation of trade, and encouraged the production of an extensive literature. Although his ephemeral empire gave way to Kassite tribes after his death, Hammurabi left for posterity the famous Code of Hammurabi, the earliest major collection of laws in history currently extant. Consisting of 282 case laws inscribed in the Akkadian (Semitic) language and presented in a series of horizontal bands on a massive diorite slab (discovered in 1901 at Susa, Iran, and now in the Louvre), the code represented no attempt by Hammurabi to produce a codification of existing statute and/or common laws into a formal legal system. Rather, it was a formal collection of select decisions rendered by Hammurabi, the "just" judge, on a variety of isolated cases intended for public dissemination that represented recommended rules of justice. As amendments to the Babylonian common law, the code omitted many important areas in the law and virtually ignored procedural law and the judiciary. Extant legal documents and reports indicate that neither judges nor litigants viewed laws in the code as binding or enforceable in Babylonian courts.

Despite the fact that Hammurabi's compilation represents only a minor con-

Reprinted from *The Babylonian Laws*, edited and translated by G. R. Driver and John C. Miles (1955) by permission of Oxford University Press. Vol. II, pp. 13, 15, 21, 51, 53, 77, 79, 81.

tribution to the advancement of law and jurisprudence, his laws offer historians important insights into Babylonian social structure, real and personal property, land tenure, trade and commerce, marriage and the family, agriculture, wages and prices, slaves, and the professions.

Writing down and maintaining formal law is one of the chief functions of any organized government, but while certain acts are almost always defined as crimes, other definitions—and related punishments—varied greatly from one culture to the next. Judging by the following passages, what kind of social and family relations was the Babylonian state trying to uphold? How did it define crime and punishment?

When Marduk commanded me to give justice to the people of the land and to let (them) have (good) governance, I set forth truth and justice throughout the land (and) prospered the people.

At that time:

§1

If a man has accused a man and has charged him with manslaughter and then has not proved (it against) him, his accuser shall be put to death.

§2

If a man has charged a man with sorcery and then has not proved (it against) him, he who is charged with the sorcery shall go to the holy river; he shall leap into the holy river and, if the holy river overwhelms him, his accuser shall take and keep his house; if the holy river proves that man clear (of the offence) and he comes back safe, he who has charged him with sorcery shall be put to death; he who leapt into the holy river shall take and keep the house of his accuser.

§§3–4

[§3]   If a man has come forward in a case to bear witness to a felony and then has not proved the statement that he has made, if that case (is) a capital one, that man shall be put to death.

[§4]   If he has come forward to bear witness to (a claim for) corn or money, he shall remain liable for the penalty for that suit.

§5

If a judge has tried a suit, given a decision, caused a sealed tablet to be executed, (and) thereafter varies his judgement, they shall convict that judge of varying (his) judgement and he shall pay twelve-fold the claim in that suit; then they shall remove him from his place on the bench of judges in the assembly, and he shall not (again) sit in judgement with the judges.

. . .

§§22–4

[§22]   If a man has committed robbery and is caught, that man shall be put to death.

[§23]   If the robber is not caught, the man who has been robbed shall formally declare whatever he has lost before a god, and the city and the mayor in whose territory or district the robbery has been committed shall replace whatever he has lost for him.

[§24]   If (it is) the life (of the owner that is lost), the city or the mayor shall pay one maneh of silver to his kinsfolk.

·   ·   ·

§127

If a man has caused a finger to be pointed at a high-priestess or a married lady and has then not proved (what he has said), they shall flog that man before the judges and shave half his head.

§128

If a man has taken a (woman to) wife and has not drawn up a contract for her, that woman is not a wife.

§129

If a married lady is caught lying with another man, they shall bind them and cast them into the water; if her husband wishes to let his wife live, then the king shall let his servant live.

§130

If a man has stopped the cries of(?) a married lady, who has not known a man and is dwelling in her father's house, and has then lain in her bosom and they catch him, that man shall be put to death; that woman then goes free.

§§131–2

[§131]   If the husband of a married lady has accused her but she is not caught lying with another man, she shall take an oath by the life of a god and return to her house.

[§132]   If a finger has been pointed at the married lady with regard to another man and she is not caught lying with the other man, she shall leap into the holy river for her husband.

§§133–5

[§133a]   If a man takes himself off and there is not the (necessary) maintenance in his house, his wife [so long as] her [husband is delayed], shall keep [herself chaste; she shall not] enter [another man's house].

[§133b] If that woman has not kept herself chaste but enters another man's house, they shall convict that woman and cast her into the water.

[§134] If the man has taken himself off and there is not the (necessary) maintenance in his house, his wife may enter another man's house; that woman shall suffer no punishment.

[§135] If the man takes himself off and there is not the (necessary) maintenance in his house, (and) before his return his wife enters another man's house and then bears sons, (if) her husband afterwards returns and regains his city, that woman shall return to her first husband; the sons shall follow their (respective) fathers.

.   .   .

§194

If a man has given his son to a nurse to be suckled and that son has then died in the charge of the nurse, (if) the nurse then binds another child (to her breast) without (the knowledge of) its father or its mother, they shall convict her, and, because she has bound another child (to her breast) without (the knowledge of) its father or its mother, they shall cut off her breast(s).

§195

If a son strikes his father, they shall cut off his fore-hand.

§§196–205

[§196] If a man has put out the eye of a free man, they shall put out his eye.

[§197] If he breaks the bone of a (free) man, they shall break his bone.

[§198] If he puts out the eye of a villein or breaks the bone of a villein, he shall pay 1 maneh of silver.

[§199] If he puts out the eye of a (free) man's slave or breaks the bone of a (free) man's slave, he shall pay half his price.

[§200] If a man knocks out the tooth of a (free) man equal (in rank) to him(self), they shall knock out his tooth.

[§201] If he knocks out the tooth of a villein, he shall pay ⅓ maneh of silver.

[§202] If a man strikes the cheek of a (free) man who is superior (in rank) to him(self), he shall be beaten with sixty stripes with a whip of ox-hide in the assembly.

[§203] If the man strikes the cheek of a free man equal to him(self in rank), he shall pay 1 maneh of silver.

[§204] If a villein strikes the cheek of a villein, he shall pay 10 shekels of silver.

[§205] If the slave of a (free) man strikes the cheek of a free man, they shall cut off his ear.

§§206–8

[§206] If a man strikes a (free) man in an affray and inflicts a wound on him, that man may swear 'Surely I did not strike (him) wittingly', and he shall pay the surgeon.

[§207]   If he dies of the striking, he may swear likewise; if (the victim is) a (free) man, he shall pay ½ maneh of silver.

[§208]   If (he is) a villein, he shall pay ⅓ maneh of silver.

§§209–14

[§209]   If a man strikes the daughter of a (free) man (and) causes her to lose the fruit of her womb, he shall pay 10 shekels of silver for the fruit of her womb.

[§210]   If that woman dies, they shall put his daughter to death.

[§211]   If he causes the daughter of a villein to lose the fruit of her womb by striking her, he shall pay 5 shekels of silver.

[§212]   If that woman dies, he shall pay ½ maneh of silver.

[§213]   If he has struck the slave-girl of a (free) man and causes her to lose the fruit of her womb, he shall pay 2 shekels of silver.

[§214]   If that slave-girl dies, he shall pay ⅓ maneh of silver.

§§215–20

[§215]   If a surgeon has made a deep incision in (the body of) a (free) man with a lancet(?) of bronze and saves the man's life or has opened the caruncle(?) in (the eye of) a man with a lancet(?) of bronze and saves his eye, he shall take 10 shekels of silver.

[§216]   If (the patient is) a villein, he shall take 5 shekels of silver.

[§217]   If (the patient is) the slave of a (free) man, the master of the slave shall give 2 shekels of silver to the surgeon.

[§218]   If the surgeon has made a deep incision in (the body of) a (free) man with a lancet(?) of bronze and causes the man's death or has opened the caruncle(?) in (the eye of) a man and so destroys the man's eye, they shall cut off his fore-hand.

[§219]   If the surgeon has made a deep incision in (the body of) a villein's slave with a lancet(?) of bronze and causes (his) death, he shall replace slave for slave.

[§220]   If he has opened his caruncle(?) with a lancet(?) of bronze and destroys his eye, he shall pay half his price in silver.

3

Ancient Egypt

The best account describing the customs and history of Egypt in ancient world texts is Book II of Herodotus's *History,* covering the Persian Wars. In his historical account of the Graeco-Persian struggle, this famous Greek historian (ca. 484–425 B.C.) provided his readers a historical background for the wars as well as a detailed survey describing the evolution of the Persian Empire. Incorporating six of nine books in the *History,* this background material was derived principally from data and firsthand observations the "father of history" had collected in travels throughout the eastern Mediterranean and Black Sea regions, including visits to the Near East and Egypt. In his account of the extension of Persian hegemony over Egypt, Herodotus included a long and fascinating digression on the geography, ethnology, and customs of Egypt as well as on the region's early history and its relations to Greece.

His perceptive and colorful observations on the Egyptians and their country, some of which appear in the selection below, were based on personal impressions Herodotus had during business travels to Lower Egypt and southward to Elephantine around 450 B.C. Modern scholarship confirms that most of his details are accurate and unbiased, but they represent only a selective vantage on ancient Egypt. By contrast, modern Egyptologists have uncovered numerous factual and chronological faults in Herodotus's accompanying dynastic history of Egypt for the period preceding 663 B.C. In fact, they view that part of his text as of little worth. Defects in his treatment owed mainly to Herodotus's ignorance of the

Egyptian language and official archival materials and to his dependence on the limited, incomplete, and faulty data native interpreters and informers provided him.

Even for his own period, which was late in the lifespan of Egyptian civilization, Herodotus obviously represents a somewhat indirect source. Travelers' accounts, however, are often extremely useful because they provide an appreciation for what was distinctive, which participants in a civilization can easily take for granted. What does Herodotus find striking about Egyptian values and institutions? How does he justify his observation that Egyptians were an unusually religious people?

As the Egyptians have a climate peculiar to themselves, and their river is different in its nature from all other rivers, so have they made all their customs and laws of a kind contrary for the most part to those of all other men. Among them, the women buy and sell, the men abide at home and weave; and whereas in weaving all others push the woof upwards, the Egyptians push it downwards. Men carry burdens on their heads, women on their shoulders. Women make water standing, men sitting. They relieve nature indoors, and eat out of doors in the streets, giving the reason, that things unseemly but necessary should be done in secret, things not unseemly should be done openly. No woman is dedicated to the service of any god or goddess; men are dedicated to all deities male or female. Sons are not compelled against their will to support their parents, but daughters must do so though they be unwilling.

36. Everywhere else, priests of the gods wear their hair long; in Egypt they are shaven. With all other men, in mourning for the dead those most nearly concerned have their heads shaven; Egyptians are shaven at other times, but after a death they let their hair and beard grow. The Egyptians are the only people who keep their animals with them in the house. Whereas all others live on wheat and barley, it is the greatest disgrace for an Egyptian so to live; they make food from a coarse grain which some call spelt. They knead dough with their feet, and gather mud and dung with their hands. The Egyptians and those who have learnt it from them are the only people who practise circumcision. Every man has two garments, every woman only one. The rings and sheets of sails are made fast elsewhere outside the boat, but inside it in Egypt. The Greeks write and calculate by moving the hand from left to right; the Egyptians do contrariwise; yet they say that their way of writing is towards the right, and the Greek way towards the left. They use two kinds of writing; one is called sacred, the other common.

37. They are beyond measure religious, more than any other nation; and these are among their customs:—They drink from cups of bronze, which they cleanse out daily; this is done not by some but by all. They are especially careful ever to wear newly-washed linen raiment. They practise circumcision for cleanliness' sake; for they set cleanness above seemliness. Their priests shave the whole body every other day, that no lice or aught else that is foul may infest them in their service of the gods. The priests wear a single linen garment and sandals of papyrus: they may take no other kind of clothing or footwear. Twice a day and twice every night they wash in cold water. Their religious observances are, one may say, innumerable. But also they receive many

benefits: they neither consume nor spend aught of their own; sacred food is cooked for them, to each man is brought every day flesh of beeves and geese in great abundance, and wine of grapes too is given to them. They may not eat fish. The Egyptians sow no beans in their country; if any grow, they will not eat them either raw or cooked; the priests cannot endure even to see them, considering beans an unclean kind of pulse. Many (not one alone) are dedicated to the service of each god. One of these is the high priest; and when a high priest dies his son succeeds to his office.

. . .

47. Swine are held by the Egyptians to be unclean beasts. Firstly, if an Egyptian touch a hog in passing by, he goes to the river and dips himself in it, clothed as he is; and secondly, swineherds, native born Egyptians though they be, are alone of all men forbidden to enter any Egyptian temple; nor will any give a swineherd his daughter in marriage, nor take a wife from their women; but swineherds intermarry among themselves. Nor do the Egyptians think right to sacrifice swine to any god save the Moon and Dionysus; to these they sacrifice their swine at the same time, in the same season of full moon; then they eat of the flesh. The Egyptians have an account of the reason why they sacrifice swine at this festival, yet abominate them at others; I know it, but it is not fitting that I should relate it. But this is how they sacrifice swine to the Moon: the sacrificer lays the end of the tail and the spleen and the caul together and covers them up with all the fat that he finds about the belly, then burns all with fire; as for the rest of the flesh, they eat it at the time of full moon when they sacrifice the victim; but they will not taste it on any other day. Poor men, having but slender means, mould swine of dough, which they then bake and sacrifice.

. . .

77. Among the Egyptians themselves, those who dwell in the cultivated country are the most careful of all men to preserve the memory of the past, and none whom I have questioned have so many chronicles. I will now speak of the manner of life which they use. For three following days in every month they purge themselves, pursuing after health by means of emetics and drenches; for they think it is from the food which they eat that all sicknesses come to men. Even without this, the Egyptians are the healthiest of all men, next to the Libyans; the reason of which to my thinking is that the climate in all seasons is the same; for change is the great cause of men's falling sick, more especially changes of seaons. They eat bread, making loaves which they call "cyllestis" of coarse grain. For wine, they use a drink made of barley; for they have no vines in their country. They eat fish uncooked, either dried in the sun or preserved with brine. Quails and ducks and small birds are salted and eaten raw; all other kinds of birds, as well as fish (except those that the Egyptians hold sacred) are eaten roast and boiled.

. . .

80. There is a custom too which no Greeks save the Lacedaemonians have in common with the Egyptians:—younger men, when they meet their elders, turn aside and give place to them in the way, and rise from their seats when an older man approaches. But they have another custom which is nowhere known in Greece: passersby do not address each other, but salute by lowering the hand to the knee.

. . .

84. The practice of medicine is so divided among them, that each physician is a healer of one disease and no more. All the country is full of physicians, some of the

eye, some of the teeth, some of what pertains to the belly, and some of the hidden diseases.

85. They mourn and bury the dead as I will show. Whenever a man of note is lost to his house by death, all the womenkind of the house daub their faces or heads with mud; then, with all the women of their kin, they leave the corpse in the house, and roam about the city lamenting, with their garments girt round them and their breasts showing; and the men too lament in their place, with garments girt likewise. When this is done, they take the dead body to be embalmed.

86. There are men whose whole business this is and who have this special craft. These, when a dead body is brought to them, show the bringers wooden models of corpses, painted in exact imitation; the most perfect manner of embalming belongs, they say, to One whose name it were profane for me to speak in treating of such matters; the second way, which they show, is less perfect than the first, and cheaper, and the third is the least costly of all. Having shown these, they ask the bringers of the body in which fashion they desire to have it prepared. The bearers, having agreed in a price, go their ways, and the workmen, left behind in their place, embalm the body. If they do this in the most perfect way, they first draw out part of the brain through the nostrils with an iron hook, and inject certain drugs into the rest. Then, making a cut near the flank with a sharp knife of Ethiopian stone, they take out all the intestines, and clean the belly, rinsing it with palm wine and bruised spices; and presently, filling the belly with pure ground myrrh and casia and any other spices, save only frankincense, they sew up the anus. Having done this, they conceal the body for seventy days, embalmed in saltpetre; no longer time is allowed for the embalming; and when the seventy days are past they wash the body and wrap the whole of it in bandages of fine linen cloth, anointed with gum, which the Egyptians mostly use instead of glue; which done, they give back the dead man to his friends. These make a hollow wooden figure like a man, in which they enclose the corpse, shut it up, and preserve it safe in a coffin-chamber, placed erect against a wall.

87. This is how they prepare the dead who have wished for the most costly fashion; those whose wish was for the middle and less costly way are prepared in another fashion. The embalmers charge their syringes with cedar oil and therewith fill the belly of the dead man, making no cut, nor removing the intestines, but injecting the drench through the anus and checking it from returning; then they embalm the body for the appointed days; on the last day they let the oil which they poured in pass out again. It has so great power that it brings away the inner parts and intestines all dissolved; the flesh is eaten away by the saltpetre, and in the end nothing is left of the body but skin and bone. Then the embalmers give back the dead body with no more ado.

88. When they use the third manner of embalming, which is the preparation of the poorer dead, they cleanse the belly with a purge, embalm the body for the seventy days and then give it back to be taken away.

4

Judaism

The principal gift of the ancient Hebrews to the world cultural bank was their "national" monotheistic religion, which today thrives as a major world religion, and in the past served as an essential ingredient for the successor religions of Christianity and Islam. Stressing complete submission to the laws and commands of their omnipotent and omnipresent Yahweh, a deity whom Hebrews perceived as outside of nature and comprehensible in intellectual and abstract terms, the religion focused on Yahweh's covenant with the Hebrews and the history of their special relationship. As lawgiver and universal upholder of moral order, Yahweh is depicted in the Holy Writ of Israel (Old Testament) as beneficent and loving but also as a stern and vengeful overseer who unhesitatingly punishes those who refuse to comply. The evolution of their unique covenant theology and their laws receive prominent treatment in this canonical text, which offers a history of the ancient Hebrews and serves as a remarkable literary masterpiece as well.

Fundamental to the above developments was the contribution of Moses, who around 1300–1250 B.C. successfully led the exodus of enslaved émigré Hebrews from Egypt to the Sinai, where he persuaded the polytheistic Hebrews to worship Yahweh exclusively. In the following passage from Exodus, Moses's strategic role in the evolution of the Hebrew religion is explicit. For at Mount Sinai, Yahweh not only revealed the Ten Commandments and the laws to Moses, but also used the prophet as the instrument for communicating them and forging a divine covenant with the entire Hebrew nation. These gifts and their observances occupy a strategic place in Hebrew monotheism, and they established the foundations for Hebrew law and social order. After receiving them, Moses spent the remaining years of his life in pursuit of unifying the Hebrew tribes into a confederation and in promoting the Yahwist cult.

How did the religion of Moses compare with those of Egypt or Mesopotamia? In what ways were its purposes and principles similar to other early religions and in what ways different?

In the third month after Israel had left Egypt, they came to the wilderness of Sinai. They set out from Rephidim and entered the wilderness of Sinai, where they encamped, pitching their tents opposite the mountain. Moses went up the mountain of God, and the LORD called to him from the mountain and said, "Speak thus to the house of Jacob, and tell this to the sons of Israel: You have seen with your own eyes what I did to Egypt, and how I have carried you on eagles' wings and brought you here to me. If only you will now listen to me and keep my covenant, then out of all peoples you shall become my special possession; for the whole earth is mine. You shall be my kingdom of priests, my holy nation. These are the words you shall speak to the Israelites."

Moses came and summoned the elders of the people and set before them all these commands which the LORD had laid upon him. The people all answered together, "Whatever the LORD has said we will do." Moses brought this answer back to the LORD. The LORD said to Moses, "I am now coming to you in a thick cloud, so that I may speak to you in the hearing of the people, and their faith in you may never fail." Moses told the LORD what the people had said, and the LORD said to him, "Go to the people and hallow them today and tomorrow and make them wash their clothes. They must be ready by the third day, because on the third day the LORD will descend upon Mount Sinai in the sight of all the people. You must put barriers round the mountain and say, 'Take care not to go up the mountain or even to touch the edge of it.' Any man who touches the mountain must be put to death. No hand shall touch him; he shall be stoned or shot dead: neither man nor beast may live. But when the ram's horn sounds, they may go up the mountain." Moses came down from the mountain to the people. He hallowed them and they washed their clothes. He said to the people, "Be ready by the third day; do not go near a woman." On the third day, when morning came, there were peals of thunder and flashes of lightning, dense cloud on the mountain and a loud trumpet blast; the people in the camp were all terrified.

Moses brought the people out from the camp to meet God, and they took their stand at the foot of the mountain. Mount Sinai was all smoking because the LORD had come down upon it in fire; the smoke went up like the smoke of a kiln; all the people were terrified, and the sound of the trumpet grew ever louder. Whenever Moses spoke, God answered him in a peal of thunder. The LORD came down upon the top of Mount Sinai and summoned Moses to the mountain-top, and Moses went up. The LORD said to Moses, "Go down; warn the people solemnly that they must not force their way through to the LORD to see him, or many of them will perish. Even the priests, who have access to the LORD, must hallow themselves, for fear that the LORD may break out against them." Moses answered the LORD, "The people cannot come up Mount Sinai, because thou thyself didst solemnly warn us to set a barrier to the mountain and so to keep it holy." The LORD therefore said to him, "Go down; then come up and bring Aaron with you, but let neither priests nor people force their way up to the LORD, for fear that he may break out against them." So Moses went down to the people and spoke to them.

God spoke, and these were his words:

I am the LORD your God who brought you out of Egypt, out of the land of slavery.

You shall have no other god to set against me.

You shall not make a carved image for yourself nor the likeness of anything in the heavens above, or on the earth below, or in the waters under the earth.

You shall not bow down to them or worship them; for I, the LORD your God, am a jealous god. I punish the children for the sins of the fathers to the third and fourth generations of those who hate me. But I keep faith with thousands, with those who love me and keep my commandments.

You shall not make wrong use of the name of the LORD your God; the LORD will not leave unpunished the man who misuses his name.

Remember to keep the sabbath day holy. You have six days to labour and do all your work. But the seventh day is a sabbath of the LORD your God; that day you shall not do any work, you, your son or your daughter, your slave or your slave-girl, your cattle or the alien within your gates; for in six days the LORD made heaven and earth, the sea, and all that is in them, and on the seventh day he rested. Therefore the LORD blessed the sabbath day and declared it holy.

Honour your father and your mother, that you may live long in the land which the LORD your God is giving you.

You shall not commit murder.

You shall not commit adultery.

You shall not steal.

You shall not give false evidence against your neighbour.

You shall not covet your neighbour's house; you shall not covet your neighbour's wife, his slave, his slave-girl, his ox, his ass, or anything that belongs to him.

When all the people saw how it thundered and the lightning flashed, when they heard the trumpet sound and saw the mountain smoking, they trembled and stood at a distance. "Speak to us yourself," they said to Moses, "and we will listen; but if God speaks to us we shall die." Moses answered, "Do not be afraid. God has come only to test you, so that the fear of him may remain with you and keep you from sin." So the people stood at a distance, while Moses approached the dark cloud where God was.

THE LORD SAID TO MOSES, Say this to the Israelites: You know now that I have spoken to you from heaven. You shall not make gods of silver to be worshipped as well as me, nor shall you make yourselves gods of gold. You shall make an altar of earth for me, and you shall sacrifice on it both your whole-offerings and your shared-offerings, your sheep and your cattle. Wherever I cause my name to be invoked, I will come to you and bless you. If you make an altar of stones for me, you must not build it of hewn stones, for if you use a chisel on it, you will profane it. You must not mount up to my altar by steps, in case your private parts be exposed on it.

These are the laws you shall set before them:

When you buy a Hebrew slave, he shall be your slave for six years, but in the seventh year he shall go free and pay nothing.

If he comes to you alone, he shall go away alone; but if he is married, his wife shall go away with him.

If his master gives him a wife, and she bears him sons or daughters, the woman and her children shall belong to her master, and the man shall go away alone. But if the slave should say, "I love my master, my wife, and my children; I will not go free," then his master shall bring him to God: he shall bring him to the door or the door-post, and his master shall pierce his ear with an awl, and the man shall be his slave for life.

When a man sells his daughter into slavery, she shall not go free as a male slave may. If her master has not had intercourse with her and she does not please him, he shall let her be ransomed. He has treated her unfairly and therefore has no right to sell her to strangers. If he assigns her to his son, he shall allow her the rights of a daughter. If he takes another woman, he shall not deprive the first of meat, clothes, and conjugal rights. If he does not provide her with these three things, she shall go free without any payment.

Whoever strikes another man and kills him shall be put to death. But if he did not act with intent, but they met by act of God, the slayer may flee to a place which I will appoint for you. But if a man has the presumption to kill another by treachery, you shall take him even from my altar to be put to death.

Whoever strikes his father or mother shall be put to death.

Whoever kidnaps a man shall be put to death, whether he has sold him, or the man is found in his possession.

Whoever reviles his father or mother shall be put to death.

When men quarrel and one hits another with a stone or with a spade, and the man is not killed but takes to his bed; if he recovers so as to walk about outside with a stick, then the one who struck him has no liability, except that he shall pay for loss of time and shall see that he is cured.

When a man strikes his slave or his slave-girl with a stick and the slave dies on the spot, he must be punished. But he shall not be punished if the slave survives for one day or two, because he is worth money to his master.

When, in the course of a brawl, a man knocks against a pregnant woman so that she has a miscarriage but suffers no further hurt, then the offender must pay whatever fine the woman's husband demands after assessment.

Wherever hurt is done, you shall give life for life, eye for eye, tooth for tooth, hand for hand, foot for foot, burn for burn, bruise for bruise, wound for wound.

When a man strikes his slave or slave-girl in the eye and destroys it, he shall let the slave go free in compensation for the eye. When he knocks out the tooth of a slave or a slave-girl, he shall let the slave go free in compensation for the tooth.

When an ox gores a man or a woman to death, the ox shall be stoned, and its flesh may not be eaten; the owner of the ox shall be free from liability. If, however, the ox has for some time past been a vicious animal, and the owner has been duly warned but has not kept it under control, and the ox kills a man or a woman, then the ox shall be stoned, and the owner shall be put to death as well. If, however, the penalty is commuted for a money payment, he shall pay in redemption of his life whatever is imposed upon him. If the ox gores a son or a daughter, the same rule shall apply. If the ox gores a slave or slave-girl, its owner shall pay thirty shekels of silver to their master, and the ox shall be stoned.

When a man removes the cover of a well or digs a well and leaves it uncovered, then if an ox or an ass falls into it, the owner of the well shall make good the loss. He shall repay the owner of the beast in silver, and the dead beast shall be his.

When one man's ox butts another's and kills it, they shall sell the live ox, share the price and also share the dead beast. But if it is known that the ox has for some time past been vicious and the owner has not kept it under control, he shall make good the loss, ox for ox, but the dead beast is his.

When a man steals an ox or a sheep and slaughters or sells it, he shall repay five beasts for the ox and four sheep for the sheep. He shall pay in full; if he has no means, he shall be sold to pay for the theft. But if the animal is found alive in his possession, be it ox, ass, or sheep, he shall repay two.

If a burglar is caught in the act and is fatally injured, it is not murder; but if he breaks in after sunrise and is fatally injured, then it is murder.

When a man burns off a field or a vineyard and lets the fire spread so that it burns another man's field, he shall make restitution from his own field according to the yield expected; and if the whole field is laid waste, he shall make restitution from the best part of his own field or vineyard.

When a fire starts and spreads to a heap of brushwood, so that sheaves, or standing corn, or a whole field is destroyed, he who started the fire shall make full restitution.

When one man gives another silver or chattels for safe keeping, and they are stolen from that man's house, the thief, if he is found, shall restore twofold. But if the thief is not found, the owner of the house shall appear before God, to make a declaration that he has not touched his neighbour's property. In every case of law-breaking involving an ox, an ass, or a sheep, a cloak, or any lost property which may be claimed, each party shall bring his case before God; he whom God declares to be in the wrong shall restore twofold to his neighbour.

When a man gives an ass, an ox, a sheep or any beast into his neighbour's keeping, and it dies or is injured or is carried off, there being no witness, the neighbour shall swear by the LORD that he has not touched the man's property. The owner shall accept this, and no restitution shall be made. If it has been stolen from him, he shall make restitution to the owner. If it has been mauled by a wild beast, he shall bring it in as evidence; he shall not make restitution for what has been mauled.

When a man borrows a beast from his neighbour and it is injured or dies while its owner is not with it, the borrower shall make full restitution; but if the owner is with it, the borrower shall not make restitution. If it was hired, only the hire shall be due.

When a man seduces a virgin who is not yet betrothed, he shall pay the bride-price for her to be his wife. If her father refuses to give her to him, the seducer shall pay in silver a sum equal to the bride-price for virgins.

You shall not allow a witch to live.

Whoever has unnatural connection with a beast shall be put to death.

Whoever sacrifices to any god but the LORD shall be put to death under solemn ban.

You shall not wrong an alien, or be hard upon him; you were yourselves aliens in Egypt. You shall not ill-treat any widow or fatherless child. If you do, be sure that I will listen if they appeal to me; my anger will be roused and I will kill you with the sword; your own wives shall become widows and your children fatherless.

If you advance money to any poor man amongst my people, you shall not act like a money-lender: you must not exact interest in advance from him.

If you take your neighbour's cloak in pawn, you shall return it to him by sunset, because it is his only covering. It is the cloak in which he wraps his body; in what else can he sleep? If he appeals to me, I will listen, for I am full of compassion.

You shall not revile God, nor curse a chief of your own people.

You shall not hold back the first of your harvest, whether corn or wine. You shall give me your first-born sons. You shall do the same with your oxen and your sheep. They shall stay with the mother for seven days; on the eighth day you shall give them to me.

You shall be holy to me: you shall not eat the flesh of anything in the open country killed by beasts, but you shall throw it to the dogs.

You shall not spread a baseless rumour. You shall not make common cause with a wicked man by giving malicious evidence.

You shall not be led into wrongdoing by the majority, nor, when you give evidence in a lawsuit, shall you side with the majority to pervert justice; nor shall you favour the poor man in his suit.

When you come upon your enemy's ox or ass straying, you shall take it back to him. When you see the ass of someone who hates you lying helpless under its load, however unwilling you may be to help it, you must give him a hand with it.

You shall not deprive the poor man of justice in his suit. Avoid all lies, and do not cause the death of the innocent and the guiltless; for I the LORD will never acquit the guilty. You shall not accept a bribe, for bribery makes the discerning man blind and the just man give a crooked answer.

You shall not oppress the alien, for you know how it feels to be an alien; you were aliens yourselves in Egypt.

For six years you may sow your land and gather its produce; but in the seventh year you shall let it lie fallow and leave it alone. It shall provide food for the poor of your people, and what they leave the wild animals may eat. You shall do likewise with your vineyard and your olive-grove.

For six days you may do your work, but on the seventh day you shall abstain from work, so that your ox and your ass may rest, and your homeborn slave and the alien may refresh themselves.

Be attentive to every word of mine. You shall not invoke other gods: your lips shall not speak their names.

Three times a year you shall keep a pilgrim-feast to me. You shall celebrate the pilgrim-feast of Unleavened Bread for seven days; you shall eat unleavened cakes as I have commanded you, at the appointed time in the month of Abib, for in that month you came out of Egypt.

No one shall come into my presence empty-handed. You shall celebrate the pilgrim-feast of Harvest, with the firstfruits of your work in sowing the land, and the pilgrim-feast of Ingathering at the end of the year, when you bring in the fruits of all your work on the land. These three times a year shall all your males come into the presence of the Lord GOD.

You shall not offer the blood of my sacrifice at the same time as anything leavened.

The fat of my festal offering shall not remain overnight till morning.

You shall bring the choicest firstfruits of your soil to the house of the LORD your God.

You shall not boil a kid in its mother's milk.

And now I send an angel before you to guard you on your way and to bring you to the place I have prepared. Take heed of him and listen to his voice. Do not defy him; he will not pardon your rebelliousness, for my authority rests in him. If you will only listen to his voice and do all I tell you, then I will be an enemy to your enemies, and I will harass those who harass you. My angel will go before you and bring you to the Amorites, the Hittites, the Perizzites, the Canaanites, the Hivites, and the Jebusites, and I will make an end of them. You are not to bow down to their gods, nor worship them, nor observe their rites, but you shall tear down all their images and smash their sacred pillars. Worship the LORD your God, and he will bless your bread and your water. I will take away all sickness out of your midst. None shall miscarry or be barren in your land. I will grant you a full span of life.

I will send my terror before you and throw into confusion all the peoples whom you find in your path. I will make all your enemies turn their backs. I will spread panic before you to drive out in front of you the Hivites, the Canaanites and the Hittites. I will not drive them out all in one year, or the land would become waste and the wild beasts too many for you. I will drive them out little by little until your numbers have grown enough to take possession of the whole country. I will establish your frontiers from the Red Sea to the sea of the Philistines, and from the wilderness to the River. I will give the inhabitants of the country into your power, and you shall drive them out before you. You shall make no covenant with them and their gods. They shall not stay in your land for fear they make you sin against me; for then you would worship their gods, and in this way you would be ensnared.

two

THE CLASSICAL PERIOD, 1000 B.C. TO A.D. 500

Basic political, cultural, and social traditions develop in China, India, and the Mediterranean world.

5

Key Chinese Values: Confucianism

Many Chinese beliefs were formed early, as civilization emerged along the Yellow River. One such belief stressed the importance of harmony in and with nature around the concept of the Way. More formal systems of thought developed later, in the sixth and fifth centuries B.C., during a divided and troubled period of Chinese politics. Various thinkers sought means to shore up a strong political system or live without one. Of the resulting philosophies or religions, Confucianism proved the most durable and significant.

Deemed by students a "Divine Sage," Confucius (K'ung Fu-tzu) (ca. 551–479 B.C.) was founder of a humanistic school of philosophy that offered Chou China a social and political ethos derived from idealized values of the past. As a remedy for the political chaos of his age, the famous teacher abandoned the decadent aristocratic code and offered in its place an ethical system focused on individual moral conduct, propriety, ritual, and benevolence. Arguing that the foundations of good government and the well-being of society rested on individual ethical conduct, Confucius urged the emperor and his assistants, the *chun-tzu* (gentlemen), to provide moral examples for society at large. Confucius believed the appointment of modest, wise, polite, and virtuous gentlemen scholars was essential for good government and that this was the best means for eliminating the immorality and amorality that undermined law and order. Idealistic gentlemen could restore the conditions prevailing under the early Chou dynasty, whose government Confucius viewed as a perfect form. In the selection from the *Analects*,

From Confucius, *The Analects of Confucius*, translated and annotated by Arthur Waley (London: George Allen and Unwin, Ltd., 1938), pp. 85, 90–1, 104, 105, 106, 121, 131, 152, 163, 167, 177, 178, 181, 187, 188, 197, 199, 200, 205–7, 233.

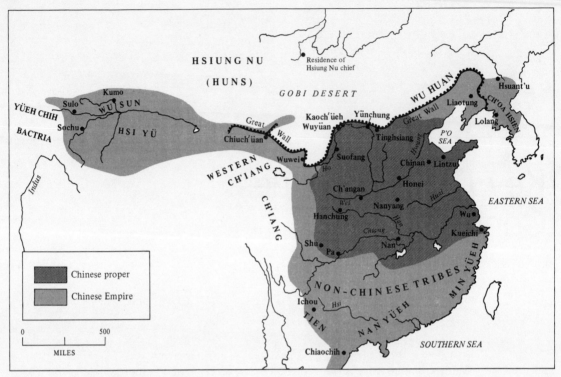

China Under Emperor Wu, About 100 B.C.

which is a collection of sayings attributed to the "Master" and set down long after his death, one finds his views of gentlemen. Since scholars doubt that Confucius put his ideas into writing, it is impossible to determine whether these views are authentically his own or those of later Confucianists.

Confucian theories of government were adopted as state ideology during the Han dynasty, and many of his concepts proved fundamental to Chinese philosophy more generally. From the following passages, consider what the main interests and values of Confucianism were. Compare these to leading values systems—typically religious systems—in other ancient and classical civilizations. How do they compare to Judaism or to Hindu or Buddhist concepts developing during the same time period in India?

The Master said, If a gentleman is frivolous, he will lose the respect of his inferiors and lack firm ground upon which to build up his education. First and foremost he must learn to be faithful to his superiors, to keep promises, to refuse the friendship of all who are not like him. And if he finds he has made a mistake, then he must not be afraid of admitting the fact and amending his ways.

Tzu-kung asked about the true gentleman. The Master said, He does not preach what he practises till he has practised what he preaches.

The Master said, A gentleman can see a question from all sides without bias. The small man is biased and can see a question only from one side.

The Master said, A gentleman in his dealings with the world has neither enmities nor affections; but wherever he sees Right he ranges himself beside it.

The Master said, A gentleman takes as much trouble to discover what is right as lesser men take to discover what will pay.

The Master said, A gentleman covets the reputation of being slow in word but prompt in deed.

The Master said, A gentleman who is widely versed in letters and at the same time knows how to submit his learning to the restraints of ritual is not likely, I think, to go far wrong.

The Master said, A true gentleman is calm and at ease; the Small Man is fretful and ill at ease.

At home in his native village his manner is simple and unassuming, as though he did not trust himself to speak. But in the ancestral temple and at Court he speaks readily, though always choosing his words with care.

At Court when conversing with the Under Ministers his attitude is friendly and affable; when conversing with the Upper Ministers, it is restrained and formal. When the ruler is present it is wary, but not cramped.

When the ruler summons him to receive a guest, a look of confusion comes over his face and his legs seem to give beneath his weight. When saluting his colleagues he passes his right hand to the left, letting his robe hang down in front and behind; and as he advances with quickened step, his attitude is one of majestic dignity.

When the guest has gone, he reports the close of the visit, saying, "The guest is no longer looking back."

On entering the Palace Gate he seems to shrink into himself, as though there were not room. If he halts, it must never be in the middle of the gate, nor in going through does he ever tread on the threshold. As he passes the Stance a look of confusion comes over his face, his legs seem to give way under him and words seem to fail him. While, holding up the hem of his skirt, he ascends the Audience Hall, he seems to double up and keeps in his breath, so that you would think he was not breathing at all. On coming out, after descending the first step his expression relaxes into one of satisfaction and relief. At the bottom of the steps he quickens his pace, advancing with an air of majestic dignity. On regaining his place he resumes his attitude of wariness and hesitation.

When carrying the tablet of jade, he seems to double up, as though borne down by its weight. He holds it at the highest as though he were making a bow, at the lowest, as though he were proffering a gift. His expression, too, changes to one of dread and his feet seem to recoil, as though he were avoiding something. When presenting ritual-presents, his expression is placid. At the private audience his attitude is gay and animated.

A gentleman does not wear facings of purple or mauve, nor in undress does he use pink or roan. In hot weather he wears an unlined gown of fine thread loosely woven, but puts on an outside garment before going out-of-doors. With a black robe he wears black lambskin; with a robe of undyed silk, fawn. With a yellow robe, fox fur. On his undress robe the fur cuffs are long; but the right is shorter than the left. His bedclothes must be half as long again as a man's height. The thicker kinds of fox and badger are for home wear. Except when in mourning, he wears all his girdle-ornaments. Apart from his Court apron, all his skirts are wider at the bottom than at the waist. Lambskin dyed black and a hat of dark-dyed silk must not be worn when making visits of condolence. At the Announcement of the New Moon he must go to Court in full Court dress.

When preparing himself for sacrifice he must wear the Bright Robe, and it must be of linen. He must change his food and also the place where he commonly sits. But there is no objection to his rice being of the finest quality, nor to his meat being finely minced. Rice affected by the weather or turned he must not eat, nor fish that is not sound, nor meat that is high. He must not eat anything discoloured or that smells bad. He must not eat what is overcooked nor what is undercooked, nor anything that is out of season. He must not eat what has been crookedly cut, nor any dish that lacks its proper seasoning. The meat that he eats must at the very most not be enough to make his breath smell of meat rather than of rice. As regards wine, no limit is laid down; but he must not be disorderly. He may not drink wine bought at a shop or eat dried meat from the market. He need not refrain from such articles of food as have ginger sprinkled over them; but he must not eat much of such dishes.

After a sacrifice in the ducal palace, the flesh must not be kept overnight. No sacrificial flesh may be kept beyond the third day. If it is kept beyond the third day, it may no longer be eaten. While it is being eaten, there must be no conversation, nor any word spoken while lying down after the repast. Any article of food, whether coarse rice, vegetables, broth or melon, that has been used as an offering must be handled with due solemnity.

He must not sit on a mat that is not straight.

When the men of his village are drinking wine he leaves the feast directly the village-elders have left. When the men of his village hold their Expulsion Rite, he puts on his Court dress and stands on the eastern steps.

When sending a messenger to enquire after someone in another country, he prostrates himself twice while speeding the messenger on his way. When K'ang-tzu sent him some medicine he prostrated himself and accepted it; but said, As I am not acquainted with its properties, I cannot venture to taste it.

When the stables were burnt down, on returning from Court, he said, Was anyone hurt? He did not ask about the horses.

When his prince sends him a present of food, he must straighten his mat and be the first to taste what has been sent. When what his prince sends is a present of uncooked meat, he must cook it and make a sacrificial offering. When his prince sends a live animal, he must rear it. When he is waiting upon his prince at meal-times, while his prince is making the sacrificial offering, he (the gentleman) tastes the dishes. If he is ill and his prince comes to see him, he has himself laid with his head to the East with his Court robes thrown over him and his sash drawn across the bed. When the prince commands his presence he goes straight to the palace without waiting for his carriage to be yoked.

On entering the Ancestral Temple, he asks about every detail.

If a friend dies and there are no relatives to fall back on, he says, "The funeral is my affair." On receiving a present from a friend, even a carriage and horses, he does not prostrate himself. He does so only in the case of sacrificial meat being sent.

In bed he avoids lying in the posture of a corpse. When at home he does not use ritual attitudes. When appearing before anyone in mourning, however well he knows him, he must put on an altered expression, and when appearing before anyone in sacrificial garb, or a blind man, even informally, he must be sure to adopt the appropriate attitude. On meeting anyone in deep mourning he must bow across the bar of his chariot; he also bows to people carrying planks. When confronted with a particularly choice dainty at a banquet, his countenance should change and he should rise to his feet. Upon hearing a sudden clap of thunder or a violent gust of wind, he must change countenance.

When mounting a carriage, he must stand facing it squarely and holding the mounting-cord. When riding he confines his gaze, does not speak rapidly or point with his hands.

(The gentleman) rises and goes at the first sign, and does not "settle till he has hovered." (A song) says:

The hen-pheasant of the hill-bridge,
Knows how to bide its time, to bide its time!
When Tzu-lu made it an offering,
It sniffed three times before it rose.

Ssu-ma Niu asked about the meaning of the term Gentleman. The Master said, The Gentleman neither grieves nor fears. Ssu-ma Niu said, So that is what is meant by being a gentleman — neither to grieve nor to fear? The Master said, On looking within himself he finds no taint; so why should he either grieve or fear?

The Master said, The gentleman calls attention to the good points in others; he does not call attention to their defects. The small man does just the reverse of this.

The Master said, The true gentleman is conciliatory but not accommodating. Common people are accommodating but not conciliatory.

The Master said, The true gentleman is easy to serve, yet difficult to please. For if you try to please him in any manner inconsistent with the Way, he refuses to be pleased; but in using the services of others he only expects of them what they are capable of performing. Common people are difficult to serve, but easy to please. Even though you try to please them in a manner inconsistent with the Way, they will still be pleased; but in using the services of others they expect them (irrespective of their capacities) to do any work that comes along.

The Master said, The gentleman is dignified, but never haughty; common people are haughty, but never dignified.

The Master said, It is possible to be a true gentleman and yet lack Goodness. But there has never yet existed a Good man who was not a gentleman.

When the Master said, He who holds no rank in a State does not discuss its policies, Master Tsêng said, "A true gentleman, even in his thoughts, never departs from what is suitable to his rank."

The Master said, A gentleman is ashamed to let his words outrun his deeds.

The Master said, The Ways of the true gentleman are three. I myself have met with success in none of them. For he that is really Good is never unhappy, he that is really wise is never perplexed, he that is really brave is never afraid. Tzu-kung said, That, Master, is your own Way!

The Master said, (A gentleman) does not grieve that people do not recognize his merits; he grieves at his own incapacities.

The Master said, The gentleman who takes the right as his material to work upon and ritual as the guide in putting what is right into practice, who is modest in setting out his projects and faithful in carrying them to their conclusion, he indeed is a true gentleman.

The Master said, A gentleman is distressed by his own lack of capacity; he is never distressed at the failure of others to recognize his merits.

The Master said, A gentleman has reason to be distressed if he ends his days without making a reputation for himself.

The Master said, "The demands that a gentleman makes are upon himself; those that a small man makes are upon others."

The Master said, A gentleman is proud, but not quarrelsome, allies himself with individuals, but not with parties.

The Master said, A gentleman does not accept men because of what they say, nor reject sayings, because the speaker is what he is.

The Master said, A gentleman, in his plans, thinks of the Way; he does not think how he is going to make a living. Even farming sometimes entails times of shortage; and even learning may incidentally lead to high pay. But a gentleman's anxieties concern the progress of the Way; he has no anxiety concerning poverty.

The Master said, It is wrong for a gentleman to have knowledge of menial matters and proper that he should be entrusted with great responsibilities. It is wrong for a small man to be entrusted with great responsibilities, but proper that he should have a knowledge of menial matters.

The Master said, From a gentleman consistency is expected, but not blind fidelity.

Master K'ung said, There are three things against which a gentleman is on his guard. In his youth, before his blood and vital humours have settled down, he is on his guard against lust. Having reached his prime, when the blood and vital humours have finally hardened, he is on his guard against strife. Having reached old age, when the blood and vital humours are already decaying, he is on his guard against avarice.

Master K'ung said, There are three things that a gentleman fears: he fears the will of Heaven, he fears great men, he fears the words of the Divine Sages. The small man does not know the will of Heaven and so does not fear it. He treats great men with contempt, and scoffs at the words of the Divine Sages.

Master K'ung said, The gentleman has nine cares. In seeing he is careful to see clearly, in hearing he is careful to hear distinctly, in his looks he is careful to be kindly; in his manner to be respectful, in his words to be loyal, in his work to be diligent. When in doubt he is careful to ask for information; when angry he has a care for the consequences, and when he sees a chance of gain, he thinks carefully whether the pursuit of it would be consonant with the Right.

The Master said, He who does not understand the will of Heaven cannot be regarded as a gentleman. He who does not know the rites cannot take his stand. He who does not understand words, cannot understand people.

6

Legalism:
An Alternative System

A student of the Confucian Xun Zi, Han Fei-Tzu (d. 233 B.C.) was the principal theoretician of legalism, a school of philosophy adopted by the Ch'in after unifying China in 256 B.C. This former Confucian adopted the pragmatic view that the Chinese, perceived as antisocial and inherently evil, must be firmly controlled by an authoritative central government through strictly applied punitive laws. This harsh but effective solution for resolving the chaotic conditions that plagued the Chou dynasty included the introduction of new managerial techniques, an improved bureaucracy, enhanced communications, land reforms, and standardization of weights, measures, and coinage. Han Fei-Tzu, who served as an official for the powerful but short-lived Ch'in dynasty (that gave China its name), died from poison at the hands of Li Ssu, a jealous legalist rival. Han Fei-Tzu authored twenty books and was honored by the grand historian, Ssu-ma Ch'ien, with a biographical sketch.

How did legalism differ from Confucianism in its view of human nature and the proper organization of the state? Officially, legalism died with the demise of the Ch'in and the renewed interest in Confucian values. In fact, though, the Chinese state continued to combine Confucian ideals with the harsher policelike approach urged by legalists—so this division of political approach was of more than passing importance. Both legalism and Confucianism, somewhat ironically, promoted a strong state.

If orders are made trim, laws never deviate; if laws are equable, there will be no culprit among the officials. Once the law is fixed, nobody can damage it by means of virtuous

From Han Fei-Tzu, *The Complete Works*, 2 vols., translated by W. K. Liao (London: Arthur Probsthain, 1959), Vol. II, pp. 322–33. Copyright © 1959 by Arthur Probsthain. Reprinted by permission.

words. If men of merit are appointed to office, the people will have little to say; if men of virtue are appointed to office the people will have much to talk about. The enforcement of laws depends upon the method of judicial administration. Who administers judicial affairs with ease . . . attains supremacy. . . . Whoever procrastinates in creating order, will see his state dismembered.

Govern by penalties; wage war by rewards; and enlarge the bounties so as to put the principles of statecraft into practice. If so, there will be no wicked people in the state nor will there by any wicked trade at the market. If things are many and trifles are numerous, and if farming is relaxed and villainy prevails, the state will certainly be dismembered.

If the people have a surplus of food, make them receive rank by giving grain to the state. If only through their own effort they can receive rank, then farmers will not idle.

If a tube three inches long has no bottom, it can never be filled. Conferring office and rank or granting profit and bounty without reference to merit, is like a tube having no bottom.

If the state confers office and bestows rank, it can be said to devise plans with complete wisdom and wage war with complete courage. Such a state will find a rival. Again, if the state confers office and bestows rank according to merit, then rules will be simplified and opponents barred; this can be said to abolish government by means of government, abolish words by means of words, and bestow rank according to merit. Therefore the state will have much strength and none else in All-under-Heaven will dare to invade it. When its soldiers march out, they will take the objective and, having taken it, will certainly be able to hold it. When it keeps its soldiers in reserve and does not attack, it will certainly become rich.

The affairs of the government, however small, should never be abandoned. For instance, office and rank are always obtained according to the acquired merit; though there may be flattering words, it will be impossible thereby to make any interference in the state affairs. This is said to be "government by figures." For instance, in attacking with force, ten points are taken for every point given out; but in attacking with words, one hundred are lost for every one marched out. If a state is fond of force, it is called hard to attack; if a state is fond of words, it is called easy to attack.

If the ability of the official is equal to his post, if his duty is lightened and he never reserves any surplus energy in mind, and if he does not shift any responsibility of additional offices back to the ruler, then there will be no hidden grudge inside. If the intelligent ruler makes the state affairs never mutually interfere, there will be no dispute; if he allows no official to hold any kind of additional post, everybody will develop his talent or skill; and if he allows no two persons to share the same meritorious achievement, there will be no quarrel.

If penalties are heavy and rewards are few, it means that the superior loves the people, wherefore the people will die for rewards. If rewards are many and penalties are light, it means that the superior does not love the people, wherefore the people will never die for rewards.

If the profit issues from one outlet only, the state will have no rival; if it issues from two outlets, its soldiers will be half useful; and if the profit comes from ten outlets, the people will not observe the law. If heavy penalties are clear and if the people are always well disciplined and then if men are engaged in case of emergency, the superior will have all the advantage.

In inflicting penalties light offences should be punished severely; if light offences do not appear, heavy offences will not come. This is said to be to abolish penalties by means of penalties. And the state will certainly become strong. If crimes are serious but penalties are light, light penalties breed further troubles. This is said to create penalties through penalties, and such a state will infallibly be dismembered.

The sage in governing the people considers their springs of action, never tolerates their wicked desires, but seeks only for the people's benefit. Therefore, the penalty he inflicts is not due to any hatred for the people but to his motive of loving the people. If penalty triumphs, the people are quiet; if reward over-flows, culprits appear. Therefore the triumph of penalty is the beginning of order; the overflow of reward, the origin of chaos.

Indeed, it is the people's nature to delight in disorder and detach themselves from legal restraints. Therefore, when the intelligent sovereign governs the state, if he makes rewards clear, the people will be encouraged to render meritorious services; if he makes penalties severe, the people will attach themselves to the law. If they are encouraged to render meritorious services, public affairs will not be obstructed; if they attach themselves to the law, culprits will not appear. Therefore, he who governs the people should nip the evil in the bud; he who commands troops, should inculcate warfare in the people's mind. If prohibitions can uproot causes of villainy, there will always be order; if soldiers can imagine warfare in mind, there will always be victory. When the sage is governing the people, he attains order first, wherefore he is strong; he prepares for war first, wherefore he wins.

Indeed, the administration of the state affairs requires the attention to the causes of human action so as to unify the people's mental trends; the exclusive elevation of public welfare so as to stop self-seeking elements; the reward for denunciation of crime so as to suppress culprits; and finally the clarification of laws so as to facilitate governmental procedures. Whoever is able to apply these four measures, will become strong; whoever is unable to apply these four measures, will become weak. Indeed, the strength of the state is due to the administration of its political affairs; the honour of the sovereign is due to his supreme power. Now, the enlightened ruler possesses the supreme power and the administrative organs; the ignoble ruler possesses both the supreme power and the administrative organs, too. Yet the results are not the same, because their standpoints are different. Thus, as the enlightened ruler has the supreme power in his grip, the superior is held in high esteem; as he unifies the administrative organs, the state is in order. Hence law is the origin of supremacy and penalty is the beginning of love.

Indeed, it is the people's nature to abhor toil and enjoy ease. However, if they pursue ease, the land will waste; if the land wastes, the state will not be in order. If the state is not orderly, it will become chaotic. If reward and penalty take no effect among the inferiors, government will come to a deadlock. Therefore, he who wants to accomplish a great achievement but hesitates to apply his full strength, can not hope for the accomplishment of the achievement; he who wants to settle the people's disorder but hesitates to change their traditions, can not hope to banish the people's disorder.

Hence there is no constant method for the government of men. The law alone leads to political order. If laws are adjusted to the time, there is good government. If government fits the age, there will be great accomplishment. Therefore, when the people are naive, if you regulate them with fame, there will be good government; when everybody in the world is intelligent, if you discipline them with penalties, they will obey. While time is moving on, if laws do not shift accordingly, there will be misrule; while abilities are diverse, if prohibitions are not changed, the state will be dismembered. Therefore, the sage in governing the people makes laws move with time and prohibitions change with abilities. Who can exert his forces to land-utilization, will become rich; who can rush his forces at enemies, will become strong. The strong man not obstructed in his way will attain supremacy.

Therefore, the way to supremacy lies in the way of shutting culprits off and the way of blocking up wicked men. Who is able to block up wicked men, will eventually attain supremacy. The policy of attaining supremacy relies not on foreign states' abstention from disturbing your state, but on their inability to disturb your state. Who has to rely on foreign powers' abstention from disturbing his state before he can maintain his own independence, will see his state dismembered; who relies on their inability to disturb his state and willingly enacts the law, will prosper.

Therefore, the worthy ruler in governing the state follows the statecraft of invulnerability. When rank is esteemed, the superior will increase his dignity. He will accordingly bestow rewards on men of merit, confer ranks upon holders of posts, and appoint wicked men to no office. Who devotes himself to practical forces, gets a high rank. If the rank is esteemed, the superior will be honoured. The superior, if honoured, will attain supremacy. On the contrary, if the state does not strive after practical forces but counts on private studies, its rank will be lowered. If the rank is lowered, the superior will be humbled. If the superior is humbled, the state will be dismembered. Therefore, if the way of founding the state and using the people can shut off foreign invaders and block up self-seeking subjects, and if the superior relies on himself, supremacy will be attained. . . .

In general, wherever the state is extensive and the ruler is honourable, there laws are so strict that whatever is ordered works and whatever is prohibited stops. Therefore, the ruler of men who distinguishes between ranks and regulates bounties, makes laws severe and thereby makes the distinction strict.

Indeed, if the state is orderly, the people are safe; if affairs are confused, the country falls into peril. Who makes laws strict, hits on the true nature of mankind; who makes prohibitions lenient, misses the apparent fact. Moreover, everybody is, indeed, gifted with desperate courage. To exert desperate courage to get what one wants, is human nature. Yet everybody's likes and dislikes should be regulated by the superior. Now the people like to have profit and bounty and hate to be punished; if the superior catches their likes and dislikes and thereby holds their desperate courage under control, he will not miss the realities of affairs.

However, if prohibitions are lenient and facts are missed, reward and penalty will be misused. Again, when governing the people, if you do not regard conformity to law as right, you will eventually observe no law. Therefore, the science and philosophy of politics should by all means emphasize the distinction between degrees of penalty and of reward.

Who governs the state, should always uphold the law. In life there are ups and downs. If any ruler goes down, it is because in regulating rewards and penalties he makes no distinction between different degrees. Who governs the state, always distinguishes between reward and punishment. Therefore, some people might regard the distinction between reward and punishment as distinction, which should not be called distinction in the strict sense.

As regards the distinction made by the clear-sighted ruler, it is the distinction between different grades of reward and of punishment. Therefore, his subjects respect laws and fear prohibitions. They try to avoid crime rather than dare to expect any reward. Hence the saying: "Without expecting penalty and reward the people attend to public affairs."

For this reason, the state at the height of order is able to take the suppression of villainy for its duty. Why? Because its law comprehends human nature and accords with the principles of government.

If so, how to get rid of delicate villainy? By making the people watch one another in their hidden affairs. Then how to make them watch one another? By implicating the people of the same hamlet in one another's crime. When everyone knows that the penalty or reward will directly affect him, if the people of the same hamlet fail to watch one another, they will fear they may not be able to escape the implication, and those who are evil-minded, will not be allowed to forget so many people watching them. Were such the law, everybody would mind his own doings, watch everybody else, and disclose the secrets of any culprit. For, whosoever denounces a criminal offence, is not held guilty but is given a reward; whosoever misses any culprit, is definitely censured and given the same penalty as the culprit. Were such the law, all types of culprits would be detected. If the minutest villainy is not tolerated, it is due to the system of personal denunciation and mutual implication.

Indeed, the most enlightened method of governing a state is to trust measures and not men. For this reason, the tactful state is never mistaken if it does not trust the empty fame of men. If the land within the boundary is always in order it is because measures are employed. If any falling state lets foreign soldiers walk all over its territory and can neither resist nor prevent them, it is because that state trusts men and uses no measures. Men may jeopardize their own country, but measures can invade others' countries. Therefore, the tactful state spurns words and trusts laws.

Broadly speaking, it is hard to uncover a crooked merit that appears to fulfil the promise; it is hard to disclose the feature of the fault that is ornamented with beautiful words. Therefore, penalty and reward are often misled by double-dealers. What is alleged to be fulfilling the promise but is hard to uncover, is a villainous merit. Any minister's fault is hard to disclose, because its motive is missed. However, if by following reason you can not disclose the false merit and by analyzing feelings you are still deceived by the villainous motive, then can both reward and punishment have no mistake respectively?

For such reasons, false scholars establish names inside, while itinerants devise plans outside, till the stupid and the coward mix themselves with the brave and the clever. Inasmuch as the false path is customary, they are tolerated by their age. There-fore, their law does not work and their penalty affects nobody. If so, both reward and penalty have to be double-dealings.

Therefore, concrete facts have their limits of extension, but abstract principles involve no accurate measures. The absence of such measures is due not to the law but to the abandonment of law and the dependence on cleverness. If the law is abandoned and cleverness is employed, how can the appointee to office perform his duty? If duty and office are not equivalent to each other, then how can the law evade mistakes and how can penalty evade troubles? For this reason reward and punishment will be thrown into confusion and disorder, and the state policy will deviate and err, because neither penalty nor reward has any clear distinction of degree as in the difference between black and white.

7

Chinese Politics in Practice:
A Historian's View

The following brief passage suggests how Chinese intellectuals interpreted their own politics. Written by Ssu-ma Ch'ien (ca. 145–90 B.C.), the "grand historian of China," it served as praise to the Han dynasty by suggesting its divine origins, its favorable astrological signs (Ssu-ma Ch'ien was also court astrologer), but also its embodiment of traditional political virtues. The "grand historian" did a great deal of research for his work, but he was also concerned that it be morally instructive — with more than a trace of the Confucian definition of political morality. What reasons does Ssu-ma Ch'ien give for devoted loyalty to the Han dynasty?

Hsiang Yü was violent and tyrannical, while the king of Han practiced goodness and virtue. In anger he marched forth from Shu and Han, returning to conquer the three kingdoms of Ch'in. He executed Hsiang Yü and became an emperor, and all the world was brought to peace. He changed the statutes and reformed the ways of the people. Thus I made The Basic Annals of Emperor Kao-tsu.

Kao-tsu was a native of the community of Chung-yang in the city of Feng, the district of P'ei. His family name was Liu and his polite name Chi. His father was known as the "Venerable Sire" and his mother as "Dame Liu."

Before he was born, Dame Liu was one day resting on the bank of a large pond

From *Records of the Grand Historian of China, from the Shi Chi of Ssu-ma Ch'ien*, Vol. I: *Early Years of the Han Dynasty 209 to 141* B.C., edited and translated by Burton Watson (New York: Columbia University Press, 1961), pp. 77–79, 118–121, 381. Copyright ©1961, Columbia University Press. Reprinted by permission.

when she dreamed that she encountered a god. At this time the sky grew dark and was filled with thunder and lightning. When Kao-tsu's father went to look for her, he saw a scaly dragon over the place where she was lying. After this she became pregnant and gave birth to Kao-tsu.

Kao-tsu had a prominent nose and a dragonlike face, with beautiful whiskers on his chin and cheeks; on his left thigh he had seventy-two black moles. He was kind and affectionate with others, liked to help people, and was very understanding. He always had great ideas and paid little attention to the business the rest of his family was engaged in.

When he grew up he took the examination to become an official and was made village head of Ssu River. He treated all the other officials in the office with familiarity and disdain. He was fond of wine and women and often used to go to Dame Wang's or old lady Wu's and drink on credit. When he got drunk and lay down to sleep, the old women, to their great wonder, would always see something like a dragon over the place where he was sleeping. Also, whenever he would drink and stay at their shops, they would sell several times as much wine as usual. Because of these strange happenings, when the end of the year came around the old women would always destroy Kao-tsu's credit slips and clear his account.

Kao-tsu was once sent on *corvée* labor to the capital city of Hsien-yang and happened to have an opportunity to see the First Emperor of Ch'in. When he saw him he sighed and said, "Ah, this is the way a great man should be."

· · ·

[An important dignitary, Master Lü, gives a party which Kao-tsu, a proud village official, bribed his way into, taking a seat of honor.]

When the drinking was nearly over, Master Lü glanced at Kao-tsu in such a way as to indicate that he should stay a while longer, and so Kao-tsu dawdled over his wine. "Since my youth," said Master Lü, "I have been fond of reading faces. I have read many faces, but none with signs like yours. You must take good care of yourself, I beg you. I have a daughter whom I hope you will do me the honor of accepting as your wife."

When the party was over, Dame Lü was very angry with her husband. "You have always idolized this girl and planned to marry her to some person of distinction," she said. "The magistrate of P'ei is a friend of yours and has asked for her, but you would not give your consent. How can you be so insane as to give her to Liu Chi?"

"This is not the sort of thing women and children can understand!" replied Master Lü. Eventually he married the girl to Kao-tsu, and it was this daughter of Master Lü who became Empress Lü and gave birth to Emperor Hui and Princess Yüan of Lu. . . .

Kao-tsu had eight sons. The oldest, a son by a concubine, was Fei, the king of Ch'i, posthumously titled King Tao-hui. The second, a son by Empress Lü, became Emperor Hui. The third, son of Lady Ch'i, was Ju-i, the king of Chao, posthumously titled King Yin. The fourth was Heng, the king of Tai, who later became Emperor Wen the Filial; he was a son of Empress Dowager Po. The fifth was Hui, the king of Liang, who in the reign of Empress Lü was transferred to the position of king of Chao; he was given the posthumous title of King Kung. The sixth was Yu, the king of Huai-yang, whom Empress Lü made the king of Chao; his posthumous title was King Yu.

The seventh was Ch'ang, who became King Li of Huai-nan, and the eighth was Chien, the king of Yen.

The Grand Historian remarks: The government of the Hsia dynasty was marked by good faith, which in time deteriorated until mean men had turned it into rusticity. Therefore the men of Shang who succeeded to the Hsia reformed this defect through the virtue of piety. But piety degenerated until mean men had made it a superstitious concern for the spirits. Therefore the men of Chou who followed corrected this fault through refinement and order. But refinement again deteriorated until it became in the hands of the mean a mere hollow show. Therefore what was needed to reform this hollow show was a return to good faith, for the way of the Three Dynasties of old is like a cycle which, when it ends, must begin over again.

It is obvious that in late Chou and Ch'in times the earlier refinement and order had deteriorated. But the government of Ch'in failed to correct this fault, instead adding its own harsh punishments and laws. Was this not a grave error?

Thus when the Han rose to power it took over the faults of its predecessors and worked to change and reform them, causing men to be unflagging in their efforts and following the order properly ordained. . . .

In ancient times, when Shun and Yü became rulers, they had first to accumulate goodness and merit for twenty or thirty years, impress the people with their virtue, prove that they could in practice handle the affairs of government, and meet the approval of Heaven before they were able to ascend the throne. Again, when Kings T'ang and Wu founded the Shang and Chou dynasties, they had behind them over ten generations of ancestors, stretching back to Hsieh and Hou Chi respectively, who had been distinguished for their just and virtuous conduct. Yet, though eight hundred nobles appeared unsummoned to aid King Wu at the Meng Ford, he still did not venture to move; it was only later that he assassinated the tyrant Chou, and only after similar cautious delay that King T'ang banished the tyrant Chieh. Ch'in first rose to prominence under Duke Hsiang and achieved eminence under Dukes Wen and Mu. From the reigns of Dukes Hsieh and Hsiao on, it gradually swallowed up the Six States until, after a hundred years or so, the First Emperor was able to bring all the noblemen under his power. Thus, even with the virtue of Shun, Yü, T'ang, and Wu, or the might of the First Emperor, it is, as one can see, an extremely difficult task to unite the empire in one rule!

After the Ch'in ruler had assumed the title of emperor, he was fearful lest warfare should continue because of the presence of feudal lords. Therefore he refused to grant so much as a foot of land in fief, but instead destroyed the fortifications of the principal cities, melted down the lance and arrow points, and ruthlessly wiped out the brave men of the world, hoping thus to ensure the safety of his dynasty for countless generations to come. Yet from the lanes of the common people there arose a man with the deeds of a king whose alliances and campaigns of attack surpassed those of the three dynasties of Hsia, Shang, and Chou. Ch'in's earlier prohibitions against feudalism and the possession of arms, as it turned out, served only to aid worthy men and remove from their path obstacles they would otherwise have encountered. Therefore Kao-tsu had but to roar forth his indignation to become a leader of the world. Why should people say that one cannot become a king unless he possesses land? Was this man not what the old books term a "great sage"? Surely this was the work of Heaven! Who but a great sage would be worthy to receive the mandate of Heaven and become emperor? . . .

When Empress Dowager Lü passed away she was buried with her husband, Emperor Kao-tsu, at Ch'ang-ling. Lü Lu, Lü Ch'an, and others of the Lü family, fearing punishment for their usurpations of power, plotted a revolt, but the great ministers overthrew them. Thus did Heaven guide the imperial line and in the end wipe out the Lü clan. Only the empress of Emperor Hui was spared, being sent to live in the Northern Palace. The king of Tai was invited to come and take the throne, and it was he, Emperor Wen, who with due reverence carried on the service of the ancestral temples of the Han. Was this not the work of Heaven? Who but one destined by Heaven for rule could assume such a charge?

8

Women in Classical China: Pan Chao

Pan Chao (ca. A.D. 45–120), China's "foremost woman scholar," served unofficially as imperial historian to Emperor Ho (A.D. 89–105) while acting as an instructor in history, classical writing, astronomy, and mathematics to the Empress Teng and her ladies-in-waiting. Summoned to complete the historical books (*Han Shu*) of her deceased brother, Ku, the scholarly and talented widow is the only woman in China to have served in that capacity. Her success in overcoming contemporary restraints on women was due to an exceptional education, which she attributed to her scholarly parents. As a historian, moralist, and royal servant, Pan Chao authored numerous literary works, including narrative poems, commemorative verses, eulogies, and her famous *Lessons for Women*. This brief educational treatise, written expressly for women and the first of its kind in world history, offers interesting insights into the Chinese perceptions of the ideal woman as well as first-century Chinese customs. It contains advice in matters of customs and manners for girls in her family so that they might not "humiliate both your ancestors and your clan."

How does Pan Chao define womanhood and women's roles? How do these definitions relate to other aspects of Chinese society such as Confucianism?

From Pan Chao, "Lessons for Women," in *Pan Chao: Foremost Woman Scholar of China* by Nancy Lee Swann (New York: The Century Co., 1932), pp. 82–87.

Chinese peasants transplanting rice seedlings. [Bulloz]

LESSONS FOR WOMEN

Introduction

I, the unworthy writer, am unsophisticated, unenlightened, and by nature unintelligent, but I am fortunate both to have received not a little favor from my scholarly father, and to have had a (cultured) mother and instructresses upon whom to rely for a literary education as well as for training in good manners. More than forty years have passed since at the age of fourteen I took up the dustpan and the broom in the Ts'ao family. During this time with trembling heart I feared constantly that I might disgrace my parents, and that I might multiply difficulties for both the women and the men (of my husband's family). Day and night I was distressed in heart, (but) I labored without confessing weariness. Now and hereafter, however, I know how to escape (from such fears).

Being careless, and by nature stupid, I taught and trained (my children) without system. Consequently I fear that my son Ku may bring disgrace upon the Imperial Dynasty by whose Holy Grace he has unprecedentedly received the extraordinary privilege of wearing the Gold and the Purple, a privilege for the attainment of which (by my son, I) a humble subject never even hoped. Nevertheless, now that he is a man and able to plan his own life, I need not again have concern for him. But I do grieve that you, my daughters, just now at the age for marriage, have not at this time had gradual training and advice; that you still have not learned the proper customs for married women. I fear that by failure in good manners in other families you will humiliate both your ancestors and your clan. I am now seriously ill, life is uncertain. As I have thought of you all in so untrained a state, I have been uneasy many a time for you. At hours of leisure I have composed in seven chapters these instructions under the title, "Lessons for Women." In order that you may have something wherewith to benefit your persons, I wish every one of you, my daughters, each to write out a copy for yourself.

From this time on every one of you strive to practise these (lessons).

Chapter I
Humility

On the third day after the birth of a girl the ancients observed three customs: (first) to place the baby below the bed; (second) to give her a potsherd with which to play; and (third) to announce her birth to her ancestors by an offering. Now to lay the baby below the bed plainly indicated that she is lowly and weak, and should regard it as her primary duty to humble herself before others. To give her potsherds with which to play indubitably signified that she should practise labor and consider it her primary duty to be industrious. To announce her birth before her ancestors clearly meant that she ought to esteem as her primary duty the continuation of the observance of worship in the home.

These three ancient customs epitomize a woman's ordinary way of life and the teachings of the traditional ceremonial rites and regulations. Let a woman modestly yield to others; let her respect others; let her put others first, herself last. Should she do something good, let her not mention it; should she do something bad, let her not deny it. Let her bear disgrace; let her even endure when others speak or do evil to her. Always let her seem to tremble and to fear. (When a woman follows such maxims as these,) then she may be said to humble herself before others.

Let a woman retire late to bed, but rise early to duties; let her not dread tasks by day or by night. Let her not refuse to perform domestic duties whether easy or difficult. That which must be done, let her finish completely, tidily, and systematically. (When a woman follows such rules as these,) then she may be said to be industrious.

Let a woman be correct in manner and upright in character in order to serve her husband. Let her live in purity and quietness (of spirit), and attend to her own affairs. Let her love not gossip and silly laughter. Let her cleanse and purify and arrange in order the wine and the food for the offerings to the ancestors. (When a woman observes such principles as these,) then she may be said to continue ancestral worship.

No woman who observes these three (fundamentals of life) has ever had a bad reputation or has fallen into disgrace. If a woman fail to observe them, how can her name be honored; how can she but bring disgrace upon herself?

Chapter II
Husband and Wife

The Way of husband and wife is intimately connected with *Yin* and *Yang*, and relates the individual to gods and ancestors. Truly it is the great principle of Heaven and Earth, and the great basis of human relationships. Therefore the "Rites" honor union of man and woman; and in the "Book of Poetry" the "First Ode" manifests the principle of marriage. For these reasons the relationship cannot but be an important one.

If a husband be unworthy then he possesses nothing by which to control his wife. If a wife be unworthy, then she possesses nothing with which to serve her husband. If a husband does not control his wife, then the rules of conduct manifesting his authority are abandoned and broken. If a wife does not serve her husband, then the proper relationship (between men and women) and the natural order of things are neglected and destroyed. As a matter of fact the purpose of these two (the controlling of women by men, and the serving of men by women) is the same.

Now examine the gentlemen of the present age. They only know that wives must be controlled, and that the husband's rules of conduct manifesting his authority must be established. They therefore teach their boys to read books and (study) histories. But they do not in the least understand that husbands and masters must (also) be served, and that the proper relationship and the rites should be maintained.

Yet only to teach men and not to teach women,—is that not ignoring the essential relation between them? According to the "Rites," it is the rule to begin to teach children to read at the age of eight years, and by the age of fifteen years they ought then to be ready for cultural training. Only why should it not be (that girls' education as well as boys' be) according to this principle?

Chapter III
Respect and Caution

As *Yin* and *Yang* are not of the same nature, so man and woman have different characteristics. The distinctive quality of the *Yang* is rigidity; the function of the *Yin* is yielding. Man is honored for strength; a woman is beautiful on account of her gentleness. Hence there arose the common saying: "A man though born like a wolf may, it is feared, become a weak monstrosity; a woman though born like a mouse may, it is feared, become a tiger."

Now for self-culture nothing equals respect for others. To counteract firmness nothing equals compliance. Consequently it can be said that the Way of respect and acquiescence is woman's most important principle of conduct. So respect may be defined as nothing other than holding on to that which is permanent; and acquiescence nothing other than being liberal and generous. Those who are steadfast in devotion know that they should stay in their proper places; those who are liberal and generous esteem others, and honor and serve (them).

If husband and wife have the habit of staying together, never leaving one another, and following each other around within the limited space of their own rooms, then they will lust after and take liberties with one another. From such action improper language will arise between the two. This kind of discussion may lead to licentiousness. Out of licentiousness will be born a heart of disrespect to the husband. Such a result comes from not knowing that one should stay in one's proper place.

Furthermore, affairs may be either crooked or straight; words may be either right or wrong. Straightforwardness cannot but lead to quarreling; crookedness cannot but lead to accusation. If there are really accusations and quarrels, then undoubtedly there will be angry affairs. Such a result comes from not esteeming others, and not honoring and serving (them).

(If wives) suppress not contempt for husbands, then it follows (that such wives) rebuke and scold (their husbands). (If husbands) stop not short of anger, then they are certain to beat (their wives). The correct relationship between husband and wife is based upon harmony and intimacy, and (conjugal) love is grounded in proper union. Should actual blows be dealt, how could matrimonial relationship be preserved? Should sharp words be spoken, how could (conjugal) love exist? If love and proper relationship both be destroyed, then husband and wife are divided.

Chapter IV
Womanly Qualifications

A woman (ought to) have four qualifications: (1) womanly virtue; (2) womanly words; (3) womanly bearing; and (4) womanly work. Now what is called womanly virtue need not be brilliant ability, exceptionally different from others. Womanly words need be neither clever in debate nor keen in conversation. Womanly appearance requires neither a pretty nor a perfect face and form. Womanly work need not be work done more skilfully than that of others.

To guard carefully her chastity; to control circumspectly her behavior; in every motion to exhibit modesty; and to model each act on the best usage, this is womanly virtue.

To choose her words with care; to avoid vulgar language; to speak at appropriate times; and not to weary others (with much conversation), may be called the characteristics of womanly words.

To wash and scrub filth away; to keep clothes and ornaments fresh and clean; to wash the head and bathe the body regularly, and to keep the person free from disgraceful filth, may be called the characteristics of womanly bearing.

With whole-hearted devotion to sew and to weave; to love not gossip and silly laughter; in cleanliness and order (to prepare) the wine and food for serving guests, may be called the characteristics of womanly work.

These four qualifications characterize the greatest virtue of a woman. No woman can afford to be without them. In fact they are very easy to possess if a woman only treasure them in her heart. The ancients had a saying: "Is Love afar off? If I desire love, then love is at hand!" So can it be said of these qualifications.

Chapter V
Whole-hearted Devotion

Now in the "Rites" is written the principle that a husband may marry again, but there is no Canon that authorizes a woman to be married the second time. Therefore it is said of husbands as of Heaven, that as certainly as people cannot run away from Heaven, so surely a wife cannot leave (a husband's home).

If people in action or character disobey the spirits of Heaven and of Earth, then Heaven punishes them. Likewise if a woman errs in the rites and in the proper mode of conduct, then her husband esteems her lightly. The ancient book, "A Pattern for Women," (*Nü Hsien*) says: "To obtain the love of one man is the crown of a woman's life; to lose the love of one man is to miss the aim in woman's life." For these reasons a woman cannot but seek to win her husband's heart. Nevertheless, the beseeching wife need not use flattery, coaxing words, and cheap methods to gain intimacy.

Decidedly nothing is better (to gain the heart of a husband) than whole-hearted devotion and correct manners. In accordance with the rites and the proper mode of conduct, (let a woman) live a pure life. Let her have ears that hear not licentiousness; and eyes that see not depravity. When she goes outside her own home, let her not be conspicuous in dress and manners. When at home let her not neglect her dress. Women should not assemble in groups, nor gather together, (for gossip and silly laughter). They should not stand watching in the gateways. (If a woman follows) these rules, she may be said to have whole-hearted devotion and correct manners.

If, in all her actions, she is frivolous, she sees and hears (only) that which pleases herself. At home her hair is dishevelled, and her dress is slovenly. Outside the home she emphasizes her femininity to attract attention; she says what ought not to be said; and she looks at what ought not to be seen. (If a woman does such as) these, (she may be) said to be without whole-hearted devotion and correct manners.

9

The Four Noble Truths
of Buddhism

One of the most important developments in classical India was the emergence of Buddhism as a major religion on the subcontinent. Prince Gautama (563–483 B.C.), the future Buddha or "Enlightened One," grew up on the mountainous frontier between India and Nepal. After marrying and fathering a son, the prince renounced worldly things and embarked on a search for truth. Following years as a wandering holy man, he found illumination under the *bodhi* (wisdom) tree at Gaya. The Buddha then turned to teaching, to which he devoted the rest of his life. His disciples continued spreading the new faith after the Buddha's death, ultimately carrying the message throughout South and East Asia.

The four noble truths are the core of Buddhism; they are the essence of what the Buddha realized while sitting under the *bodhi* tree. Like all of the Buddha's teaching, they were initially transmitted orally and only put into written form several hundred years after his death.

In reading the four noble truths, keep in mind the following questions. What basic problem do they address? How is this problem defined? What is the solution? Are there characteristics of the four noble truths that seem distinctively Indian? Compare Buddhist values, for example, with Chinese Confucianism. What is it about the four noble truths that might make them appealing beyond the borders of India?

From *Buddhism in Translations: Passages Selected from the Buddhist Sacred Books*, translated by Henry Clarke Warren (Cambridge, Mass.: Harvard University Press, 1953), pp. 368–74.

THE FOUR NOBLE TRUTHS OF BUDDHISM

1. The Truth Concerning Misery

And how, O priests, does a priest live, as respects the elements of being, observant of the elements of being in the four noble truths?

Whenever, O priest, a priest knows the truth concerning misery, knows the truth concerning the origin of misery, knows the truth concerning the cessation of misery, knows the truth concerning the path leading to the cessation of misery.

And what, O priests, is the noble truth of misery?

Birth is misery; old age is misery; disease is misery; death is misery; sorrow, lamentation, misery, grief, and despair are misery; to wish for what one cannot have is misery; in short, all the five attachment-groups are misery. . . .

This, O priests, is called the noble truth of misery.

2. The Truth of the Origin of Misery

And what, O priests, is the noble truth of the origin of misery?

It is desire leading to rebirth, joining itself to pleasure and passion, and finding delight in every existence,—desire, namely, for sensual pleasure, desire for permanent existence, desire for transitory existence.

But where, O priests, does this desire spring up and grow? where does it settle and take root?

Where anything is delightful and agreeable to men, there desire springs up and grows, there it settles and takes root.

And what is delightful and agreeable to men, where desire springs up and grows, where it settles and takes root?

The eye is delightful and agreeable to men; there desire springs up and grows, there it settles and takes root.

The ear . . . the nose . . . the tongue . . . the body . . . the mind is delightful and agreeable to men; there desire springs up and grows, there it settles and takes root.

The Six Organs of Sense.

Forms . . . sounds . . . odors . . . tastes . . . things tangible . . . ideas are delightful and agreeable to men; there desire springs up and grows, there it settles and takes root.

The Six Objects of Sense.

Eye-consciousness . . . ear-consciousness . . . nose-consciousness . . . tongue-consciousness . . . body-consciousness . . . mind-consciousness is delightful and agreeable to men; there desire springs up and grows, there it settles and takes root.

The Six Consciousnesses.

Contact of the eye . . . ear . . . nose . . . tongue . . . body . . . mind is delightful and agreeable to men; there desire springs up and grows, there it settles and takes root.

The Six Contacts.

Sensation produced by contact of the eye . . . ear . . . nose . . . tongue . . .

body . . . mind is delightful and agreeable to men; there desire springs up and grows, there it settles and takes root.

The Six Sensations.

Perception of forms . . . sounds . . . odors . . . tastes . . . things tangible . . . ideas is delightful and agreeable to men; there desire springs up and grows, there it settles and takes root.

The Six Perceptions.

Thinking on forms . . . sounds . . . odors . . . tastes . . . things tangible . . . ideas is delightful and agreeable to men; there desire springs up and grows, there it settles and takes root.

The Six Thinkings.

Desire for forms . . . sounds . . . odors . . . tastes . . . things tangible . . . ideas is delightful and agreeable to men; there desire springs up and grows, there it settles and takes root.

The Six Desires.

Reasoning on forms . . . sounds . . . odors . . . tastes . . . things tangible . . . ideas is delightful and agreeable to men; there desire springs up and grows, there it settles and takes root.

The Six Reasonings.

Reflection on forms . . . sounds . . . odors . . . tastes . . . things tangible . . . ideas is delightful and agreeable to men; there desire springs up and grows, there it settles and takes root.

The Six Reflections.

This, O priests, is called the noble truth of the origin of misery.

3. The Truth of the Cessation of Misery

And what, O priests, is the noble truth of the cessation of misery?

It is the complete fading out and cessation of this desire, a giving up, a losing hold, a relinquishment, and a nonadhesion.

But where, O priests, does this desire wane and disappear? where is it broken up and destroyed?

Where anything is delightful and agreeable to men; there desire wanes and disappears, there it is broken up and destroyed.

And what is delightful and agreeable to men, where desire wanes and disappears, where it is broken up and destroyed?

The eye is delightful and agreeable to men; there desire wanes and disappears, there it is broken up and destroyed.

[Similarly respecting the other organs of sense, the six objects of sense, the six consciousnesses, the six contacts, the six sensations, the six perceptions, the six thinkings, the six desires, the six reasonings, and the six reflections.]

This, O priests, is called the noble truth of the cessation of misery.

4. The Truth of the Path Leading to the Cessation of Misery

And what, O priests, is the noble truth of the path leading to the cessation of misery?

It is this noble eightfold path, to wit, right belief, right resolve, right speech, right behavior, right occupation, right effort, right contemplation, right concentration.

And what, O priests, is right belief?

The knowledge of misery, O priests, the knowledge of the origin of misery, the knowledge of the cessation of misery, and the knowledge of the path leading to the cessation of misery, this, O priests, is called "right belief."

And what, O priests, is right resolve?

The resolve to renounce sensual pleasures, the resolve to have malice towards none, and the resolve to harm no living creature, this, O priests, is called "right resolve."

And what, O priests, is right speech?

To abstain from falsehood, to abstain from backbiting, to abstain from harsh language, and to abstain from frivolous talk, this, O priests, is called "right speech."

And what, O priests, is right behavior?

To abstain from destroying life, to abstain from taking that which is not given one, and to abstain from immorality, this, O priests, is called "right behavior."

And what, O priests, is right occupation?

Whenever, O priests, a noble disciple, quitting a wrong occupation, gets his livelihood by a right occupation, this, O priests, is called "right occupation."

And what, O priests, is right effort?

Whenever, O priests, a priest purposes, makes an effort, heroically endeavors, applies his mind, and exerts himself that evil and demeritorious qualities not yet arisen may not arise; purposes, makes an effort, heroically endeavors, applies his mind, and exerts himself that evil and demeritorious qualities already arisen may be abandoned; purposes, makes an effort, heroically endeavors, applies his mind, and exerts himself that meritorious qualities not yet arisen may arise; purposes, makes an effort, heroically endeavors, applies his mind, and exerts himself for the preservation, retention, growth, increase, development, and perfection of meritorious qualities already arisen, this, O priest, is called "right effort."

And what, O priests, is right contemplation?

Whenever, O priests, a priest lives, as respects the body, observant of the body, strenuous, conscious, contemplative, and has rid himself of lust and grief; as respects sensations, observant of sensations, strenuous, conscious, contemplative, and has rid himself of lust and grief; as respects the mind, observant of the mind, strenuous, conscious, comtemplative, and has rid himself of lust and grief; as respects the elements of being, observant of the elements of being, strenuous, conscious, contemplative, and has rid himself of lust and grief, this, O priests, is called "right contemplation."

And what, O priests, is right concentration?

Whenever, O priests, a priest, having isolated himself from sensual pleasures, having isolated himself from demeritorious traits, and still exercising reasoning, still exercising reflection, enters upon the first trance which is produced by isolation and characterized by joy and happiness; when, through the subsidence of reasoning and reflection, and still retaining joy and happiness, he enters upon the second trance, which is an interior tranquilization and intentness of the thoughts, and is produced by concentration; when, through the paling of joy, indifferent, contemplative, conscious, and in the experience of bodily happiness—that state which eminent men describe when they say, "Indifferent, contemplative, and living happily"—he enters upon the third trance; when, through the abandonment of happiness, through the abandonment of misery, through the disappearance of all antecedent gladness and grief, he enters upon the fourth trance, which has neither misery nor happiness, but is contemplation as refined by indifference, this, O priests, is called "right concentration."

This, O priests, is called the noble truth of the path leading to the cessation of misery.

10

State and Society in Classical India

There were numerous efforts to build stable and enduring states in early classical India, most notably on the Ganges Plain. This region served as the base of the first true Indian empire, that of the Mauryan rulers who governed most of the subcontinent from 321 to 181 B.C. The Mauryan state was founded by King Chandragupta (ruled 321–301 B.C.). He was the leader who first brought northern India under centralized rule. This paved the way for his successors, including the famous Ashoka (ruled 269–232 B.C.), who extended Mauryan authority to the south.

The Mauryan Empire was one of the largest states in the classical world, rivaling the empires of the Romans and the Han Chinese. What held it together? Tradition assigns an important role to the policies favored by Chandragupta's advisor, Kautilya, the author of the *Arthashastra* (*Treatise on Material Gain*), the great Indian text on practical politics. While we may doubt whether the ideas of one person could explain the success of a great empire, the *Arthashastra* is nonetheless an enormously important source for the historian of classical India. It makes clear that early on, in addition to being a center of important religious and philosophical ideas, India was also the home of advanced political thought. In addition, the *Arthashastra* is valuable for the light it sheds on Mauryan economic and social life.

According to the passages from the *Arthashastra* that follow, what is it that a ruler must do in order to be successful in domestic policy and foreign relations?

From William H. McNeill and Jean W. Sedlar, eds., *Classical India* (New York: Oxford University Press, 1969), pp. 20–22, 24–27, 32–33, 35–36. Copyright © 1969 by Oxford University Press. Reprinted by permission.

What evidence is there in the *Arthashastra* regarding the economy and society of the Mauryan period?

Chapter 10: On Spies

Advised and assisted by a tried council of officers, the ruler should proceed to institute spies.

Spies are in the guise of pseudo-student, priest, householder, trader, saint practising renunciation, classmate or colleague, desperado, poisoner and woman mendicant.

An artful person, capable of reading human nature, is a pseudo-student. Such a person should be encouraged with presents and purse and be told by the officer: "Sworn to the ruler and myself you shall inform us what wickedness you find in others."

One initiated in scripture and of pure character is a priest-spy. This spy should carry on farming, cattle culture and commerce with resources given to him. Out of the produce and profit accrued, he should encourage other priests to live with him and send them on espionage work. The other priests also should send their followers on similar errands.

A householder-spy is a farmer fallen in his profession but pure in character. This spy should do as the priest [above].

A trader-spy is a merchant in distress but generally trustworthy. This spy should carry on espionage, in addition to his profession.

A person with proper appearance and accomplishments as an ascetic is a saint-spy. He surrounds himself with followers and may settle down in the suburb of a big city and may pretend prayer and fasting in public. Trader-spies may associate with this class of spies. He may practise fortune-telling, palmistry, and pretend supernatural and magical powers by predictions. The followers will adduce proof for the predictions of their saint. He may even foretell official rewards and official changes, which the officers concerned may substantiate by reciprocating.

Rewarded by the rulers with money and titles, these five institutions of espionage should maintain the integrity of the country's officers.

Chapter 14: Administrative Councils

Deliberation in well-constituted councils precedes administrative measures. The proceedings of a council should be in camera and deliberations made top secret so that not even a bird can whisper. The ruler should be guarded against disclosure.

Whoever divulges secret deliberations should be destroyed. Such guilt can be detected by physical and attitudinal changes of ambassadors, ministers and heads.

Secrecy of proceedings in the council and guarding of officers participating in the council must be organised.

The causes of divulgence of counsels are recklessness, drink, talking in one's sleep and infatuation with women which assail councillors.

He of secretive nature or who is not regarded well will divulge council matters. Disclosure of council secrets is of advantage to persons other than the ruler and his high officers. Steps should be taken to safeguard deliberations. . . .

Chapter 20: Personal Security

The ruler should employ as his security staff only such persons as have noble and proven ancestry and are closely related to him and are well trained and loyal. No foreigners, or anonymous persons, or persons with clouded antecedents are to be employed as security staff for the ruler.

In a securely guarded chamber, the chief should supervise the ruler's food arrangements.

Special precautions are to be taken against contaminated and poisoned food. The following reveal poison: rice sending out deep blue vapour; unnaturally coloured and artificially dried-up and hard vegetables; unusually bright and dull vessels; foamy vessels; streaky soups, milk and liquor; white streaked honey; strange-tempered food; carpets and curtains stained with dark spots and threadbare; polishless and lustreless metallic vessels and gems.

The poisoner reveals himself by parched and dry mouth, hesitating talk, perspiration, tremour, yawning, evasive demeanour and nervous behaviour.

Experts in poison detection should be in attendance on the ruler. The physicians attending the ruler should satisfy themselves personally as to the purity of the drugs which they administer to the ruler. The same precaution is indicated for liquor and beverages which the ruler uses. Scrupulous cleanliness should be insisted on in persons in charge of the ruler's dress and toilet requisites. This should be ensured by seals.
. . .

In any entertainment meant for the amusement of the ruler, the actors should not use weapons, fire and poison. Musical instruments and accoutrements for horses, elephants and vehicles should be secured in the palace.

The ruler should mount beasts and vehicles only after the traditional rider or driver has done so. If he has to travel in a boat, the pilot should be trustworthy and the boat itself secured to another boat. There should be a proper convoy on land or water guarding the ruler. He should swim only in rivers which are free of larger fishes and crocodiles and hunt in forests free from snakes, man-eaters and brigands.

He should give private audience only attended by his security guards. He should receive foreign ambassadors in his full ministerial council. While reviewing his militia, the ruler should also attend in full battle uniform and be on horseback or on the back of an elephant. When he enters or exits from the capital city, the path of the ruler should be guarded by staffed officers and cleared of armed men, mendicants and the suspicious. He should attend public performances, festivals, processions or religious gatherings accompanied by trained bodyguards. The ruler should guard his own person with the same care with which he secures the safety of those around him through espionage arrangements.

Chapter 21: Building of Villages

The ruler may form villages either on new sites or on old sites, either by shifting population from heavily populated areas in his own state or by causing population to immigrate into his state.

Villages should consist of not less than a hundred and not more than five hundred families of cultivators of the service classes. The villages should extend from about one and a half miles to three miles each [in circumference] and should be capable of defending each other. Village boundaries may consist of rivers, hills, forests, hedges, caves, bridges and trees.

Each eight hundred villages should have a major fort. There should be a capital city for every four hundred villages, a market town for every two hundred villages, and an urban cluster for every ten villages.

The frontiers of the state should have fortifications protected by internal guards, manning the entrances to the state. The interior of the state should be guarded by huntsmen, armed guards, forest tribes, fierce tribes and frontier men.

Those who do social service by sacrifices, the clergy, and the intellectuals should be settled in the villages on tax-free farms.

Officers, scribes, cattlemen, guards, cattle doctors, physicians, horse-trainers and news purveyors should be given life interest in lands.

Lands fit for cultivation should be given to tenants only for life. Land prepared for cultivation by tenants should not be taken away from them.

Lands not cultivated by the landholders may be confiscated and given to cultivators. Or they may be cultivated through hired labourers or traders to avoid loss to the state. If cultivators pay their taxes promptly, they may be supplied with grains, cattle and money.

The ruler should give to cultivators only such farms and concessions as will replenish the treasury and avoid denuding it.

A denuded exchequer is a grave threat to the security of the state. Only on rare occasions like settlement of new areas or in grave emergencies should tax-remissions be granted. The ruler should be benevolent to those who have conquered the crisis by remission of taxes.

He should facilitate mining operations. He should encourage manufacturers. He should help exploitation of forest wealth. He should provide amenities for cattle breeding and commerce. He should construct highways both on land and on water. He should plan markets.

He should build dikes for water either perennial or from other sources. He should assist with resources and communications those who build reservoirs or construct works of communal comfort and public parks.

All should share in corporate work, sharing the expenditure but not claiming profit.

The ruler should have suzerainty over all fishing, transport and grain trade, reservoirs and bridges.

Those who do not recognise the rights of their servants, hirelings and relatives should be made to do so.

The ruler should maintain adolescents, the aged, the diseased and the orphans. He should also provide livelihood to deserted women with prenatal care and protection for the children born to them. . . .

The ruler should abstain from taking over any area which is open to attack by enemies and wild tribes and which is visited by frequent famines and pests. He should also abstain from extravagant sports.

He should protect cultivation from heavy taxes, slave labour and severe penalties, herds of cattle from cattle lifters, wild animals, venomous creatures and diseases.

He should clear highways of the visitation of petty officials, workmen, brigands and guards. He should not only conserve existing forests, buildings and mines, but also develop new ones.

Chapter 41: Decay, Stabilisation, and Progress of States

A state should always observe such a policy as will help it strengthen its defensive fortifications and life-lines of communications, build plantations, construct villages, and exploit the mineral and forest wealth of the country, while at the same time preventing fulfilment of similar programmes in the rival state.

Any two states hostile to each other, finding that neither has an advantage over the other in fulfilment of their respective programmes, should make peace with each other.

When any two states which are rivals expect to acquire equal possessions over the same span of time, they should keep peace with each other.

A state can indulge in armed invasion only:

Where, by invasion, it can reduce the power of an enemy without in any way reducing its own potential, by making suitable arrangements for protection of its own strategic works. . . .

Chapter 54: Restoration of Lost Balance of Power

When an invader is assailed by an alliance of his enemies, he should try to purchase the leader of the alliance with offers of gold and his own alliance and by diplomatic camouflage of the threat of treachery from the alliance of powers. He should instigate the leader of the allied enemies to break up his alliance.

The invader should also attempt to break the allied enemies' formation by setting up the leader of the alliance against the weaker of his enemies, or attempt to forge a combination of the weaker allies against their leader. He may also form a pact with the leader through intrigue, or offer of resources. When the confederation is shattered, he may form alliances with any of his former enemies.

If a state is weak in treasury or in striking power, attention should be directed to strengthen both through stabilisation of authority. Irrigational projects are a source of agricultural prosperity. Good highways should be constructed to facilitate movements of armed might and merchandise. Mines should be developed, as they supply ammunition. Forests should be conserved, as they supply material for defence, communication and vehicles. Pasture lands are the source of cattle wealth.

Thus, a state should build up its striking power through development of the exchequer, the army and wise counsel; and, till the proper time, should conduct itself as a weak power towards its neighbours, to evade conflict or envy from enemy or allied states. If the state is deficient in resources, it should acquire them from related or allied states. It should attract to itself capable men from corporations, from wild and ferocious tribes, and foreigners, and organise espionage that will damage hostile powers.

11

Caste and Moral Duty
in Classical India

The Aryan conquest of northern India, beginning around 1500 B.C., set in motion the forces that led to the creation of the fourfold system of castes on the subcontinent. During the first millennium B.C. the lines between priests, warriors, merchants, and peasants (as well as the outcastes or "untouchables") became increasingly well defined. This system was based on the military victories of the Aryan warriors, but it soon received religious sanction. Hindu priests came to insist that each caste had its own sacred or moral duty (*dharma*) to perform.

The idea of *dharma* is vividly illustrated in the most famous of all Hindu texts, the *Bhagavad Gita* (*Song of God*), which, in its present form, dates from the second century B.C. The *Gita,* as it is called, is a portion of a much larger work, the *Mahabharata,* the epic tale of a war between two branches of the same family in northern India following the Aryan conquest.

The central theme of the *Gita* is the dilemma faced by the warrior Arjuna on the eve of a great battle. Arjuna is torn between his love for his family, many of whom are on the opposing side, and his duty as a warrior to fight. Unable to go into battle, Arjuna enters into a long dialogue with the driver of his chariot, Krishna, who is actually the great Hindu deity, Vishnu. Krishna (Vishnu) urges Arjuna to fight; ultimately the warrior does so, secure in the knowledge that he is doing God's will.

The following passages from the *Gita* (in which a third character, Sanjaya, appears as the narrator) illustrate Arjuna's dilemma and the response of Krishna.

From *The Bhagavad Gita,* translated by Juan Mascaro (Baltimore, Md.: Penguin Books, 1962), pp. 45–51. Copyright ©1962 by Juan Mascaro. Reproduced by permission of Penguin Books Ltd.

Why is Arjuna reluctant to fight? Note that he gives more than one reason. What are Krishna's reasons for urging Arjuna into battle? What is Krishna's attitude toward warriors? How do these passages illustrate the importance of the caste system?

THE GITA

Chapter 1

. . .

Arjuna

21 Drive my chariot, Krishna immortal, and place it between the two armies.

22 That I may see those warriors who stand there eager for battle, with whom I must now fight at the beginning of this war.

23 That I may see those who have come here eager and ready to fight, in their desire to do the will of the evil son of Dhrita-rashtra.

Sanjaya

24 When Krishna heard the words of Arjuna he drove their glorious chariot and placed it between the two armies.

25 And facing Bhishma and Drona and other royal rulers he said: "See, Arjuna, the armies of the Kurus, gathered here on this field of battle."

26 Then Arjuna saw in both armies fathers, grandfathers,

27 sons, grandsons; fathers of wives, uncles, masters;

28 brothers, companions and friends.
   When Arjuna thus saw his kinsmen face to face in both lines of battle, he was overcome by grief and despair and thus he spoke with a sinking heart.

Arjuna

When I see all my kinsmen, Krishna, who have come here on this field of battle,

29 Life goes from my limbs and they sink, and my mouth is sear and dry; a trembling overcomes my body, and my hair shudders in horror;

30 My great bow Gandiva falls from my hands, and the skin of my flesh is burning; I am no longer able to stand, because my mind is whirling and wandering.

31 And I see forebodings of evil, Krishna. I cannot foresee

any glory if I kill my own kinsmen in the sacrifice of battle.

32 Because I have no wish for victory, Krishna, nor for a kingdom, nor for its pleasures. How can we want a kingdom, Govinda, or its pleasures or even life,

33 When those for whom we want a kingdom, and its pleasures, and the joys of life, are here in this field of battle about to give up their wealth and their life?

34 Facing us in the field of battle are teachers, fathers and sons; grandsons, grandfathers, wives' brothers; mothers' brothers and fathers of wives.

35 These I do not wish to slay, even if I myself am slain. Not even for the kingdom of the three worlds: how much less for a kingdom of the earth!

36 If we kill these evil men, evil shall fall upon us: what joy in their death could we have, O Janardana, mover of souls?

37 I cannot therefore kill my own kinsmen, the sons of king Dhrita-rashtra, the brother of my own father. What happiness could we ever enjoy, if we killed our own kinsmen in battle?

38 Even if they, with minds overcome by greed, see no evil in the destruction of a family, see no sin in the treachery to friends;

39 Shall we not, who see the evil of destruction, shall we not refrain from this terrible deed?

40 The destruction of a family destroys its rituals of righteousness, and when the righteous rituals are no more, unrighteousness overcomes the whole family.

41 When unrighteous disorder prevails, the women sin and are impure; and when women are not pure, Krishna, there is disorder of castes, social confusion.

42 This disorder carries down to hell the family and the destroyers of the family. The spirits of their dead suffer in pain when deprived of the ritual offerings.

43 Those evil deeds of the destroyers of a family, which cause this social disorder, destroy the righteousness of birth and the ancestral rituals of righteousness.

44 And have we not heard that hell is waiting for those whose familiar rituals of righteousness are no more?

45 O day of darkness! What evil spirit moved our minds when for the sake of an earthly kingdom we came to this field of battle ready to kill our own people?

46 Better for me indeed if the sons of Dhrita-rashtra, with arms in hand, found me unarmed, unresisting, and killed me in the struggle of war.

Sanjaya

47 Thus spoke Arjuna in the field of battle, and letting fall
his bow and arrows he sank down in his chariot, his soul
overcome by despair and grief.

Chapter 2

Sanjaya

1 Then arose the Spirit of Krishna and spoke to Arjuna, his
friend, who with eyes filled with tears, thus had sunk into
despair and grief.

Krishna

2 Whence this lifeless dejection, Arjuna, in this hour, the
hour of trial? Strong men know not despair, Arjuna, for
this wins neither heaven nor earth.

3 Fall not into degrading weakness, for this becomes not a
man who is a man. Throw off this ignoble discourage-
ment, and arise like a fire that burns all before it.

Arjuna

4 I owe veneration to Bhishma and Drona. Shall I kill with
my arrows my grandfather's brother, great Bhishma?
Shall my arrows in battle slay Drona, my teacher?

5 Shall I kill my own masters who, though greedy of my
kingdom, are yet my sacred teachers? I would rather eat
in this life the food of a beggar than eat royal food tasting
of their blood.

6 And we know not whether their victory or ours be better
for us. The sons of my uncle and king, Dhrita-rashtra,
are here before us: after their death, should we wish
to live?

7 In the dark night of my soul I feel desolation. In my self-
pity I see not the way of righteousness. I am thy disciple,
come to thee in supplication: be a light unto me on the
path of my duty.

8 For neither the kingdom of the earth, nor the kingdom of
the gods in heaven, could give me peace from the fire of
sorrow which thus burns my life.

Sanjaya

9 When Arjuna the great warrior had thus unburdened his
heart, "I will not fight, Krishna," he said, and then fell
silent.

10 Krishna smiled and spoke to Arjuna—there between the
two armies the voice of God spoke these words:

Krishna

11 Thy tears are for those beyond tears; and are thy words
words of wisdom? The wise grieve not for those who
live; and they grieve not for those who die—for life and
death shall pass away.

12 Because we all have been for all time: I, and thou, and
those kings of men. And we all shall be for all time, we
all for ever and ever.

13 As the Spirit of our mortal body wanders on in childhood,
and youth and old age, the Spirit wanders on to a new
body: of this the sage has no doubts.

14 From the world of the senses, Arjuna, comes heat and
comes cold, and pleasure and pain. They come and they
go: they are transient. Arise above them, strong soul.

15 The man whom these cannot move, whose soul is one,
beyond pleasure and pain, is worthy of life in Eternity.

16 The unreal never is: the Real never is not. This truth
indeed has been seen by those who can see the true.

17 Interwoven in his creation, the Spirit is beyond destruction. No one can bring to an end the Spirit which is everlasting.

18 For beyond time he dwells in these bodies, though these
bodies have an end in their time; but he remains immea-
surable, immortal. Therefore, great warrior, carry on thy
fight.

19 If any man thinks he slays, and if another thinks he is
slain, neither knows the ways of truth. The Eternal in
man cannot kill: the Eternal in man cannot die.

20 He is never born, and he never dies. He is in Eternity: he
is for evermore. Never-born and eternal, beyond times
gone or to come, he does not die when the body dies.

21 When a man knows him as never-born, everlasting, never-
changing, beyond all destruction, how can that man kill
a man, or cause another to kill?

22 As a man leaves an old garment and puts on one that is
new, the Spirit leaves his mortal body and then puts on
one that is new.

23 Weapons cannot hurt the Spirit and fire can never burn
him. Untouched is he by drenching waters, untouched
is he by parching winds.

24 Beyond the power of sword and fire, beyond the power
of waters and winds, the Spirit is everlasting, omnipresent, never-changing, never-moving, ever One.

25 Invisible is he to mortal eyes, beyond thought and beyond change. Know that he is, and cease from sorrow.

26 But if he were born again and again, and again and again he were to die, even then, victorious man, cease thou from sorrow.

27 For all things born in truth must die, and out of death in truth comes life. Face to face with what must be, cease thou from sorrow.

28 Invisible before birth are all beings and after death invisible again. They are seen between two unseens. Why in this truth find sorrow?

29 One sees him in a vision of wonder, and another gives us words of his wonder. There is one who hears of his wonder; but he hears and knows him not.

30 The Spirit that is in all beings is immortal in them all: for the death of what cannot die, cease thou to sorrow.

31 Think thou also of thy duty and do not waver. There is no greater good for a warrior than to fight in a righteous war.

32 There is a war that opens the doors of heaven, Arjuna! Happy the warriors whose fate is to fight such war.

33 But to forgo this fight for righteousness is to forgo thy duty and honour: is to fall into transgression.

34 Men will tell of thy dishonour both now and in times to come. And to a man who is in honour, dishonour is more than death.

35 The great warriors will say that thou hast run from the battle through fear; and those who thought great things of thee will speak of thee in scorn.

36 And thine enemies will speak of thee in contemptuous words of ill-will and derision, pouring scorn upon thy courage. Can there be for a warrior a more shameful fate?

37 In death thy glory in heaven, in victory thy glory on earth. Arise therefore, Arjuna, with thy soul ready to fight. . . .

12

Gender Relations in Classical India: Two Hindu Tales

Classical India, like the other civilizations of Eurasia, had a strongly patriarchal social order. The *Laws of Manu,* a law code composed between the first century B.C. and the third century A.D., clearly indicates the extent to which the male domination of females was the ideal on the subcontinent: "A father protects a woman in her youth, her husband in her middle years, and her son in old age; a woman is never fit for independence" (*Manu* 9:3). "If a wife is obedient to her husband, that alone will assure her birth in heaven" (*Manu* 5:155).

Did these patriarchal ideals prevail in gender relations among ordinary people? Unfortunately, the evidence that would enable historians to answer this question with confidence is not easy to find. Commoners, mainly preliterate peasants, did not leave diaries and letters for later scholars to examine. Thus we must turn to evidence that is often only indirect and suggestive rather than conclusive. One interesting possibility is folktales, the popular stories passed from generation to generation by both elites and commoners. Two examples follow, both dating from the same period as the *Laws of Manu.* "The Carpenter's Wife" comes from the *Panchatantra,* a famous collection of Indian fables. "Savatri and the God of Death" is from the great Indian epic, the *Mahabharata,* and has been popular since classical times.

Does the image of women in these stories mesh with what one would expect to find in a society that produced the *Laws of Manu?* In what ways do the carpenter's wife and Savatri differ from one another? Based on your reading of these

From Roy C. Amore and Larry D. Shinn, *Lustful Maidens and Ascetic Kings: Buddhist and Hindu Stories of Life* (New York: Oxford University Press, 1981), pp. 27–30, 32–33. Copyright © 1981 by Oxford University Press. Reprinted by permission.

stories, what can you conclude (however tentatively) about gender relations in classical India? How do they compare with classical China? (See selection 8.)

THE CARPENTER'S WIFE

In a small town there was a carpenter whose lovely wife was as unfaithful as the carpenter's friends and family reported. In order to determine the truth of these rumors, the carpenter said to his wife one day, "My dear, there is a palace to be constructed in a distant city and I must go there to work. I will leave tomorrow and will spend a number of days there. Please make some food for my journey." The carpenter's wife joyfully prepared the provisions her husband requested. Early in the morning while it was still dark, the carpenter took his knapsack of provisions and said to his wife, "I am going, my dear, please lock the door." Instead of leaving, the carpenter circled his house, came in the back door and situated himself and his apprentice under his own bed.

The carpenter's wife was overjoyed at the thought that she could meet her paramour with no fear of being caught by her husband. She quickly summoned her lover through a close friend and the lovers ate and drank a meal together as though they were children freed from parental guidance. When they climbed into bed the wife's foot brushed against her husband's knee as he lay coiled up under the bed. Terrified, the wife thought, "Without a doubt, that must be my husband! What can I do?" Just then her lover asked, "Tell me dear, whom do you love more, me or your husband?"

The quick-witted wife responded, "What a silly question to ask. As you know, we women are accused of being immoral creatures who resort to all kinds of activities to satisfy our natural longings. In fact, some men would claim that we women would eat cow dung if we did not have noses to smell. But I would die on the spot if I should hear of any harm coming to my dear husband."

The carpenter was deceived by the lying words of his shameless wife, and he said to his apprentice, "Long live my beloved and fully devoted wife! I will praise her before all the people of the town." As he spoke, the carpenter rose up with the bed on his back, bearing his wife and her lover through the streets of the town proclaiming his wife to be devoted and honorable. And all of the people of the town laughed at the foolish carpenter.

SAVATRI AND THE GOD OF DEATH

Ashvapati, the virtuous king of Madras, grew old without offspring to continue his royal family. Desiring a son, Ashvapati took rigid vows and observed long fasts to accumulate merit. It is said that he offered 10,000 oblations to the goddess Savatri in hopes of having a son. After eighteen years of constant devotion, Ashvapati was granted his wish for an offspring even though the baby born was a girl.

The king rejoiced at his good fortune and named the child Savatri in honor of the goddess who gave him this joy to brighten his elder years.

Savatri was both a beautiful and an intelligent child. She was her father's delight and grew in wisdom and beauty as the years passed. As the age approached for Savatri to be given in marriage as custom demanded, no suitor came forward to ask her father for her hand—so awed were all the princes by the beauty and intellect of this unusual maiden. Her father became concerned lest he not fulfill his duty as father and incur disgrace for his failure to provide a suitable husband for his daughter. At last, he instructed Savatri herself to lead a procession throughout the surrounding kingdoms and handpick a man suitable for her.

Savatri returned from her search and told her father that she had found the perfect man. Though he was poor and an ascetic of the woods, he was handsome, well educated, and of kind temperament. His name was Satyavan and he was actually a prince whose blind father had been displaced by an evil king. Ashvapati asked the venerable sage Narada whether Satyavan would be a suitable spouse for Savatri. Narada responded that there was no one in the world more worthy than Satyavan. However, Narada continued, Satyavan had one unavoidable flaw. He was fated to live a short life and would die exactly one year from that very day. Ashvapati then tried to dissuade Savatri from marrying Satyavan by telling her of the impending death of her loved one. Savatri held firm to her choice, and the king and Narada both gave their blessings to this seemingly ill-fated bond.

After the marriage procession had retreated from the forest hermitage of Savatri's new father-in-law, Dyumatsena, the bride removed her wedding sari and donned the ocher robe and bark garments of her ascetic family. As the days and weeks passed, Savatri busied herself by waiting upon the every need of her new family. She served her husband, Satyavan, cheerfully and skillfully. Satyavan responded with an even-tempered love which enhanced the bond of devotion between Savatri and himself. Yet the dark cloud of Narada's prophecy cast a shadow over this otherwise blissful life.

When the fateful time approached, Savatri began a fast to strengthen her wifely resolve as she kept nightly vigils while her husband slept. The day marked for the death of Satyavan began as any other day at the hermitage. Satyavan shouldered his axe and was about to set off to cut wood for the day's fires when Savatri stopped him to ask if she could go along saying, "I cannot bear to be separated from you today." Satyavan responded, "You've never come into the forest before and the paths are rough and the way very difficult. Besides, you've been fasting and are surely weak." Savatri persisted, and Satyavan finally agreed to take her along. Savatri went to her parents-in-law to get their permission saying she wanted to see the spring blossoms which now covered the forest. They too expressed concern over her health but finally relented out of consideration for her long period of gracious service to them.

Together Satyavan and Savatri entered the tangled woods enjoying the beauty of the flowers and animals which betoken spring in the forest. Coming to a fallen tree, Satyavan began chopping firewood. As he worked, he began to perspire heavily and to grow weak. Finally, he had to stop and lie down telling Savatri to wake him after a short nap. With dread in her heart, Savatri took Satyavan's head in her lap and kept a vigil knowing Satyavan's condition to be more serious than rest could assuage. In a short time, Savatri saw approaching a huge figure clad in red and carrying a small noose. Placing Satyavan's head upon the ground, Savatri arose and asked the stranger of his mission. The lord of death replied, "I am Yama and your husband's days are finished. I speak to you, a mortal, only because of your extreme merit. I have come personally instead of sending my emissaries because of your husband's righteous life."

Without a further word, Yama then pulled Satyavan's soul out of his body with the small noose he was carrying. The lord of death then set off immediately for the realm of the dead in the south. Grief stricken and yet filled with wifely devotion, Savatri followed Yama at a distance. Hours passed yet hunger and weariness could not slow Savatri's footsteps. She persisted through thorny paths and rocky slopes to follow Yama and his precious burden. As Yama walked south he thought he heard a woman's anklets tingling on the path behind him. He turned around to see Savatri in the distance following without pause. He called out to her to return to Satyavan's body and to perform her wifely duties of cremating the dead. Savatri approached Yama and responded, "It is said that those who walk seven steps together are friends. Certainly we have traveled farther than that together. Why should I return to a dead body when you possess the soul of my husband?"

Yama was impressed by the courage and wisdom of this beautiful young woman. He replied, "Please stop following me. Your wise words and persistent devotion for your husband deserve a boon. Ask of me anything except that your husband's life be restored, and I will grant it." Savatri asked that her blind father-in-law be granted new sight. Yama said that her wish would be granted, and then he turned to leave only to find that Savatri was about to continue following. Yama again praised her devotion and offered a second, and then a third boon. Savatri told Yama of the misfortune of her father-in-law's lost kingdom and asked that Yama assist in ousting the evil king from Dyumatsena's throne. Yama agreed. Then Savatri utilized her third boon to ask that her own father be given one hundred sons to protect his royal line, and that too was granted by Yama.

Yama then set off in a southerly direction only to discover after a short while that Savatri still relentlessly followed him. Yama was amazed at the thoroughly self-giving attitude displayed by Savatri and agreed to grant one last boon if Savatri would promise to return home. Yama again stipulated that the bereaved wife could not ask for her husband's soul. Savatri agreed to the two conditions and said, "I only ask for myself one thing, and that is that I may be granted one hundred sons to continue Satyavan's royal family." Yama agreed only to realize, upon prompting from Savatri, that the only way Satyavan's line could be continued would be for him to be restored to life. Although he had been tricked by the wise and thoughtful Savatri, Yama laughed heartily and said, "So be it! Auspicious and chaste lady, your husband's soul is freed by me." Loosening his noose Yama permitted the soul of Satyavan to return to its earthly abode and Savatri ran without stopping back to the place where Satyavan had fallen asleep. Just as Savatri arrived at the place where her husband lay, he awoke saying, "Oh, I have slept into the night, why did you not waken me?"

13

The Greek Political Tradition

As with all the classical civilizations, the culture that developed along Europe's Mediterranean shores produced important political institutions and principles. The key political form, in Greece and later in republican Rome, was the city-state. Within its bounds, the portion of the population with political rights was supposed to participate actively in the affairs of state, to which they owed loyalty and service. Within this context, however, a variety of political structures arose. Some evolved toward democracy (though with many residents excluded from rights). In this Athens led the way, providing not only participant assemblies, but also considerable support for individual freedom and legal rights. Other Greek city-states, however, stressed the power of government. Sparta, which would finally clash with Athens in the Peloponnesian War, set up a rigid militaristic regime designed to transform each male or female citizen into an absolute servant of the government. When Athens and Sparta warred at the end of the fifth century, the conflict involved not only power, but also two clashing views of political life.

The Spartan system, described in the first selection, was set up by the lawmaker Lycurgus after 650 B.C., in large part to keep a vast slave population under control. The description comes from the writings of Plutarch [ca. A.D. 45–125], in a biography of Lycurgus. The contrasting Athenian ideal was articulated by its great leader Pericles during the fifth century B.C., in the early stages of the Peloponnesian War, as part of a famous funeral oration that appears in the history of Thucydides.

Selection I from Plutarch, *The Library of Original Sources: II: The Greek World*, Oliver J. Thatcher, ed. (University Research Extension Co., Milwaukee, Wis., n.d.), pp. 118–19, 122, 128. Selection II from Thucydides, *History of the Peloponnesian War* (London, 1896), Book 2, translated by Richard Crawley.

The two selections thus allow a clear comparison between the ideals of the two city-states. It is important to realize that most articulate Greeks (including both Thucydides and Plutarch) preferred Spartan values; why might this be so? Are there any shared features beneath the obvious contrasts of Athens and Sparta? What resulted, in classical Greece itself and in the later Greek heritage, from such sharply differentiated systems within a common culture?

I. SPARTA

In order to [promote] the good education of their youth (which . . . he thought the most important and noblest work of a lawgiver), he went so far back as to take into consideration their very conception and birth, by regulating their marriages. For Aristotle is wrong in saying, that, after he had tried all ways to reduce the women to more modesty and sobriety, he was at last forced to leave them as they were, because that, in the absence of their husbands, who spent the best part of their lives in the wars, their wives, whom they were obliged to leave absolute mistresses at home, took great liberties and assumed the superiority; and were treated with overmuch respect and called by the title of lady or queen. The truth is, he took in their case, also, all the care that was possible; he ordered the maidens to exercise themselves with wrestling, running, throwing the quoit, and casting the dart, to the end that the fruit they conceived might, in strong and healthy bodies, take firmer root and find better growth, and withal that they, with this greater vigor, might be the more able to undergo the pains of child-bearing. And to the end he might take away their overgreat tenderness and fear of exposure to the air, and all acquired womanishness, he ordered that the young women should go naked in the processions, as well as the young men, and dance, too, in that condition, at certain solemn feasts, singing certain songs, whilst the young men stood around, seeing and hearing them. On these occasions, they now and then made, by jests, a befitting reflection upon those who had misbehaved themselves in the wars; and again sang encomiums upon those who had done any gallant action, and by these means inspired the younger sort with an emulation of their glory. Those that were thus commended went away proud, elated, and gratified with their honor among the maidens; and those who were rallied were as sensibly touched with it as if they had been formally reprimanded; and so much the more, because the kings and the elders, as well as the rest of the city, saw and heard all that passed. Nor was there anything shameful in this nakedness of the young women; modesty attended them, and all wantonness was excluded. It taught them simplicity and a care for good health, and gave them some taste of higher feelings, admitted as they thus were to the field of noble action and glory. Hence it was natural for them to think and speak as Gorgo, for example, the wife of Leonidas, is said to have done, when some foreign lady, as it would seem, told her that the women of Lacedæmon were the only women of the world who could rule men; "With good reason," she said, "for we are the only women who bring forth men."

These public processions of the maidens, and their appearing naked in their exercises and dancings, were incitements to marriage, operating upon the young with the rigor and certainty, as Plato says, of love, if not of mathematics. But besides all this, to promote it yet more effectually, those who continued bachelors were in a degree disfranchised by law; for they were excluded from the sight of those public processions in which the young men and maidens danced naked, and, in winter-time, the officers compelled them to march naked themselves round the market-place, singing as they went a certain song to their own disgrace, that they justly suffered this punishment for disobeying the laws. Moreover, they were denied that respect and observance which the younger men paid their elders; and no man, for example, found fault with what was said to Dercyllidas, though so eminent a commander; upon whose approach one day, a young man, instead of rising, retained his seat, remarking, "No child of yours will make room for me." . . .

Nor was it lawful, indeed, for the father himself to breed up the children after his own fancy; but as soon as they were seven years old, they were to be enrolled in certain companies and classes, where they all lived under the same order and discipline, doing their exercises and taking their play together. Of these, he who showed the most conduct and courage was made captain; they had their eyes always upon him, obeyed his orders, and underwent patiently whatsoever punishment he inflicted; so that the whole course of their education was one continued exercise of a ready and perfect obedience. The old men, too, were spectators of their performances, and often raised quarrels and disputes among them, to have a good opportunity of finding out their different characters, and of seeing which would be valiant, which a coward, when they should come to more dangerous encounters. Reading and writing they gave them, just enough to serve their turn; their chief care was to make them good subjects, and to teach them to endure pain and conquer in battle. To this end, as they grew in years, their discipline was proportionately increased; their heads were close-clipped, they were accustomed to go bare-foot, and for the most part to play naked.

After they were twelve years old, they were no longer allowed to wear any under-garment; they had one coat to serve them a year; their bodies were hard and dry, with but little acquaintance of baths and unguents; these human indulgences they were allowed only on some few particular days in the year. They lodged together in little bands upon beds made of the rushes which grew by the banks of the river Eurotas, which they were to break off with their hands without a knife; if it were winter, they mingled some thistle-down with their rushes, which it was thought had the property of giving warmth. By the time they were come to this age, there was not any of the more hopeful boys who had not a lover to bear him company. The old men, too, had an eye upon them, coming often to the grounds to hear and see them contend either in wit or strength with one another, and this as seriously and with as much concern as if they were their fathers, their tutors, or their magistrates; so that there scarcely was any time or place without some one present to put them in mind of their duty, and punish them if they had neglected it. . . .

Their discipline continued still after they were full-grown men. No one was allowed to live after his own fancy; but the city was a sort of camp, in which every man had his share of provisions and business set out, and looked upon himself not so much born to serve his own ends as the interest of his country. Therefore, if they were commanded nothing else, they went to see the boys perform their exercises, to teach them something useful, or to learn it themselves of those who knew better. And, indeed, one of the greatest and highest blessings Lycurgus procured his people was the abundance of leisure, which proceeded from his forbidding to them the exercise of any mean and mechanical trade. Of the money-making that depends on troublesome going about and seeing people and doing business, they had no need at all in a state where wealth obtained no honor or respect. The Helots tilled their ground for them, and paid them yearly in kind the appointed quantity, without any trouble of theirs. To this purpose there goes a story of a Lacedæmonian who, happening to be at Athens when the courts were sitting, was told of a citizen that had been fined for living an idle life, and was being escorted home in much distress of mind by his condoling friends; the Lacedæmonian was much surprised at it, and desired his friend to show him the man who was condemned for living like a freeman. So much beneath them did they esteem the frivolous devotion of time and attention to the mechanical arts and to money-making.

II. PERICLEAN ATHENS

Our constitution does not copy the laws of neighbouring states; we are rather a pattern to others than imitators ourselves. Its administration favours the many instead of the few; this is why it is called a democracy. If we look to the laws, they afford equal justice to all in their private differences; if to social standing, advancement in public life falls to reputation for capacity, class considerations not being allowed to interfere with merit; nor again does poverty bar the way, if a man is able to serve the state, he is not hindered by the obscurity of his condition. The freedom which we enjoy in our government extends also to our ordinary life. There, far from exercising a jealous sur-veillance over each other, we do not feel called upon to be angry with our neighbour for doing what he likes, or even to indulge in those injurious looks which cannot fail to be offensive, although they inflict no positive penalty. But all this ease in our private relations does not make us lawless as citizens. Against this fear is our chief safeguard, teaching us to obey the magistrates and the laws, particularly such as regard the pro-tection of the injured, whether they are actually on the statute book, or belong to that code which, although unwritten, yet cannot be broken without acknowledged disgrace.

Further, we provide plenty of means for the mind to refresh itself from business. We celebrate games and sacrifices all the year round, and the elegance of our private establishments forms a daily source of pleasure and helps to banish the spleen; while the magnitude of our city draws the produce of the world into our harbour, so that to the Athenian the fruits of other countries are as familiar a luxury as those of his own.

If we turn to our military policy, there also we differ from our antagonists. We throw open our city to the world, and never by alien acts exclude foreigners from any opportunity of learning or observing, although the eyes of an enemy may occasionally profit by our liberality; trusting less in system and policy than to the native spirit of our citizens; while in education, where our rivals from their very cradles by a painful discipline seek after manliness, at Athens we live exactly as we please, and yet are just as ready to encounter every legitimate danger. In proof of this it may be noticed that the Lacedæmonians do not invade our country alone, but bring with them all their confederates; while we Athenians advance unsupported into the territory of a neighbour, and fighting upon a foreign soil usually vanquish with ease men who are defending their homes. Our united force was never yet encountered by an enemy, because we have at once to attend to our marine and to despatch our citizens by land upon a hundred different services; so that, wherever they engage with some such fraction of our strength, a success against a detachment is magnified into a victory over the nation, and a defeat into a reverse suffered at the hands of our entire people. And yet if with habits not of labour but of ease, and courage not of art but of nature, we are still willing to encounter danger, we have the double advantage of escaping the experience of hardships in anticipation and of facing them in the hour of need as fearlessly as those who are never free from them.

Nor are these the only points in which our city is worthy of admiration. We cultivate refinement without extravagance and knowledge without effeminacy; wealth we employ more for use than for show, and place the real disgrace of poverty not in owning to the fact but in declining the struggle against it. Our public men have, besides politics, their private affairs to attend to, and our ordinary citizens, though occupied with the pursuits of industry, are still fair judges of public matters; for, unlike any other nation, regarding him who takes no part in these duties not as unambitious but as useless, we Athenians are able to judge at all events if we cannot originate, and instead of looking on discussion as a stumbling-block in the way of action, we think it an indispensable preliminary to any wise action at all. Again, in our enterprises we present the singular spectacle of daring and deliberation, each carried to its highest point, and both united in the same persons; although usually decision is the fruit of ignorance, hesitation of reflexion. But the palm of courage will surely be adjudged most justly to those who best know the difference between hardship and pleasure and yet are never tempted to shrink from danger. In generosity we are equally singular, acquiring our friends by conferring not by receiving favours. Yet, of course, the doer of the favour is the firmer friend of the two, in order by continued kindness to keep the recipient in his debt; while the debtor feels less keenly from the very consciousness that the return he makes will be a payment, not a free gift. And it is only the Athenians who, fearless of consequences, confer their benefits not from calculations of expediency, but in the confidence of liberality.

In short, I say that as a city we are the school of Hellas; while I doubt if the world can produce a man, who where he has only himself to depend upon, is equal to so many emergencies, and graced by so happy a versatility as the Athenian. And that this is no mere boast thrown out for the occasion, but plain matter of fact, the power of the state acquired by these habits proves. For Athens alone of her contemporaries is found when tested to be greater than her reputation, and alone gives no occasion to her assailants to blush at the antagonist by whom they have been worsted, or to her subjects to question her title by merit to rule. Rather, the admiration of the present and succeeding ages will be ours, since we have not left our power without witness, but have shown it by mighty proofs; and far from needing a Homer for our panegyrist, or others of his craft whose verses might charm for the moment only for the impression they gave to melt at the touch of fact, we have forced every sea and land to be the highway of our daring, and everywhere, whether for evil or for good, have left imperishable monuments behind us. Such is the Athens for which these men, in the assertion of their resolve not to lose her, nobly fought and died; and well may every one of their survivors be ready to suffer in her cause.

14

Greek Science

One of the leading features of Greek culture, and of the later Hellenistic world in the Middle East and North Africa, was the attempt to explain the physical world in purely rational terms. Greek science, which brought dramatic progress in the fields of medicine, physics, astronomy, and mathematics, required a strict methodology based on logic, which could extend empirical data gained from observation into more general laws about nature's workings. More than Asian scientists of the classical period and later, the Greeks insisted on generalizing. More than modern scientific practitioners, they favored the deductive approach over the inductive. They often made use of insufficient observational data and testing.

Greek and Hellenistic science built on the work of many outstanding figures, but it was most deeply indebted to Aristotle (383–322 B.C.), who formulated logic into a discipline while gathering and categorizing a host of observations about nature.

The following selections from Aristotle's *Nicomachean Ethics* and the *De Caelo* provide Aristotle's definition of pure science and illustrate his scientific approach through arguments about the shape and size of the earth. Like most Hellenes, Aristotle accepted the notion that the spherical earth was the stationary center of the universe and that all the planets and stars moved uniformly in perfect circles around it. His errors here were accepted in Western science until the sixteenth century, so powerful was the example of Greek thought. But while

Selection I from Aristotle, *Nicomachean Ethics,* translated by Martin Ostwald (New York: Bobbs-Merrill, 1962), pp. 154–55. Copyright 1962, The Bobbs-Merrill Company. Reprinted by permission. Selection II from *A Source Book in Greek Science,* Morris R. Cohen and I. E. Drabkin, eds. (New York: McGraw-Hill, 1948), pp. 143–48. Copyright © 1948, The McGraw-Hill Book Company. Reprinted by permission.

Aristotle's facts were wrong, his argument was exceedingly important, for it showed the power of the rationalist concept; this too would be a heritage for later centuries. How does Aristotle "prove" his scientific beliefs? What view of the relationship between the human mind and physical nature does his method suggest?

I. NICOMACHEAN ETHICS

Since pure science or scientific knowledge is a basic conviction concerning universal and necessary truths, and since everything demonstrable and all pure science begins from fundamental principles (for science proceeds rationally), the fundamental principle or starting point for scientific knowledge cannot itself be the object either of science, of art, or of practical wisdom. For what is known scientifically is demonstrable, whereas art and practical wisdom are concerned with things that can be other than they are. Nor are these fundamental principles the objects of theoretical wisdom: for it is the task of a man of theoretical wisdom to have a demonstration for certain truths. Now, if scientific knowledge, practical wisdom, theoretical wisdom, and intelligence are the faculties by which we attain truth and by which we are never deceived both in matters which can and in those matters which cannot be other than they are; and if three of these — I am referring to practical wisdom, scientific knowledge, and theoretical wisdom — cannot be the faculty in question, we are left with the conclusion that it is intelligence that apprehends fundamental principles.

II. *DE CAELO*

There are similar disputes about the *shape* of the earth. Some think it is spherical, others that it is flat and drum-shaped. For evidence they bring the fact that, as the sun rises and sets, the part concealed by the earth shows a straight and not a curved edge, whereas if the earth were spherical the line of section would have to be circular. In this they leave out of account the great distance of the sun from the earth and the great size of the circumference, which, seen from a distance on these apparently small circles, appears straight. Such an appearance ought not to make them doubt the circular shape of the earth. But they have another argument. They say that because it is at rest, the earth must necessarily have this shape. For there are many differnt ways in which the movement or rest of the earth has been conceived.

The difficulty must have occurred to every one. It would indeed be a complacent mind that felt no surprise that, while a little bit of earth, let loose in mid-air, moves and will not stay still, and the more there is of it the faster it moves, the whole earth, free in mid-air, should show no movement at all. Yet here is this great weight of earth and it is at rest. And again, from beneath one of these moving fragments of earth, before it falls, take away the earth, and it will continue its downward movement with nothing to stop it. The difficulty then, has naturally passed into a commonplace of philosophy; and one may well wonder that the solutions offered are not seen to involve greater absurdities than the problem itself.

By these considerations some have been led to assert that the earth below us is infinite, saying, with Xenophanes of Colophon, that it has "pushed its roots to infinity" in order to save the trouble of seeking for the cause. Hence the sharp rebuke of Empedocles, in the words "if the deeps of the earth are endless and endless the ample ether — such is the vain tale told by many a tongue, poured from the mouths of those who have seen but little of the whole." Others say that the earth rests upon water. This, indeed, is the oldest theory that has been preserved and is attributed to Thales of Miletus. It was supposed to stay still because it floated like wood and other similar substances, which are so constituted as to rest upon water but not upon air. As if the same account had not to be given of the water which carries the earth as of the earth itself! It is not the nature of water, any more than of earth, to stay in mid-air: it must have something to rest upon. Again, as air is lighter than water, so is water than earth: how then can they think that the naturally lighter substance lies below the heavier? Again, if the earth as a whole is capable of floating upon water, that must obviously be the case with any part of it. But observation shows that this is not the case. Any piece of earth goes to the bottom, the quicker the larger it is. These thinkers seem to push their inquiries some way into the problem, but not so far as they might. It is what we are all inclined to do, to direct our inquiry not by the matter itself, but by the views of our opponents: and even when interrogating oneself one pushes the inquiry only to the point at which one can no longer offer any opposition. Hence a good inquirer will be one who is [as] ready in bringing forward the objections proper to the genus, . . . [as] he will be when he has gained an understanding of all the differences.

Anaximenes and Anaxagoras and Democritus give the flatness of the earth as the cause of its staying still. Thus, they say, it does not cut, but covers like a lid, the air beneath it. This seems to be the way of flat-shaped bodies: for even the wind can scarcely move them because of their power of resistance. The same immobility, they say, is produced by the flatness of the surface which the earth presents to the air which underlies it; while the air, not having room enough to change its place because it is underneath the earth, stays there in a mass, like the water in the case of the water-clock. And they adduce an amount of evidence to prove that air, when cut off and at rest, can bear a considerable weight. . . .

Let us first decide the question whether the earth moves or is at rest. For, as we said, there are some who make it one of the stars, and others who, setting it at the centre, suppose it to be "rolled" and in motion about the pole as axis. That both views are untenable will be clear if we take as our starting-point the fact that the earth's motion, whether the earth be at the centre or away from it, must needs be a constrained motion. It cannot be the movement of the earth itself. If it were, any portion of it would have this movement; but in fact every part moves in a straight line to the centre. Being, then, constrained and unnatural, the movement could not be eternal. But the order of the universe is eternal. Again, everything that moves with the circular movement, except the first sphere, is observed to be passed, and to move with more than one motion. The earth, then, also, whether it move about the centre or as stationary at it, must necessarily move with two motions. But if this were so, there would have to be passings and turnings of the fixed stars. Yet no such thing is observed. The same stars always rise and set in the same parts of the earth.

Further, the natural movement of the earth, part and whole alike, is to the centre of the whole — whence the fact that it is now actually situated at the centre — but it might be questioned, since both centres are the same, which centre it is that portions of earth and other heavy things move to. Is this their goal because it is the centre of the earth or because it is the centre of the whole? The goal, surely, must be the centre of the whole. For fire and other light things move to the extremity of the area which contains the centre. It happens, however, that the centre of the earth and of the whole is the same. Thus they do move to the centre of the earth, but accidentally, in virtue of the fact that the earth's centre lies at the centre of the whole. That the centre of the earth is the goal of their movement is indicated by the fact that heavy bodies moving towards the earth do not move parallel but so as to make equal angles, and thus to a single centre, that of the earth. It is clear, then, that the earth must be at the centre and immovable, not only for the reasons already given, but also because heavy bodies forcibly thrown quite straight upward return to the point from which they started, even if they are thrown to an infinite distance. From these considerations then it is clear that the earth does not move and does not lie elsewhere than at the centre.

From what we have said the explanation of the earth's immobility is also apparent. If it is the nature of earth, as observation shows, to move from any point to the centre, as of fire contrariwise to move from the centre to the extremity, it is impossible that any portion of earth should move away from the centre except by constraint. For a single thing has a single movement, and a simple thing a simple: contrary movements cannot belong to the same thing, and movement away from the centre is the contrary of movement to it. If then no portion of earth can move away from the centre, obviously still less can the earth as a whole so move. For it is the nature of the whole to move to the point to which the part naturally moves. Since, then, it would require a force greater than itself to move it, it must needs stay at the centre. This view is further supported by the contributions of mathematicians to astronomy, since the observations made as the shapes change, by which the order of the stars is determined, are fully accounted for on the hypothesis that the earth lies at the centre. Of the position of the earth and of the manner of its rest or movement, our discussion may here end.

Its shape must necessarily be spherical. For every portion of earth has weight until it reaches the centre, and the jostling of parts greater and smaller would bring about not a waved surface, but rather compression and convergence of part and part until the centre is reached. The process should be conceived by supposing the earth to come into being in the way that some of the natural philosophers describe. Only they attribute the downward movement to constraint, and it is better to keep to the truth and say that the reason of this motion is that a thing which possesses weight is naturally endowed with a centripetal movement. When the mixture, then, was merely potential, the things that were separated off moved similarly from every side towards the centre. Whether the parts which came together at the centre were distributed at the extremities evenly, or in some other way, makes no difference. If, on the one hand, there were a similar movement from each quarter of the extremity to the single centre, it is obvious that the resulting mass would be similar on every side. For if an equal amount is added on every side the extremity of the mass will be everywhere equidistant from its centre, i.e., the figure will be spherical. But neither will it in any way affect the argument if there is not a similar accession of concurrent fragments from every side. For the greater quantity, finding a lesser in front of it, must necessarily drive it on, both having an impulse whose goal is the centre, and the greater weight driving the lesser forward till this goal is reached. In this we have also the solution of a possible difficulty. The earth, it might be argued, is at the centre and spherical in shape: if, then, a weight many times that of the earth were added to one hemisphere, the centre of the earth and of the whole will no longer be coincident. So that either the earth will not stay still at the centre, or if it does, it will be at rest without having its centre at the place to which it is still its nature to move. Such is the difficulty. A short consideration will give us an easy answer, if we first give precision to our postulate that any body endowed with weight, of whatever size, moves towards the centre. Clearly it will not stop when its edge touches the centre. The greater quantity must prevail until the body's centre occupies the centre. For that is the goal of its impulse. Now it makes no difference whether we apply this to a clod or common fragment of earth or to the earth as a whole. The fact indicated does not depend upon degrees of size but applies universally to everything that has the centripetal impulse. Therefore earth in motion, whether in a mass or in fragments, necessarily continues to move until it occupies the centre equally in every way, the less being forced to equalize itself by the greater owing to the forward drive of the impulse.

If the earth was generated, then, it must have been formed in this way, and so clearly its generation was spherical; and if it is ungenerated and has remained so always, its character must be that which the initial generation, if it had occurred, would have given it. But the spherical shape, necessitated by this argument, follows also from the fact that the motions of heavy bodies always make equal angles and are not parallel. This would be the natural form of movement towards what is naturally spherical. Either then the earth is spherical or it is at least naturally spherical. And it is right to call anything that which nature intends it to be, and which belongs to it, rather than that which it is by constraint and contrary to nature. The evidence of the senses further corroborates this. How else would eclipses of the moon show segments shaped as we see them? As it is, the shapes which the moon itself each month shows are of every kind — straight, gibbous, and concave — but in eclipses the outline is always curved: and, since it is the interposition of the earth that makes the eclipse, the form of this line will be caused by the form of the earth's surface, which is therefore spherical. Again, our observations of the stars make it evident, not only that the earth is circular, but also that it is a circle of no great size. For quite a small change of position to south or north causes a manifest alteration of the horizon. There is much change, I mean, in the stars which are overhead, and the stars seen are different, as one moves northward or southward. Indeed there are some stars seen in Egypt and in the neighbourhood of Cyprus which are not seen in the northerly regions; and stars, which in the north are never beyond the range of observation, in those regions rise and set. All of which goes to show not only that the earth is circular in shape, but also that it is a sphere of no great size: for otherwise the effect of so slight a change of place would not be so quickly apparent. Hence one should not be too sure of the incredibility of the view of those who conceive that there is continuity between the parts about the pillars of Hercules and the parts about India, and that in this way the ocean is one. As further evidence in favour of this they quote the case of elephants, a species occurring in each of these extreme regions, suggesting that the common characteristic of these extremes is explained by their continuity. Also, those mathematicians who try to calculate the size of the earth's circumference arrive at the figure 400,000 stades. This indicates not only that the earth's mass is spherical in shape, but also that as compared with the stars it is not of great size.

15

Mediterranean Social and Family Structure

In these selections, Aristotle describes some widely accepted Greek principles of social organization that also came to be current in Rome. He is obviously intent on justifying a social hierarchy; how does he divide functions? Why does he prefer that manual labor (at least in agriculture) be done by slaves? The idea of hierarchy also extends to the family, with clear divisions between men and women; were these unusual in classical civilizations? Does Aristotle's definition of the purposes of family organization differ from those in China and India?

Aristotle was an ardent defender of most Athenian political principles, including a degree of democracy as the Athenians defined it. How do his arguments for social and family hierarchy relate to Greek politics?

Social divisions existed in all the classicial civilizations, of course. Were the kinds of divisions Aristotle described comparable to social structures elsewhere in the classical world, for example, in India's caste system?

I. POLITICS

We stated above that the land ought to be possessed by those who have arms and enjoy full participation in the constitution, and why the cultivators should be different from the owners, also the nature and extent of the territory required. We must speak first about the division of the land for the purposes of cultivation and about those who will

Selection I from Aristotle, *The Politics,* T. A. Sinclair, translator (Harmmondsworth, England: Penguin Classics edition, 1962). Copyright © 1962 by the Estate of T. A. Sinclair. Reprinted by permission of Penguin Books Ltd. Selection II from Aristotle, *Economics,* Book I, in Vol. 10 of *The Oxford Translation of Aristotle,* edited by W. D. Ross (Oxford: Oxford University Press, 1921).

cultivate it, who and of what type they will be. We do not agree with those who have said that all land should be communally owned, but we do believe that there should be a friendly arrangement for sharing the usufruct and that none of the citizens should be without means of support. Next as to communal feeding, it is generally agreed that this is a very useful institution in a well-ordered society; why we too are of this opinion we will say later. In any case, where communal meals exist, all citizens should partake of them, though it is not easy for those who are badly off to pay the contribution fixed and keep a household going at the same time. Another thing that should be a charge on the whole community is the public worship of the gods. Thus it becomes necessary to divide the land into two parts, one publicly owned, the other privately. Each of these has to be further divided into two. One part of the public land will support the service of the gods, the other the communal feeding. Of the privately owned land one part will be near the frontier, the other near the city, so that every citizen will have two portions, one in each locality. This is not only in accordance with justice and equality but makes also for greater unity in the face of wars with bordering states. Without this dual ar-rangement some make too little of hostilities on the border, others too much, some underestimate the dangers of frontier quarrels, others take them too seriously, even sacrificing honour in order to avoid them. Hence in some countries it is the custom that when war against a neighbour is under consideration, those who live near to the border should be excluded from the discussion as being too closely involved to be able to give honest advice. It is therefore important that the territory should for the reasons given be divided in the manner stated. As for those who are to till the land, they should, if possible, be slaves (and we are building as we would wish). They should not be all of one stock nor men of spirit; this will ensure that they will be good workers and not prone to revolt. An alternative to slaves is foreigners settled on the countryside, men of the same type as the slaves just mentioned. They fall into two groups according to whether they work privately on the land of individual owners of property, or publicly on the common land. I hope later on to say how slaves ought to be used in agriculture and why it is a good thing that all slaves should have before them the prospect of receiving their freedom as a reward.

II. ECONOMICS

As regards the human part of the household, the first care is concerning a wife; for a common life is above all things natural to the female and to the male. For we have elsewhere laid down the principle that nature aims at producing many such forms of association, just as also it produces the various kinds of animals. But it is impossible for the female to accomplish this without the male or the male without the female, so that their common life has necessarily arisen. Now in the other animals this intercourse is not based on reason, but depends on the amount of natural instinct which they possess and is entirely for the purpose of procreation. But in the civilized and more intelligent animals the bond of unity is more perfect (for in them we see more mutual help and goodwill and co-operation), above all in the case of man, because the female and the male co-operate to ensure not merely existence but a good life. And the production of children is not only a way of serving nature but also of securing a real advantage; for the trouble which parents bestow upon their helpless children when they are themselves vigorous is repaid to them in old age when they are helpless by their children, who are then in their full vigour. At the same time also nature thus periodically provides for the perpetuation of mankind as a species, since she cannot do so individually. Thus the nature both of the man and of the woman has been preordained by the will of heaven to live a common life. For they are distinguished in that the powers which they possess are not applicable to purposes in all cases identical, but in some respects their functions are opposed to one another though they all tend to the same end. For nature has made the one sex stronger, the other weaker, that the latter through fear may be the more cautious, while the former by its courage is better able to ward off attacks; and that the one may acquire possessions outside the house, the other preserve those within. In the performance of work, she made one sex able to lead a sedentary life and not strong enough to endure exposure, the other less adapted for quiet pursuits but well constituted for outdoor activities; and in relation to offspring she has made both share in the procreation of children, but each render its peculiar service towards them, the woman by nurturing, the man by educating them.

First, then, there are certain laws to be observed towards a wife, including the avoidance of doing her any wrong; for thus a man is less likely himself to be wronged. This is inculcated by the general law, as the Pythagoreans say, that one least of all should injure a wife as being "a suppliant and seated at the hearth." Now wrong inflicted by a husband is the formation of connexions outside his own house. As regards sexual intercourse, a man ought not to accustom himself not to need it at all nor to be unable to rest when it is lacking, but so as to be content with or without it. The saying of Hesiod is a good one:

A man should marry a maiden, that habits discreet he may teach her.

For dissimilarity of habits tends more than anything to destroy affection. As regards adornment, husband and wife ought not to approach one another with false affectation in their person any more than in their manners; for if the society of husband and wife requires such embellishment, it is no better than play-acting on the tragic stage.

Of possessions, that which is the best and the worthiest subject of economics comes first and is most essential — I mean, man. It is necessary therefore first to provide oneself with good slaves. Now slaves are of two kinds, the overseer and the worker. And since we see that methods of education produce a certain character in the young, it is necessary when one has procured slaves to bring up carefully those to whom the higher duties are to be entrusted. The intercourse of a master with his slaves should be such as not either to allow them to be insolent or to irritate them. To the higher class of slaves he ought to give some share of honour, and to the workers abundance of nourishment. And since the drinking of wine makes even freemen insolent, and many nations even of freemen abstain therefrom (the Carthaginians, for instance, when they are on military service), it is clear that wine ought never to be given to slaves, or at any rate very seldom. Three things make up the life of a slave, work, punishment, and food. To give them food but no punishment and no work makes them insolent; and that they should have work and punishment but no food is tyrannical and destroys their efficiency. It remains therefore to give them work and sufficient food; for it is impossible to rule over slaves without offering rewards, and a slave's reward is his food. And just as all other men become worse when they get no advantage by being better and there are no rewards for virtue and punishments for vice, so also is it with slaves. Therefore we must take careful notice and bestow or withhold everything, whether food or clothing or leisure or punishments, according to merit, in word and deed following the practice adopted by physicians in the matter of medicine, remembering at the same time that food is not medicine because it must be given continually.

The slave who is best suited for his work is the kind that is neither too cowardly nor too courageous. Slaves who have either of these characteristics are injurious to their owners; those who are too cowardly lack endurance, while the high-spirited are not easy to control. All ought to have a definite end in view; for it is just and beneficial to offer slaves their freedom as a prize, for they are willing to work when a prize is set before them and a limit of time is defined.

16

The Grandeur of the Roman Empire

All the world's major civilizations witnessed successful programs of imperial state building in the last half of the first millennium B.C. Having mastered the entire Mediterranean world by military conquest, the republican city-state of Rome gave way to imperial rule under Octavian (31 B.C.–14 A.D.). An efficient bureaucratic reorganization, backed with professional armies and improved communications and strengthened by the unique Roman concept of citizenship, provided nearly 100 million inhabitants in the Roman Empire a long era of order, security, and economic prosperity. By means of this *pax Romana,* the Romans allowed for unrestricted diffusion and dissemination of the empire's regional cultures, including their own, as well as contact with other major regional civilizations. Consequently the Celts, Germans, Slavs, and North Africans acquired familiarity with the advanced Romano-Hellenistic civilization as the empire reached its cultural, economic, and organizational peak in the second century A.D.

Many Roman and provincial intellectuals, conscious of the blessings of imperial rule, perceived the Roman Empire as an ideal state and equated its rule with civilization itself. This perception was to survive the empire, and the imperial ideal became a formative concept in the succeeding Western civilization. The following selection from the *Roman Oration,* a rhetorical hymn of praise to the empire delivered in A.D. 143 by Aristides—a rich Greek provincial—provides such a view. Despite the fact that his observations and historical judgments are both

From Aelius Aristides, *The Roman Oration,* "The Ruling Power. A Study of the Roman Empire in the Second Century after Christ through the Roman Oration of Aelius Aristides," by James N. Oliver, *Transactions of the American Philosophical Society,* New Series, XLIII, pt. 4 (1953): 896, 898–99, 901. Copyright © 1953, American Philosophical Society. Reprinted by permission.

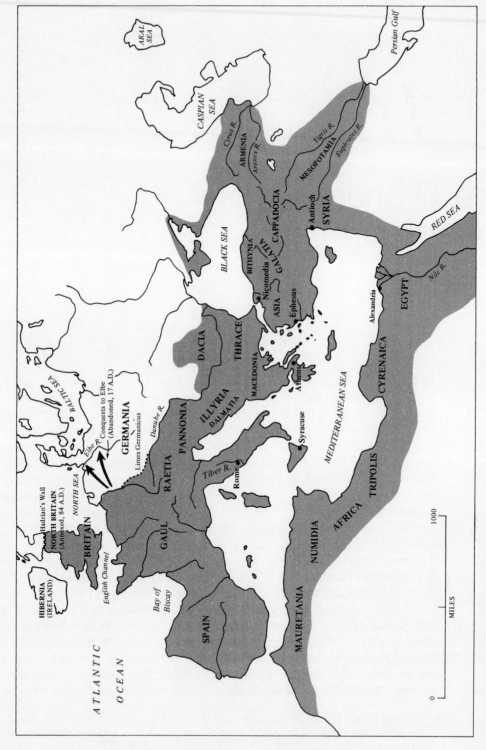

The Roman Empire at Its Greatest Extent, A.D. 98–117

Map labels:
ARAL SEA
Persian Gulf
CASPIAN SEA
Cyrus R.
Araxes R.
ARMENIA
Tigris R.
Euphrates R.
MESOPOTAMIA
CAPPADOCIA
GALATIA
BITHYNIA
Nicomedia
ASIA
Ephesus
Antioch
SYRIA
RED SEA
BLACK SEA
Nile R.
EGYPT
Alexandria
THRACE
DACIA
MACEDONIA
Athens
CYRENAICA
Conquests to Elbe
(Abandoned, 17 A.D.)
Elbe R.
GERMANIA
Limes Germanicus
Danube R.
ILLYRIA
DALMATIA
PANNONIA
RAETIA
Syracuse
MEDITERRANEAN SEA
BALTIC SEA
Hadrian's Wall
NORTH BRITAIN
(Annexed, 84 A.D.)
NORTH SEA
BRITAIN
GAUL
Tiber R.
Rome
TRIPOLIS
AFRICA
HIBERNIA
(IRELAND)
English Channel
Bay of Biscay
SPAIN
NUMIDIA
MAURETANIA
ATLANTIC OCEAN

0   1000   MILES

superficial and exaggerated, Aristides properly noted the advantages of Roman rule and attempted to provide a philosophical and historical justification for the existence of the "universal" empire. Acknowledging divine intervention in the operation of the empire, Aristides attributed the art of government to the Romans, whom he considered the first to provide true freedom, justice, and peace because they allowed fruition of the Greek way of life.

What, according to Aristides, are the key political principles of the empire? How might his ideas about politics and imperial greatness affect later civilizations, such as those of Byzantium and Russia or Western Europe, that looked back to Rome for inspiration? Did Rome's principles of empire have any connection to earlier Greek politics?

Homer says of snow that as it falls, it covers "the crest of the range and the mountain peaks and the flowering fields and the rich acres of men, and," he says, "it is poured out over the white sea, the harbors and the shores." So also of this city. Like the snow, she covers mountain peaks, she covers the land intervening, and she goes down to the sea, where the commerce of all mankind has its common exchange and all the produce of the earth has its common market. Wherever one may go in Rome, there is no vacancy to keep one from being, there also, in mid-city. And indeed she is poured out, not just over the level ground, but in a manner with which the simile cannot begin to keep pace, she rises great distances into the air, so that her height is not to be compared to a covering of snow but rather to the peaks themselves. And as a man who far surpasses others in size and strength likes to show his strength by carrying others on his back, so this city, which is built over so much land, is not satisfied with her extent, but raising upon her shoulders others of equal size, one over the other, she carries them. It is from this that she gets her name, and strength (*rômê*) is the mark of all that is hers. Therefore, if one chose to unfold, as it were, and lay flat on the ground the cities which now she carries high in air, and place them side by side, all that part of Italy which intervenes would, I think, be filled and become one continuous city stretching to the Strait of Otranto.

Though she is so vast as perhaps even now I have not sufficiently shown, but as the eye attests more clearly, it is not possible to say of her as of other cities, "There she stands." Again it has been said of the capital cities of the Athenians and the La-cedaemonians — and may no ill omen attend the comparison — that the first would in size appear twice as great as in its intrinsic power, the second far inferior in size to its intrinsic power. But of this city, great in every respect, no one could say that she has not created power in keeping with her magnitude. No, if one looks at the whole empire and reflects how small a fraction rules the whole world, he may be amazed at the city, but when he has beheld the city herself and the boundaries of the city, he can no longer be amazed that the entire civilized world is ruled by one so great.

Some chronicler, speaking of Asia, asserted that one man ruled as much land as the sun passed, and his statement was not true because he placed all Africa and Europe outside the limits where the sun rises in the East and sets in the West. It has now however turned out to be true. Your possession is equal to what the sun can pass, and the sun passes over your land. Neither the Chelidonean nor the Cyanean promontories limit your empire, nor does the distance from which a horseman can reach the sea in one day, nor do you reign within fixed boundaries, nor does another dictate to what point your control reaches; but the sea like a girdle lies extended, at once in the middle of the civilized world and of your hegemony.

Around it lie the great continents [gently] sloping, ever offering to you in full measure something of their own. Whatever the seasons make grow and whatever countries and rivers and lakes and arts of Hellenes and non-Hellenes produce are brought from every land and sea, so that if one would look at all these things, he must needs behold them either by visiting the entire civilized world or by coming to this city. For whatever is grown and made among each people cannot fail to be here at all times and in abundance. And here the merchant vessels come carrying these many products from all regions in every season and even at every equinox, so that the city appears a kind of common emporium of the world.

Cargoes from India and, if you will, even from Arabia the Blest one can see in such numbers as to surmise that in those lands the trees will have been stripped bare and that the inhabitants of these lands, if they need anything, must come here and beg for a share of their own. Again one can see Babylonian garments and ornaments from the barbarian country beyond arriving in greater quantity and with more ease than if shippers from Naxos or from Cythnos, bearing something from those islands, had but to enter the port of Athens. Your farms are Egypt, Sicily and the civilized part of Africa.

. . .

Now, however, the present empire has been extended to boundaries of no mean distance, to such, in fact, that one cannot even measure the area within them. On the contrary, for one who begins a journey westward from the point where at that period the empire of the Persian found its limit, the rest is far more than the entirety of his domain, and there are no sections which you have omitted, neither city nor tribe nor harbor nor district, except possibly some that you condemned as worthless. The Red Sea and the Cataracts of the Nile and Lake Maeotis, which formerly were said to lie on the boundaries of the earth, are like the courtyard walls to the house which is this city of yours. On the other hand, you have explored Ocean. Some writers did not believe that Ocean existed at all, or did not believe that it flowed around the earth; they thought that poets had invented the name and had introduced it into literature for the sake of entertainment. But you have explored it so thoroughly that not even the island therein has escaped you.

Vast and comprehensive as is the size of it, your empire is much greater for its perfection than for the area which its boundaries encircle. There are no pockets of the empire held by Mysians, Sacae, Pisidians, or others, land which some have occupied by force, others have detached by revolt, who cannot be captured. Nor is it merely called the land of the *King*, while really the land of all who are able to hold it. Nor do satraps fight one another as if they had no king; nor are cities at variance, some fighting against these and some against those, with garrisons being dispatched to some cities and being expelled from others. But for the eternal duration of this empire the whole civilized world prays all together, emitting, like an aulos after a thorough cleaning, one note with more perfect precision than a chorus; so beautifully is it harmonized by the leader in command.

. . .

For of all who have ever gained empire you alone rule over men who are free. . . . [N]or is the country said to be enslaved, as household of so-and-so, to whomsoever it has been turned over, a man himself not free. But just as those in states of one city appoint the magistrates to protect and care for the governed, so you, who conduct public business in the whole civilized world exactly as if it were one city state, appoint the governors, as is natural after elections, to protect and care for the governed, not to be slave masters over them. Therefore governor makes way for governor unobtrusively, when his time is up, and far from staying too long and disputing the land with his successor, he might easily not stay long enough even to meet him.

Appeals to a higher court are made . . . with no greater menace for those who make them than for those who have accepted the local verdict. Therefore one might say that the men of today are ruled by the governors who are sent out, only in so far as they are content to be ruled.

. . .

But there is that which very decidedly deserves as much attention and admiration now as all the rest together. I mean your magnificent citizenship with its grand conception, because there is nothing like it in the records of all mankind. Dividing into two groups all those in your empire — and with this word I have indicated the entire civilized world — you have everywhere appointed to your citizenship, or even to kinship with you, the better part of the world's talent, courage, and leadership, while the rest you recognized as a league under your hegemony.

Neither sea nor intervening continent are bars to citizenship, nor are Asia and Europe divided in their treatment here. In your empire all paths are open to all. No one worthy of rule or trust remains an alien, but a civil community of the World has been established as a Free Republic under one, the best, ruler and teacher of order; and all come together as into a common civic center, in order to receive each man his due.

. . .

Let this passing comment, which the subject suggested, suffice. As we were saying, you who are "great greatly" distributed your citizenship. It was not because you stood off and refused to give a share in it to any of the others that you made your citizenship an object of wonder. On the contrary, you sought its expansion as a worthy aim, and you have caused the word Roman to be the label, not of membership in a city, but of some common nationality, and this not just one among all, but one balancing all the rest. For the categories into which you now divide the world are not Hellenes and Barbarians, and it is not absurd, the distinction which you made, because you show them a citizenry more numerous, so to speak, than the entire Hellenic race. The division which you substituted is one into Romans and non-Romans. To such a degree have you expanded the name of your city.

Since these are the lines along which the distinction has been made, many in every city are fellow-citizens of yours no less than of their own kinsmen, though some of them have not yet seen this city. There is no need of garrisons to hold their citadels, but the men of greatest standing and influence in every city guard their own fatherlands for you. And you have a double hold upon the cities, both from here and from your fellow citizens in each.

. . .

Wars, even if they once occurred, no longer seem to have been real; on the contrary, stories about them are interpreted more as myths by the many who hear them. If anywhere an actual clash occurs along the border, as is only natural in the immensity of a great empire, because of the madness of Getae or the misfortune of Libyans or the wickedness of those around the Red Sea, who are unable to enjoy the blessings they have, then simply like myths they themselves quickly pass and the stories about them. So great is your peace, though war was traditional among you.

· · ·

As on holiday the whole civilized world lays down the arms which were its ancient burden and has turned to adornment and all glad thoughts with power to realize them. All the other rivalries have left the [cities], and this one contention holds them all, how each city may appear most beautiful and attractive. All localities are full of gymnasia, fountains, monumental approaches, temples, workshops, schools, and one can say that the civilized world, which had been sick from the beginning, as it were, has been brought by the right knowledge to a state of health. Gifts never cease from you to the cities, and it is not possible to determine who the major beneficiaries have been, because your kindness is the same to all.

Cities gleam with radiance and charm, and the whole earth has been beautified like a garden. Smoke rising from plains and fire signals for friend and foe have disappeared, as if a breath had blown them away, beyond land and sea. Every charming spectacle and an infinite number of festal games have been introduced instead. Thus like an ever-burning sacred fire the celebration never ends, but moves around from time to time and people to people, always somewhere, a demonstration justified by the way all men have fared. Thus it is right to pity only those outside your hegemony, if indeed there are any, because they lose such blessings. . . .

Before the rule of Zeus, as the poets say, the universe was full of strife, confusion and disorder, but when Zeus came to the rule he settled everything, and the Titans, forced back by Zeus and the gods who supported him, departed to the lowest caverns of the earth. Thus one who reflects about the world before your time and about the condition of affairs in your period would come to the opinion that before your empire there had been confusion everywhere and things were taking a random course, but when you assumed the presidency, confusion and strife ceased, and universal order entered as a brilliant light over the private and public affairs of man, laws appeared and altars of gods received man's confidence.

three

CHANGE AND EXPANSION IN TRADITIONAL CIVILIZATIONS, A.D. 500–1500

After the collapse of key classical dynasties or empires, new influences arose in many older centers—particularly with the rise of Islam and the spread of Buddhism. Civilization also expanded from older centers—thus the rise of a Japanese form of East Asian culture and the development of civilization in northwestern Europe and in Russia, with links, however, to earlier Mediterranean forms. Early civilization also arose in portions of the Americas and sub-Saharan Africa.

17

The Koran and the Family

The canonical source of Islam (*al-Islâm* meaning "surrender") is the Koran [*Qurʾ ān*], which contains revelations from Allah, "the God of Abraham, Ishmael, Isaac, and Jacob, and the Tribes [of Israel] . . . and Jesus," to the Prophet Muhammad [ca. A.D. 570–632]. Transmitted through the intermediary of the angel Gabriel during the twenty years of Muhammad's apostolate, these full and complete revelations embodied Allah's "eternal knowledge and judgment of all things" and a perfection of all previous religions. As the ultimate authority in Islam and the "supreme self-manifestation of God to His creatures," the Koran was early reduced to writing. Yet an official, authoritative edition did not appear until after the Prophet's death in A.D. 632. Divided into 114 chapters (*suras*) and containing 77,639 words, the text of the Koran is arranged in order of decreasing length with complete disregard for chronology. Internally each *sura* consists of verses ['*ayāt*' meaning "signs" or "tokens"] with post-Muhammad headings derived from key terms in the text. Written in classical Arabic, the Koran adheres to a metrical style and was designed to be heard. In the selections below from *Sura* IV ("Women") the focus is on women, children, orphans, and inheritances, with injunctions to males in the Islamic patriarchal society regarding them.

The following passages obviously invite judgments about what kind of family life and gender relations were urged in Islamic society; we can compare these with other versions of a patriarchal system in classical India and China (see selections 8 and 12, above). These passages also show how Islamic religion

---

From Arthur J. Arberry, *The Koran Interpreted*, 2 vols. (London: George Allen and Unwin, Ltd., 1955), Vol. I., pp. 100–6, 119–20. Copyright © George Allen and Unwin, 1955. Reprinted by permission.

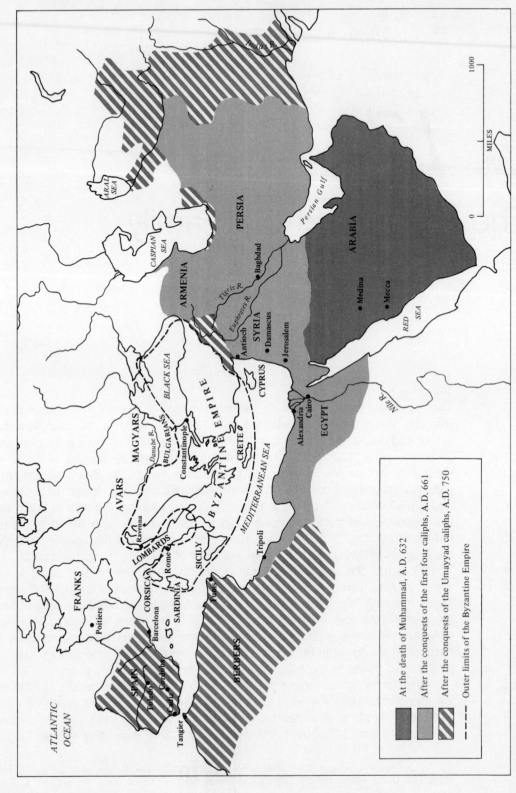

The Expansion of Islam

developed specific regulations, not just general ethics, for personal and family behavior, harking back to older Middle Eastern traditions in this area (see selections 2 and 4). Finally, the passages also show something of the Islamic view of God, in whose name men and women were to regulate their relationships.

WOMEN

In the Name of God, the Merciful, the Compassionate
· · ·

Give the orphans their property, and do not
exchange the corrupt for the good; and devour
not their property with your property; surely
  that is a great crime.
If you fear that you will not act justly
toward the orphans, marry such women
as seem good to you, two, three, four;
but if you fear you will not be equitable,
then only one, or what your right hands own;
so it is likelier you will not be partial.
And give the women their dowries as a gift
spontaneous; but if they are pleased
to offer you any of it, consume it
  with wholesome appetite.
But do not give to fools their property
that God has assigned to you to manage;
provide for them and clothe them out of it,
and speak to them honourable words.
Test well the orphans, until they reach
the age of marrying; then, if you perceive
in them right judgment, deliver to them
their property; consume it not wastefully
  and hastily
ere they are grown. If any man is rich,
let him be abstinent; if poor, let him
  consume in reason.
And when you deliver to them their property,
take witnesses over them; God suffices
  for a reckoner.

To the men a share of what parents and kinsmen
leave, and to the women a share of what
parents and kinsman leave, whether it be
little or much, a share apportioned;
and when the division is attended by
kinsmen and orphans and the poor,

make provision for them out of it,
and speak to them honourable words.
And let those fear who, if they left
behind them weak seed, would be afraid
on their account, and let them fear
God, and speak words hitting the mark.
Those who devour the property of orphans
unjustly, devour Fire in their bellies,
and shall assuredly roast in a Blaze.
God charges you, concerning your children:
to the male the like of the portion
of two females, and if they be women
above two, then for them two-thirds
of what he leaves, but if she be one
then to her a half; and to his parents
to each one of the two the sixth
of what he leaves, if he has children;
but if he has no children, and his
heirs are his parents, a third to his
mother, or, if he has brothers, to his
mother a sixth, after any bequest
he may bequeath, or any debt.
Your fathers and your sons — you know not
which out of them is nearer in profit
to you. So God apportions; surely God is
    All-knowing, All-wise.

And for you a half of what your wives
leave, if they have no children; but
if they have children, then for you of what
they leave a fourth, after any bequest
they may bequeath, or any debt.
And for them a fourth of what you leave,
if you have no children; but if you
have children, then for them of what
you leave an eighth, after any bequest
you may bequeath, or any debt.
If a man or a woman have no heir
direct, but have a brother or a sister,
to each of the two a sixth; but if they
are more numerous than that, they share
equally a third, after any bequest
he may bequeath, or any debt not
prejudicial; a charge from God. God is
    All-knowing, All-clement.

Those are God's bounds. Whoso obeys God
and His Messenger, He will admit him
to gardens underneath which rivers flow,
therein dwelling forever; that is
  the mighty triumph.
But whoso disobeys God, and His Messenger,
and transgresses His bounds, him He will
admit to a Fire, therein dwelling
forever, and for him there awaits
  a humbling chastisement.

Such of your women as commit indecency,
call four of you to witness against them;
and if they witness, then detain them
in their houses until death takes them
or God appoints for them a way.
And when two of you commit indecency,
punish them both; but if they repent
and make amends, then suffer them to be;
God turns, and is All-compassionate.
God shall turn only towards those who do
evil in ignorance, then shortly repent;
God will return towards those; God is
  All-knowing, All-wise.
But God shall not turn towards those
who do evil deeds until, when one of them
is visited by death, he says, "Indeed
now I repent," neither to those who die
disbelieving; for them We have prepared
  a painful chastisement.

O believers, it is not lawful for you
to inherit women against their will;
neither debar them, that you may go off
with part of what you have given them,
except when they commit a flagrant indecency.
Consort with them honourably; or if
you are averse to them, it is possible
you may be averse to a thing, and God set
  in it much good.
And if you desire to exchange a wife
in place of another, and you have given
to one a hundredweight, take of it nothing.
What, will you take it by way of calumny
  and manifest sin?

How shall you take it, when each of you has been
privily with the other, and they have taken from you
    a solemn compact?
And do not marry women that your fathers
married, unless it be a thing of the past;
surely that is indecent and hateful,
    an evil way.

Forbidden to you are your mothers and daughters,
your sisters, your aunts paternal and maternal,
your brother's daughters, your sister's daughters,
your mothers who have given suck to you,
your suckling sisters, your wives' mothers,
your stepdaughters who are in your care
being born of your wives you have been in to—
but if you have not yet been in to them
it is no fault in you — and the spouses
of your sons who are of your loins,
and that you should take to you two sisters
together, unless it be a thing of the past;
God is All-forgiving, All compassionate;
and wedded women, save what your right hands own.
So God prescribes for you. Lawful for you,
beyond all that, is that you may seek,
using your wealth, in wedlock and not
in licence. Such wives as you enjoy thereby,
give them their wages apportionate; it is no
fault in you in your agreeing together,
after the due apportionate. God is
    All-knowing, All-wise.

Any one of you who has not the affluence
to be able to marry believing freewomen
in wedlock, let him take believing handmaids
that your right hands own; God knows very well
your faith; the one of you is as the other.
So marry them, with their people's leave,
and give them their wages honourably
as women in wedlock, not as in licence
    or taking lovers.
But when they are in wedlock, if they
commit indecency, they shall be liable
to half the chastisement of freewomen.
That provision is for those of you who fear
fornication; yet it is better for you

to be patient. God is All-forgiving
All-compassionate.
God desires to make clear to you, and to
guide you in the institutions of those
before you, and to turn towards you; God is
All-knowing, All-wise;
and God desires to turn towards you, but
those who follow their lusts desire you
to swerve away mightily. God desires
to lighten things for you, for man was
created a weakling. . . .

Do not covet that whereby God in bounty
has preferred one of you above another.
To the men a share from what they have earned,
and to the women a share from what they
have earned. And ask God of His bounty;
God knows everything.

To everyone We have appointed heirs
of that which parents and kinsmen leave,
and those with whom you have sworn compact.
So give to them their share; God is witness
over everything.

Men are the managers of the affairs of women
for that God has preferred in bounty
one of them over another, and for that
they have expended of their property.
Righteous women are therefore obedient,
guarding the secret for God's guarding.
And those you fear may be rebellious
admonish; banish them to their couches,
and beat them. If they then obey you,
look not for any way against them; God is
All-high, All-great.
And if you fear a breach between the two,
bring forth an arbiter from his people
and from her people an arbiter, if they
desire to set things right; God will
compose their differences; surely God is
All-knowing, All-aware. . . .

If a woman fear rebelliousness or aversion
in her husband, there is no fault in them
if the couple set things right between them;

right settlement is better; and souls are very
prone to avarice. If you do good
and are godfearing, surely God is aware of
     the things you do.
You will not be able to be equitable
between your wives, be you ever so eager;
yet do not be altogether partial
so that you leave her as it were suspended.
If you set things right, and are godfearing,
God is All-forgiving, All-compassionate.
But if they separate, God will enrich
each of them of His plenty; God is
All-embracing, All-wise.

18

The Islamic Religion

Supplementing the Koran as a source for Islamic religious, social, and legal precepts is the Hadith (which means a story, tale, or report). These are collections of traditions attributed to Muhammed, his companions, and early caliphs. Consisting of rules and practical social norms (*sunnah*) formulated by the prophet and enforced by early leaders in the Islamic community, the Hadith contains prescribed rules and behaviors not offered in the Koran that guide Muslims. Proclaimed in sermons or informally before witnesses, the apostolic traditions remained unwritten until the beginning of the seventh century. In response to Caliph Oman II's orders for a formal collection of extant traditions, an Iranian savant, Abū ʿAbdallah Muhammad (b. Ismāʿīl al-Bukhārī, 810–870), traveled throughout the Islamic World, where he uncovered more than 600,000. Joined by other collectors, al-Bukhārī devised a critical scientific method to separate authentic traditions from the spurious. From this, he produced an authoritative Hadith consisting of 7,397 authentic traditions. His collection, along with those by ʾAbul Husain Muslim (819–874) and four less reliable collectors, acquired canonical status among the orthodox Sunnis and is known as the *Sahīh* ("The Genuine").

In the Hadith selections that follow, you can get a sense of what the main religious duties of a Muslim were and are and how the individual could relate to Allah. What is distinctive about Muslim religious life? Why did and do so many people find Islam such a satisfactory religion, often converting to it from other faiths?

From Arthur Jeffery, ed., *A Reader on Islam* (New York: Books for Libraries, A Division of Arno Press, 1980), pp. 81–86. Copyright © Arno Press, 1980. Reprinted by permission.

Said the Apostle of Allah—upon whom be Allah's blessing and peace—: "The [true] Muslim is he from whose tongue and whose hand [other] Muslims are safe, and the [true] Muhājir is he who has fled from those things Allah has forbidden."

Islam is built upon five things: on testifying that there is no deity save Allah and that Muhammad is his Apostle, on performing prayer, on paying the legal alms (*zakāt*), on the pilgrimage [to Mecca], and on the fast of Ramaḍān.

The Apostle of Allah—upon whom be Allah's blessing and peace—was asked which [good] work was the most excellent, and he answered: "Belief in Allah and in His Apostle." He was asked: "And then which?" He replied: "Jihād in the way of Allah." He was again asked: "And then what?" and he replied: "An acceptable pilgrimage."

No one ever bears witness that there is no deity save Allah and that Muhammad is the Apostle of Allah, [testifying to it] sincerely from his heart, but Allah will preserve him from Hell-fire.

There is no Muslim who plants a tree or cultivates a plot from which birds or man or domestic beasts [may gather food to] eat, but has therein an act of charitable alms [recorded to his merit].

If a man seizes the property of others with intent to restore it, Allah will settle with him, but if he seizes it with intent to waste it Allah will make waste of him.

If a slave serves honestly his [earthly] master and worships earnestly his [heavenly] Lord, he will have a double recompense.

He who shows concern for the widows and the unfortunate [ranks as high] as one who goes on Jihād in the way of Allah, or one who fasts by day and who rises at night [for prayer].

A [true] believer views his sins as though he were sitting beneath a mountain which he fears may fall on him, but an evil-doer views his sins as a fly that moves across his nose.

In this world be as a stranger, or as one who is just passing along the road.

In two things an old man's heart never ceases to be that of a youth, in love of this world and in hoping long.

Were a man to possess two valleys full of gold he would be wanting a third, for nothing will ever really fill man's belly but the dust.

To look at a woman is forbidden, even if it is a look without desire, so how much the more is touching her.

Said he—upon whom be Allah's blessing and peace—: "Avoid seven pernicious things." [His Companions] said: "And what are they, O Apostle of Allah?" He answered: "Associating anything with Allah, sorcery, depriving anyone of life where Allah has forbidden that save for just cause, taking usury, devouring the property of orphans, turning the back on the day of battle, and slandering chaste believing women even though they may be acting carelessly."

No one who enters Paradise will ever want to return to this world, even could he possess the earth and all that is on it, save the martyrs who desire to return to this world and be killed ten times so great is the regard in which they find themselves held.

To be stationed on the frontier for one day during Holy War is better than [to possess] this world and all that is on it. A place in Paradise the size of one of your whip-lashes is better than this world and all that is on it. A night or a day that a man spends on Holy War is better than this world and all that is on it.

The similitude of a stingy man and a generous giver of alms is that of two men wearing cloaks of mail in which the hand-pieces are fastened to the collar-piece. Whenever the generous giver starts to give an alms it stretches for him so that it is as though it were not, but when the stingy man starts to give an alms every link clings to the one next it so contracting that his hands are kept tight by his collar-bone and however much he strives it will not stretch.

It is right to "hearken and obey" so long as one is not bidden disobey [Allah], but should the command be to disobedience let there be no "hearken and obey."

Travelling is part of one's punishment, for one is deprived of one's sleeping, one's eating, one's drinking thereby, so whenever any one of you has finished what he had to do let him hurry home.

Allah desires to meet those who desire to meet with Him, but is disinclined to meet those who are disinclined to meet with Him.

The man who has the lightest punishment on the Day will be the one who has live coals placed under the soles of his feet [so hot that] his brains will boil from the heat thereof.

If a man sees something in [the conduct of] his ruler which he dislikes let him put up with it patiently, for there is no one who separates himself even a span from the community and dies [in that separation], but dies a pagan death.

When Friday comes angels take their seat over every mosque gate and write down in order those who come in, but when the prayer-leader sits they fold their sheets and come to hearken to the words.

Said the Prophet—upon whom be Allah's blessing and peace—: "I had a look into Paradise and I saw that the poor made up most of its inhabitants, and I had a look into Hell and saw that most of its inhabitants were women."

When [the month of] Ramaḍān begins the gates of heaven are set open, the gates of Hell are locked shut, and the satans are chained.

Treat women-folk kindly for woman was created of a rib. The crookedest part of a rib is its upper part. If you go to straighten it out you will break it, and if you leave it alone it will continue crooked. So treat women in kindly fashion.

Whosoever testifies that there is no deity save Allah, that Muhammad is His servant and His Apostle, that Jesus is His servant and His Apostle and His word which He cast to Mary and a Spirit from Him, that Paradise is a reality and Hell-fire a reality, him will Allah bring into Paradise in accordance with his works.

Only two men are really to be envied, namely, a man to whom Allah has given Scripture and who sits up at nights with it, and a man to whom Allah has given wealth which he distributes in charitable alms day and night.

Said the Apostle of Allah—upon whom be Allah's blessing and peace: "O band of youths, let him among you who is able to make a home get married, and let him who is not able betake himself to fasting for he will find in that a quencher [of his passions]."

The worst of foods is that of a feast to which the rich have been invited and the poor overlooked, yet anyone who overlooks an invitation is in rebellion against Allah and His Apostle.

Said the Apostle of Allah—upon whom be Allah's blessing and peace—: "Do not wear silks and satins, and do not drink from gold and silver vessels nor eat from dishes made thereof, for these things are theirs in this world but ours in the world to come."

Said the Apostle of Allah—upon whom be Allah's blessing and peace—: "Gabriel said to me: 'Whosoever of your community dies without ever having associated any other with Allah will enter Paradise' (or perhaps he said: 'will not enter Hell-fire'). Someone said: 'Even if he is an adulterer or a thief?' He replied: 'Even if.' "

The similitude of a good companion and a bad one is [that of] a man who carries musk and one who blows a blacksmith's bellows, for one who is carrying musk may give you a share, or you may purchase some of it, or in any case enjoy the delightful smell, but one who blows the blacksmith's bellows will either set your clothes on fire or accost you with an evil smell.

Said the Prophet—upon whom be Allah's blessing and peace—: "The first group to enter Paradise will have faces like the moon on the night of its fullness, will neither spit nor blow their noses or defecate therein, their utensils there will be of gold, their combs of gold and silver, their censers of aloes wood, their sweat will be musk, and each of them will have two spouses so beautiful that the marrow of their leg-bones will be visible through the flesh. There will be no differences or disputings among them for they will all be of one heart, glorifying Allah morning and evening."

'Ā'isha said: "I was stuffing a pillow for the Prophet—upon whom be Allah's blessing and peace—on which were images like those on a saddle-cushion, when he came and stood in the doorway. His countenance started to alter, so I said: 'What is it, O Apostle of Allah?' He said: 'What are you doing with this pillow?' 'It is a pillow,' I answered, 'that I have made for you on which you may recline.' Said he: 'Do you not know that angels will not enter a house in which there is a picture? On the Day makers of [such] pictures will be punished, for [Allah] will say to them: 'Give life to that which you have created.' "

Among the signs of the coming of the Hour are these: ignorance will be apparent and learning inconspicuous, fornication will be rampant and the drinking of wine, men will be few but women many so that fifty women will have but one husband between them.

Said the Prophet—upon whom be Allah's blessing and peace—: "He who drinks wine in this world and repents not of it will be forbidden it in the world to come."

There is no misfortune befalls a Muslim but Allah will atone for some sin of his thereby, even if it be only [so small a misfortune as] his being pricked by a thorn.

Said the Prophet—upon whom be Allah's blessing and peace—: "Visions are from Allah but dreams are from Satan, so if any one of you sees anything disagreeable [during sleep] let him spit three times when he wakens up and take refuge [with Allah] from its evil, and then it will do him no harm."

Said the Apostle of Allah—upon whom be Allah's blessing and peace—: "Among the greatest of mortal sins is that a man curse his parents." They said: "O Apostle of Allah, how could a man curse his parents?" He replied: "The man who reviles another man's parents is reviling his own father and mother." . . .

The Apostle of Allah—on whom be Allah's blessing and peace—once kissed al-Ḥasan the son of 'Alī while al-Aqra' b. Ḥābis of Tamīm was sitting there. Al-Aqra' said: "I have ten sons but never have kissed any one of them." The Apostle of Allah—

upon whom be Allah's blessing and peace—looked at him, and then said: "He who does not show tenderness will not have tenderness shown him."

Said the Prophet—upon whom be Allah's blessing and peace—: "Whoever casts himself down from a mountain so as to kill himself will be in Hell continually casting himself down thus for ever and ever. Whoever sips poison so as to kill himself will in Hell have poison in his hand which he will go on sipping there for ever and ever. Whoever kills himself with a knife will in Hell have a knife in his hand which he will go on continually plunging into his bowels for ever and ever."

Said he—upon whom be Allah's blessing and peace—: "Let none of you wish for death because of any hardship that has befallen him. If he needs must say something, let him say: 'Allahumma! let me live so long as life is best for me, and let me pass away when passing away is the best thing for me.' "

Said the Prophet—upon whom be Allah's blessing and peace—: "Allah made mercy in a hundred parts. Ninety-nine of these parts He kept with Himself and one single part He sent down on earth. It is by reason of this one part that creatures show mercy to one another, so that a mare carefully lifts her hoof fearing lest with it she harm her foal."

Said the Apostle of Allah—on whom be Allah's blessing and peace—: "Let him who believes in Allah and the Last Day refrain from doing harm to his neighbour. Let him who believes in Allah and the Last Day see to it that he properly honours his guest. Let him who believes in Allah and the Last Day either speak what is good or hold his tongue."

Said the Prophet—upon whom be Allah's blessing and peace—: "No one will ever experience the sweetness of faith till he loves a man solely for the sake of Allah, till he feels that he would rather be cast into Hell-fire than return to unbelief once Allah has delivered him from it, till Allah and His Apostle are dearer to him than anything besides."

Muḥammad b. Muqātil Abū'l-Ḥasan has related to me [saying]: 'Abdallah informed us on the authority of Ḥumaid b. 'Abd ar-Raḥmān, on the authority of Abū Huraira—with whom may Allah be pleased—that a man came to the Apostle of Allah—upon whom be Allah's blessing and peace—saying: "O Apostle of Allah, there is no hope for me." He replied: "Too bad for you." Said [the man]: "I had intercourse with my wife during Ramaḍān." [The Prophet] answered: "Then set free a slave." Said he: "I have none." [The Prophet] answered: "Then fast for two months on end." Said he: "But I could not." [The Prophet] answered: "Then feed sixty poor people." Said he: "I have not the wherewithall." Just then there was brought to [the Prophet] a basket of dates, so he said to the man: "Take this and distribute it as charitable alms [in expiation for your sin]." Said he: "O Apostle of Allah, [am I to distribute it] to other than my own family? when by Him in whose hand is my soul there is no one between the gateposts of the city more needy than I am." Thereat the Prophet laughed till his canine teeth showed, and he said: "Go along and take it."

19

Religious and Political Organization in the Islamic Middle East

The office of Imam, or leader, dates from Muhammed's death in 632, when a successor, or caliph, was elected. The word *imam* is also applied to local leaders of worship within a mosque. The following passage, from Al-Mawārdī's (d. 1058) *Ordinance of Government,* describes the central leadership of Islam during the centuries of Arab dominance in the office most commonly known as the caliphate. The statement of the duties and eligibility of the caliph comes from the majority, or Sunni Muslims. Minority Shiite Muslims split away in their belief that the caliphate was a divinely designated office inherited by descendants of Muhammed.

The orthodox Sunni view held that the imam or caliph was an elected and secular office that did, however, involve strict religious as well as political duties. The authority of the office was absolute so long as its holder adhered to the Koran and Hadith. Early elective procedures gave way to inheritance of the office in the Umayyad and Abbasid dynasties (661–750 and 750–1378), but the concept of the caliph's duties remained consistent. This office, then, was the chief political legacy of Islam during the centuries of Arab rule in the Middle East. In what sense was the caliphate a religious office? In what sense did it embrace nonreligious functions? What kind of government structure did the powers of the caliphate imply?

The office of Imam was set up in order to replace the office of Prophet in the defense of the faith and the government of the world. By general consensus [*ijmāʿ*], from which

From Bernard Lewis, editor and translator, *Islam from the Prophet Muhammed to the Capture of Constantinople* (New York: Harper and Row, 1974), Vol. I, pp. 150–51, 171–79. Reprinted by permission.

only al-Aṣamm dissents, the investiture of whichsoever member of the community exercises the functions of Imam is obligatory. But there is disagreement as to whether this obligation derives from reason or from Holy Law. One group says it derives from reason, since it is in the nature of reasonable men to submit to a leader who will prevent them from injuring one another and who will settle quarrels and disputes, for without rulers men would live in anarchy and heedlessness like benighted savages. . . .

Another group says that the obligation derives from the Holy Law and not from reason, since the Imam deals with matters of Holy Law to which, in reason, he would be allowed not to devote himself, since reason does not make them obligatory. All that reason requires is that a reasonable man should refrain from mutual injury and conflict with his neighbor and act equitably in mutual fairness and good relations, conducting himself in accordance with his own reason, and not with someone else's. But it is the Holy Law which intervenes to entrust these affairs to its religious representative. . . .

The obligation of the Imamate, which is thus confirmed, is a collective duty, like the Holy War and the pursuit of knowledge, so that when it is performed by those whose charge it is, the general obligation of the rest of the community lapses. If no one discharges it, then two groups of people must be distinguished from the rest; first, the electors, who choose an Imam for the community; and second, those eligible for the Imamate, one of whom must be made Imam. The rest of the community, who belong neither to the one nor to the other group, commit no sin or offense if there is a delay in filling the Imamate. When these two groups are constituted and take over the collective obligation, each group must conform to the prescribed conditions. The conditions required in the electors are three:

1. Rectitude ['adāla] in all respects.
2. The knowledge to recognize the required qualifications for the Imamate.
3. The discernment and wisdom to choose the candidate best suited to the Imamate, the most capable and the best informed of the conduct of public affairs.

He who is in the city of the Imam has no privilege or precedence, because of this, over those in other places. That those who are present in the city of the Imam undertake the appointment of the new Imam is custom, not law; this happens because they are the first to hear of his death and because those who are best qualified to succeed him are usually to be found in his city.

The conditions of eligibility for the Imamate are seven:

1. Rectitude in all respects.
2. The knowledge to exercise personal judgment [ijtihād] in cases and decisions.
3. Soundness of hearing, sight, and tongue so that he may deal accurately with those matters which can only be attained by them.
4. Soundness of limb so that he has no defect which would prevent him from moving freely and rising quickly.
5. The discernment needed to govern the subjects and conduct public affairs.
6. The courage and vigor to defend the lands of Islam and to wage holy war against the enemy.
7. Descent, that is to say, he must be of the tribe of Quraysh, as is prescribed by a text and accepted by consensus. . . .

The Imamate is conferred in two ways: one is by the choice of the electors [literally, those competent to bind and to loosen], and the other is by the nomination of the previous Imam. . . .

When the electors meet, they scrutinize the qualified candidates and proceed to appoint that one among them who is the most worthy, who best meets the required conditions, and to whom the people are most willing to give obedience. They recognize him without delay. If the exercise of their judgment leads them to choose a particular person from the community, they offer him the Imamate. If he accepts, they swear allegiance to him, and the Imamate is vested in him by this procedure. Allegiance to him and obedience to him then become binding on the entire community. If he holds back and refuses the Imamate, it cannot be imposed upon him, since it is a contract by consent and choice and may not involve compulsion or constraint. In such case the Imamate is offered to another qualified candidate.

If two candidates are equally well qualified, the elder takes precedence in choice; however, seniority, where the parties are of age, is not a necessary condition, and if the younger is appointed, it is still valid. If one is wiser and the other braver, the choice should be determined by the needs of the time. If the need for courage is more urgent because of the disorder of the frontiers and the appearance of rebels, then the braver has a better claim. If the need for wisdom is more urgent because of the quiescence of the populace and the appearance of heretics, then it is the wiser who has a better claim. . . .

The duties of the Imam in the conduct of public affairs are ten:

1. To maintain the religion according to established principles and the consensus of the first generation of Muslims. If an innovator appears or if some dubious person deviates from it, the Imam must clarify the proofs of religion to him, expound that which is correct, and apply to him the proper rules and penalties so that religion may be protected from injury and the community safeguarded from error.
2. To execute judgments given between litigants and to settle disputes between contestants so that justice may prevail and so that none commit or suffer injustice.
3. To defend the lands of Islam and to protect them from intrusion so that people may earn their livelihood and travel at will without danger to life or property.
4. To enforce the legal penalties for the protection of God's commandments from violation and for the preservation of the rights of his servants from injury or destruction.
5. To maintain the frontier fortresses with adequate supplies and effective force for their defense so that the enemy may not take them by surprise, commit profanation there, or shed the blood, either of a Muslim or an ally [mu'āhad].
6. To wage holy war [jihād] against those who, after having been invited to accept Islam, persist in rejecting it, until they either become Muslims or enter the Pact [dhimma] so that God's truth may prevail over every religion [cf. Qur'ān, ix, 33].
7. To collect the booty and the alms [ṣadaqa] in conformity with the prescriptions of the Holy Law, as defined by explicit texts and by independent judgment [ijtihād], and this without terror or oppression.
8. To determine the salaries and other sums due from the treasury, without ex-

travagance and without parsimony, and to make payment at the proper time, neither in advance nor in arrears.

9. To employ capable and trustworthy men and appoint sincere men for the tasks which he delegates to them and for the money which he entrusts to them so that the tasks may be competently discharged and the money honestly safeguarded.

10. To concern himself directly with the supervision of affairs and the scrutiny of conditions so that he may personally govern the community, safeguard the faith, and not resort to delegation in order to free himself either for pleasure or for worship, for even the trustworthy may betray and the sincere may deceive. God said, "O David, we have made you our vicegerent [*khalīfa*] on earth; therefore, judge justly among men and do not follow your caprice, which will lead you astray from God's path." [Qur'ān, xxxviii, 25]. In this, God was not content with delegation, but required a personal performance and did not excuse the following of passions, which, He says, lead astray from His path, and this, though He considered David worthy to judge in religion and to hold His vicegerency [*khilāfa*]. This is one of the duties of government of any shepherd. The Prophet of God, may God bless and save him, said, "You are all shepherds, and you are all answerable for your flocks."

. . .

The rules of the Imamate and its general jurisdiction over the interests of religion and the governance of the community, as we have described them, being established, and the investiture of an Imam being duly confirmed, the authority which comes from him to his deputies is of four kinds:

1. Those who have unlimited authority of unlimited scope. These are the viziers, for they are entrusted with all public affairs without specific attribution.

2. Those who have unlimited authority of limited scope. Such are the provincial and district governors, whose authority is unlimited within the specific areas assigned to them.

3. Those who have limited authority of unlimited scope. Such are the chief qāḍī, the commander of the armies, the commandant of the frontier fortresses, the intendant of the land tax, and the collector of the alms, each of whom has unlimited authority in the specific functions assigned to him.

4. Those with limited authority of limited scope, such as the *qāḍī* of a town or district, the local intendant of the land tax, collector of tithes, the frontier commandment, or the army commander, every one of whom has limited authority of limited scope.

20

Islamic Culture

The Islamic world built a unique and sophisticated civilization on its religion and on foundations laid by its predecessors in the classical world. Its strategic location not only allowed the Islamic world opportunity to use facets of neighboring civilizations, but also made it an important cultural bridge for the interregional exchange of ideas and technology. By 1500 Muslim creativity had resulted in significant contributions to the fields of science, medicine, mathematics, philosophy, literature, the fine arts, and history. 'Abd-ar-Raḥmân Abû Záyd ibn Muḥammad ibn Muḥammad ibn Khaldûn (1332–1406), Islam's most acclaimed medieval historian, deserves special notice because he introduced a sociological theory of history. He also pioneered the evolution of a branch in history, the philosophy of history, several centuries before Europeans did. In the famous introduction (*The Muqaddimah*) to his seven-volume universal history, *Kitâb al-'Ibar* (*The Book of Examples*), Ibn Khaldûn offers an exposition on the patterns of historical evolution and suggests reasons for the rise and fall of civilizations by means of a scientific and rational analysis of the social and economic structures in society. His unique approach, focused on Muslim dynastic history, incorporated examination of various elements, including the impact of climate and environment, religious and economic determinism, and the "laws" of social change. In the following selection from *The Muqaddimah,* Ibn Khaldûn assesses the importance of the Arabic language in Islamic culture.

From Ibn Khaldûn, *The Muqaddimah: An Introduction to History,* translated from the Arabic by Franz Rosenthal, Bollingen Series XLIII. Copyright © 1958 and 1967 by Princeton University Press. Excerpts, pp. 428–33. Reprinted by permission of Princeton University Press.

This passage shows how a degree of cultural unity was forged in the Middle East, amid ongoing diversity, even beyond the Islamic religion. In what ways did Arabs depend on other cultural traditions, and why were they so receptive? How does Ibn Khaldûn relate religion to other intellectual activities? How did the cultural boundaries of the Middle East change under Arab ascendancy?

It is a remarkable fact that, with few exceptions, most Muslim scholars both in the religious and in the intellectual sciences have been non-Arabs. When a scholar is of Arab origin, he is non-Arab in language and upbringing and has non-Arab teachers. This is so in spite of the fact that Islam is an Arab religion, and its founder was an Arab.

The reason for it is that at the beginning Islam had no sciences or crafts, because of the simple conditions and the desert attitude. The religious laws, which are the commands and prohibitions of God, were in the breasts of the authorities. They knew their sources, the Qur'ân and the Sunnah, from information they had received directly from Muḥammad himself and from the men around him. The people at that time were Arabs. They did not know anything about scientific instruction or the writing of books and systematic works. There was no incentive or need for that. This was the situation during the time of the men around Muḥammad and the men of the second generation. The persons who were concerned with knowing and transmitting the (religious laws) were called "Qur'ân readers," that is, people who were able to read the Qur'ân and were not illiterate. Illiteracy was general at that time among the men around Muḥammad, since they were Bedouins.

By the time of the reign of ar-Rashid, (oral) tradition had become far removed (from its starting point). It was thus necessary to write commentaries on the Qur'ân and to fix the traditions in writing, because it was feared that they might be lost. It was also necessary to know the chains of transmitters and to assess their reliability, in order to be able to distinguish sound chains of transmitters from inferior ones. Then, more and more laws concerning actual cases were derived from the Qur'ân and the Sunnah. Moreover, the Arabic language became corrupt, and it was necessary to lay down grammatical rules.

All the religious sciences had thus become habits connected with producing and deriving (laws and norms) and with comparison and analogical reasoning. Other, auxiliary sciences became necessary, such as knowledge of the rules of the Arabic language, (knowledge of) the rules that govern the derivation (of laws) and analogical reasoning, and defence of the articles of faith by means of arguments, because a great number of innovations and heresies (had come into existence). All these things developed into sciences with their own habits, requiring instruction (for their acquisition). Thus, they came to fall under the category of crafts.

We have mentioned before that the crafts are cultivated by sedentary people and that of all peoples the Bedouins are least familiar with the crafts. Thus, the sciences came to belong to sedentary culture, and the Arabs were not familiar with them or with their cultivation. Now, the only sedentary people at that time were non-Arabs and, what amounts to the same thing, the clients and sedentary people who followed the non-Arabs at that time in all matters of sedentary culture, including the crafts and professions. They were most versed in those things, because sedentary culture had been firmly rooted among them from the time of the Persian Empire.

Thus, the founders of grammar were Sîbawayh and, after him, al-Fârisî and az-Zajjâj. All of them were of non-Arab (Persian) descent. They were brought up in the Arabic language and acquired the knowledge of it through their upbringing and through contact with Arabs. They invented the rules of (grammar) and made it into a discipline (in its own right) for later (generations to use).

Most of the *ḥadîth* scholars who preserved traditions for the Muslims also were Persians, or Persian in language and upbringing, because the discipline was widely cultivated in the 'Irâq and the regions beyond. Furthermore, all the scholars who worked in the science of the principles of jurisprudence were Persians. The same applies to speculative theologians and to most Qur'ân commentators. Only the Persians engaged in the task of preserving knowledge and writing systematic scholarly works. Thus, the truth of the following statement by the Prophet becomes apparent: "If scholarship hung suspended in the highest parts of heaven, the Persians would attain it."

The Arabs who came into contact with that flourishing sedentary culture and exchanged their Bedouin attitude for it, were diverted from occupying themselves with scholarship and study by their leading position in the 'Abbâsid dynasty and the tasks that confronted them in government. They were the men of the dynasty, at once its protectors and the executors of its policy. In addition, at that time, they considered it a lowly thing to be a scholar, because scholarship is a craft, and political leaders are always contemptuous of the crafts and professions and everything that leads to them. Thus, they left such things to non-Arabs and persons of mixed Arab and non-Arab parentage. The latter cultivated them, and the Arabs always considered it their right to cultivate them, as they were their custom and their sciences, and never felt complete contempt for the men learned in them. The final result, however, was that when the Arabs lost power and the non-Arabs took over, the religious sciences had no place with the men in power, because the latter had no relations with (scholarship). Scholars were viewed with contempt, because the men in power saw that scholars had no contact with them and were occupying themselves with things that were of no interest to the men in power in governmental and political matters. This is why all scholars in the religious sciences, or most of them, are non-Arabs.

The intellectual sciences, as well, made their appearance in Islam only after scholars and authors had become a distinct group of people and all scholarship had become a craft. (The intellectual sciences) were then the special preserve of non-Arabs, left alone by the Arabs, who did not cultivate them.

This situation continued in the cities as long as the Persians and the Persian countries, the 'Irâq, Khurâsân, and Transoxania, retained their sedentary culture. But when those cities fell into ruin, sedentary culture, which God has devised for the attainment of sciences and crafts, disappeared from them. Along with it, scholarship altogether disappeared from among the Persians, who were now engulfed by the desert attitude. Scholarship was restricted to cities with an abundant sedentary culture. Today, no city has a more abundant sedentary culture than Cairo. It is the mother of the world, the great centre of Islam, and the mainspring of the sciences and the crafts.

A person whose first language was not Arabic finds it harder than the native speaker of Arabic to acquire the sciences

This is explained by the fact that all scientific research deals with ideas of the mind and the imagination. This applies to the religious sciences in which research is mostly concerned with the meaning of words. These are matters of the imagination. The same fact also applies to the intellectual sciences, which are matters of the mind.

Linguistic expression is merely the interpreter of ideas that are in the mind. One person conveys them to another in oral discussion, instruction, and constant scientific research. Words and expressions are media and veils between the ideas. They constitute the bonds between them and give them their final imprint. The student of ideas must extract them from the words that express them. For this he needs a knowledge of their linguistic meaning and a good (linguistic) habit. Otherwise, it is difficult for him to get (the ideas), apart from the usual difficulties inherent in mental investigation of them. When he has a firmly rooted habit as far as semantics is concerned, so that the (correct) ideas present themselves to his mind when he hears certain words used, spontaneously and naturally, the veil between the ideas and the understanding is either totally removed, or becomes less heavy, and the only task that remains is to investigate the problems inherent in the ideas.

All this applies to instruction by personal contact in the form of oral address and explanation. But when the student has to rely upon the study of books and written material and must understand scientific problems from the forms of written letters in books, he is confronted with another veil, (namely, the veil) that separates handwriting and the form of letters found in writing from the spoken words found in the imagination. The written letters have their own way of indicating the spoken words. As long as that way is not known, it is impossible to know what they express. If it is known imperfectly, (the meaning) expressed by the letters is known imperfectly. Thus, the student is confronted with another veil standing between him and his objective of attaining scientific habits, one that is more difficult to cope with than the first one. Now, if his habit, as far as the meaning of words and writing goes, is firmly established, the veils between him and the ideas are lifted. He has merely to occupy himself with understanding the problems inherent in the (ideas). The same relationship of ideas with words and writing exists in every language. The habits of students who learn these things while they are young, are more firmly established (than those of other people).

Furthermore, the Muslim realm was far-flung and included many nations. The sciences of the ancients were wiped out through the prophecy of (Islam) and its holy book. Illiteracy was the proper thing and symbol of Islam. Islam then gained royal authority and power. (Foreign) nations served the (Muslims) with their sedentary culture and refinement. The religious sciences, which had been traditional, were turned by the Muslims into crafts. Thus, (scholarly) habits originated among them. Many systematic works and books were written. The Muslims desired to learn the sciences of the foreign nations. They made them their own through translations. They pressed them into the mould of their own views. They took them over into their own language from the non-Arab languages and surpassed the achievements of the non-Arabs in them. The manuscripts in the non-Arabic language were forgotten, abandoned, and scattered. All the sciences came to exist in Arabic. The systematic works on them were written in Arabic writing. Thus, students of the sciences needed a knowledge of the meaning of Arabic words and Arabic writing. They could dispense with all other languages, because they had been wiped out and there was no longer any interest in them.

Language is a habit of the tongue. Likewise, handwriting is a craft, the habit of which is located in the hand. The tongue which had at first the habit of speaking a language other than Arabic, becomes deficient in (its mastery of) Arabic, because the person whose habit has advanced to a certain point in a particular craft is rarely able to master another one. This is obvious. If a person is deficient in his mastery of Arabic, in the meaning of its words and its writing, it is difficult for him to derive the ideas from Arabic words and (Arabic writing). Only if the early habit of speaking a non-Arab language is not yet firmly established in a person when he makes the transition from it to Arabic, as is the case with small non-Arab children who grow up with Arabs before their (habit) of speaking a non-Arab language is firmly established, only then does the Arabic language come to be like a first native language, and his ability to derive the ideas from the words of the Arabic language is not deficient. The same applies to persons who learned non-Arabic writing before Arabic writing.

This is why we find that most non-Arab scholars in their research and classes do not copy comments from books but read them aloud. In this way they are less disturbed by the veils (between words and ideas), so that they can get more easily at the ideas. When a person possesses the perfect habit as far as verbal and written expression is concerned, he does not have to (read aloud). For him, it has become like a firmly engrained natural disposition to derive an understanding of words from writing and of ideas from words. The veils between him and the ideas are lifted.

Intensive study and constant practice of the language and of writing may lead a person to a firmly rooted habit, as we find in most non-Arab scholars. However, this occurs rarely. When one compares such a person with an Arabic scholar of equal merit, the latter is the more efficient, and his habit the stronger. The non-Arab has trouble because his early use of a non-Arab language necessarily makes him inferior.

This is not in contradiction with the aforementioned fact that most Muslim scholars are non-Arabs. In that connection, "non-Arab" meant non-Arab by descent. Such non-Arabs had a lengthy sedentary culture. Being non-Arab in language is something quite different, and this is what is meant here.

It is also not in contradiction with the fact that the Greeks were highly accomplished scholars. They learned their sciences in their own native language and in their own writing, such as was customarily used among them. The non-Arab Muslim who studies to become a scholar learns his subject in a language other than his native one and from a writing other than the one whose habit he has mastered. This, then, becomes an impediment to him. This applies quite generally to all kinds of speakers of non-Arab languages, such as the Persians, the Turks, the Berbers, the European Christians, and all others whose language is not Arabic.

21

Poetry and Society in Tang China

The Tang period (618–907) was one of the great ages in the Chinese past. Changan, the remarkably well-administered Tang capital, had over a million inhabitants, making it the largest city in the world. During the seventh and eighth centuries, Tang military power penetrated deep into central Asia, while—in the opposite direction—Korea and Japan came under the cultural leadership of the Chinese. The Tang centuries were also a time when Buddhist temples and monasteries, often elaborately decorated with sculpture and wall paintings, were built throughout China. In addition, the Tang period saw a great flowering of literary culture, especially poetry.

Tang poets were amazingly prolific; they produced nearly fifty thousand poems. Two characteristics of this verse are particularly significant. First, it was often written by people who were primarily government officials. Indeed, during the Tang period the ability to write good poetry was an important criterion for the selection of imperial administrators. Second, Tang poetry—like much of Chinese

Source: "Recruiting Officer of Shih-hao," "Watching the Wheat-reapers," and "Bitter Cold, Living in the Village" translated by Irving Yucheng Lo; "The Old Man of Hsing-feng with the Broken Arm" and "An Old Charcoal Seller" translated by Eugene Eoyang; "Farmers," "On Covering the Bones of Chang Chin, the Hired Man" translated by Jan W. Walls; and "Lament of a Woman Acorn-gatherer" translated by William H. Niehauser. All poems from *Sunflower Splendor,* edited by Wu-chi Liu and Irving Yucheng Lo. Copyright © 1975 by Wu-chi Liu and Irving Lo. Reprinted by permission of Doubleday & Company, Inc.

poetry in other periods—was often concerned with the experiences of ordinary people.

It is this latter characteristic that makes the following poems so valuable to the historian of daily life. While the four authors of the poems below were all government officials, their verse — in focusing on the peasantry and rural life — illuminates the social history of the Tang period. Two of the poets reprinted here are of particular importance: Tu Fu (712–770) has long been regarded as China's greatest poet. Po Chü-yi (772–846) was China's first great popular poet; unlike the other poets of his time, he often found his poems copied on the walls of inns and monasteries.

How do these poems help us to understand the experiences of the common people during the Tang centuries? Note that these poems come from the second half of the Tang period, a time of retrenchment and decline for the ruling dynasty. What problems in Tang life do the poems point to? What is the attitude of the poet-officials toward the common people?

FROM TU FU (712–770)

Recruiting Officer of Shih-hao

At dusk I sought lodging at Shih-hao village,
When a recruiting officer came to seize men at night.
An old man scaled the wall and fled,
His old wife came out to answer the door.

How furious was the officer's shout!
How pitiable was the woman's cry!
I listened as she stepped forward to speak:
"All my three sons have left for garrison duty at Yeh;
From one of them a letter just arrived,
Saying my two sons had newly died in battle.
Survivors can manage to live on,
But the dead are gone forever.
Now there's no other man in the house,
Only a grandchild at his mother's breast.
The child's mother has not gone away;
She has only a tattered skirt for wear.
An old woman, I am feeble and weak,
But I will gladly leave with you tonight
To answer the urgent call at Ho-yang—
I can still cook morning gruel for your men."

The night drew on, but talking stopped;
It seemed I heard only half-concealed sobs.
As I got back on the road at daybreak,
Only the old man was there to see me off.

FROM PO CHÜ-YI (772–846)

Watching the Wheat-reapers

Farm families have few leisure months,
In the fifth month chores double up.
When south wind rises at night,
Fields and dikes are covered with golden wheat.

Women old and young carry baskets of food,
Children and toddlers bring out porridge in pots,
Following each other with food for the farmhands,
Those stout fellows on the southern knoll.

Their feet steamed by the sultry vapor from the soil,
Their backs scorched by the sun's burning light;
Drained of all strength to feel any heat,
Their only regret, summer days are too short.

Then there are those poor womenfolk,
Their children clinging to their side.
With their right hand they pick up leftover grains;
On their left arm dangles a broken basket.

To hear their words of complaint—
All who listen will grieve for them:
Their family land stripped clean to pay tax,
They now glean the field to fill their stomach.

What deeds of merit have I done?
I've neither farmed nor raised silkworms;
My official's salary, three hundred piculs of rice,
And at year's end there is surplus grain to eat.

Thinking of this, I feel guilty and ashamed;
All day long I cannot keep it out of my mind.

Bitter Cold, Living in the Village

In the twelfth month of this Eighth Year,
On the fifth day, a heavy snow fell.
Bamboos and cypress all perished from the freeze.
How much worse for people without warm clothes!

As I looked around the village,
Of ten families, eight or nine were in need.
The north wind was sharper than the sword,
And homespun cloth could hardly cover one's body.

Only brambles were burnt for firewood,
And sadly people sat at night to wait for dawn.

From this I know that when winter is harsh,
The farmers suffer most.
Looking at myself, during these days—
How I'd shut tight the gate of my thatched hall,
Cover myself with fur, wool, and silk,
Sitting or lying down, I had ample warmth.
I was lucky to be spared cold or hunger,
Neither did I have to labor in the field.

Thinking of that, how can I not feel ashamed?
I ask myself what kind of man am I.

The Old Man of Hsin-feng with the Broken Arm

An old man from Hsin-feng, eighty-eight years old,
Hair on his temples and his eyebrows white as snow.
Leaning on his great-great-grandson, he walks to the front of the inn,
His left arm on the boy's shoulder, his right arm broken.
I ask the old man how long has his arm been broken,
And how it came about, how it happened.
The old man said he grew up in the Hsin-feng district.
He was born during blessed times, without war or strife,
And he used to listen to the singing and dancing in the Pear Garden,
Knew nothing of banner and spear, or bow and arrow.
Then, during the T'ien-pao period, a big army was recruited:
From each family, one was taken out of every three,
And of those chosen, where were they sent?
Five months, ten thousand miles away, to Yunnan,
Where, it is said, the Lu River runs,
Where, when flowers fall from pepper trees, noxious fumes rise;
Where, when a great army fords the river, with its seething eddies,
Two or three out of ten never reach the other side.

The village, north and south, was full of the sound of wailing,
Sons leaving father and mother, husbands leaving wives.
They all said, of those who went out to fight the barbarians,
Not one out of a thousand lived to come back.
At the time, this old man was twenty-four,
And the army had his name on their roster.

"Then, late one night, not daring to let anyone know,
By stealth, I broke my arm, smashed it with a big stone.
Now I was unfit to draw the bow or carry the flag,
And I would be spared the fighting in Yunnan.

Bone shattered, muscles ached, it wasn't unpainful,
But I could count on being rejected and sent home.

"This arm has been broken now for over sixty years:
I've lost one limb, but the body's intact.
Even now, in cold nights, when the wind and rain blow,
Right up to daybreak, I hurt so much I cannot sleep,
But I have never had any regrets.
At least, now I alone have survived.
Or else, years ago at the River Lu,
I would have died, my spirit fled, and my bones left to rot:
I would have wandered, a ghost in Yunnan looking for home,
Mourning over the graves of ten thousands."
So the old man spoke: I ask you to listen.
Have you not heard the Prime Minister of the K'ai-yüan period, Sung K'ai-
    fu?
How he wouldn't reward frontier campaigns, not wanting to glorify war?
And, have you not heard of Yang Kuo-chung, the Prime Minister of the
    T'ien-pao period,
Wishing to seek favor, achieved military deeds at the frontier,
But, before he could pacify the frontier, the people became disgruntled:
Ask the old man of Hsin-feng with the broken arm!

An Old Charcoal Seller

An old charcoal seller
Cuts firewood, burns coal by the southern mountain.
His face, all covered with dust and ash, the color of smoke,
The hair at his temples is gray, his ten fingers black.
The money he makes selling coal, what is it for?
To put clothes on his back and food in his mouth.
The rags on his poor body are thin and threadbare;
Distressed at the low price of coal, he hopes for colder weather.
Night comes, an inch of snow has fallen on the city,
In the morning, he rides his cart along the icy ruts,
His ox weary, he hungry, and the sun already high.
In the mud by the south gate, outside the market, he stops to rest.
All of a sudden, two dashing riders appear;
An imperial envoy, garbed in yellow (his attendant in white),
Holding an official dispatch, he reads a proclamation.
Then turns the cart around, curses the ox, and leads it north.
One cartload of coal—a thousand or more catties!
No use appealing to the official spiriting the cart away:
Half a length of red lace, a slip of damask
Dropped on the ox—is payment in full!

FROM LIU TSUNG-YÜAN (773–819)

Farmers

Beyond the bamboo fence, cooking fire and smoke,
an evening when neighboring farmers chat.
From courtyard's edge autumn insects chirrup,
scattered hempstalks, now desolate and alone.
Silk from the worms all surrendered as tax,
loom and shuttle lean idly on the wall.
An officer passes through one night,
and is served a feast of fowl and millet.
Everyone says the official is harsh,
his language full of reprimands.
East villagers are behind in their rent
and wagon wheels sink in mire and bog.
Officials' residences are short on mercy;
where whips and rods are given fiendish rein.
We must attend cautiously to our work,
for flesh and skin are to be pitied.
We welcome now the new year's arrival,
fearing only to tread on the former tracks.

On Covering the Bones of Chang Chin, the Hired Man

The cycle of life is a worrisome thing,
a single breath that gathers and scatters again.
We come by chance into a hubbub of joy and rage
and suddenly we're taking leave again.
To be an underling is no disgrace,
neither is nobility divine;
all at once when breathing stops,
fair and ugly disappear in decay.
You slaved in my stables all your life,
cutting fodder, you never complained you were tired.
When you died we gave you a cheap coffin
and buried you at the foot of the eastern hill.
But then, alas, there came a raging flood
that left you helter-skelter by the roadside.
Dry and brittle, your hundred bones baked in the sun,
scattered about, never to join again.
Luckily an attendant told me of this,
and the vision saddened me to tears,
for even cats and tigers rate a sacrificial offering,

and dogs and horses have their ragged shrouds.
Long I stand here mourning for your soul
yet how could you know of this act?
Basket and spade bear you to the grave
which waterways will keep from further harm.
My mind is now at ease
whether you know it or not.
One should wait for spring to cover up bones,
and propitious is the time now.
Benevolence for all things is not mine to confer;
just call it a personal favor for you.

FROM P'I JIH-HSIU (ca. 833–883)

Lament of a Woman Acorn-gatherer

Deep into autumn the acorns ripen,
Scattering as they fall into the scrub on the hill.
Hunched over, a hoary-haired crone
Gathers them, treading the morning frost.
After a long time she's got only a handful,
An entire day just fills her basket.
First she suns them, then steams them,
To use in making late winter provisions.

At the foot of the mountain she has ripening rice,
From its purple spikes a fragrance pervades.
Carefully she reaps, then hulls the grain,
Kernel after kernel like a jade earring.
She takes the grain to offer as government tax,
In her own home there are no granary bins.
How could she know that well over a picul of rice
Is only five pecks in official measurement?
Those crafty clerks don't fear the law,
Their greedy masters won't shun a bribe.
In the growing season she goes into debt,
In the off season sends grain to government bin.
From winter even into spring,
With acorns she tricks her hungry innards.
                         ·   ·   ·

Aah, meeting this old woman acorn-gatherer,
Tears come uncalled to moisten my robe.

22

An Uncommon Woman in Sung China

The Sung period (960–1279) was a time of dynamic change in China, especially in economic and social life. New strains of early-ripening rice greatly increased agricultural production in the Yangtze region and led to rapid population growth. Commerce and urban growth developed swiftly; Sung China had, at various times, two of the world's most populous cities, Kaifeng and Hangchow. A great expansion of coal mining and iron smelting in eleventh-century China seemingly brought the country to the edge of industrialization. Paper money, gunpowder, and printing with movable type were other key innovations during the Sung centuries. This period was also a golden age for Chinese porcelains.

If Sung economic and social trends greatly increased the prosperity of the country, their impact on gender relations remains uncertain. We know that during the Sung centuries the urban upper classes first began to bind the feet of young girls, suggesting a decline in the position of elite women. As is often the case, however, the evidence is too fragmentary to permit us to speak with much confidence about the circumstances of ordinary women.

Nevertheless, as we have seen earlier in the case of classical India, popular tales may help shed light on gender relations among the lower classes. The following Chinese story, entitled *The Shrew,* which combines elements of realism and parody, was widely known during the Sung period. It is especially valuable for the evidence it provides on marriage and family life. While reading this story, keep the following questions in mind: Why did Ts'ui-lien get into so much trouble?

Reprinted with permission of The Free Press, a Division of Macmillan, Inc. From *Chinese Civilization and Society: A Sourcebook,* by Patricia Buckley Ebrey. Copyright © 1981 by The Free Press.

What does the story reveal about the attributes of a "good" daughter and a "good" wife? What characteristics of the Chinese family are illustrated in the story? Do you see any similarities between Ts'ui-lien and the women in the Hindu stories (selection 12)? What are the differences?

She declaims whole chapters extempore—
  let no one despise her gift!
Each speech brings her fresh enemies;
  her fate moves men to pity.
Though she lacks the persuasion of the wise Tzu-lu
May her tale yet win a laugh from you.

These lines refer to former days in the Eastern Capital, where dwelt a gentleman by the name of Chang Eminent, who had in his house much gold and silver. Of his two grown-up sons, the older was called Tiger, the younger, Wolf. The older son had already taken a wife, the younger was not yet married. In the same city was another gentleman, Li Lucky, who had a daughter named Ts'ui-lien, aged sixteen and uncommonly pretty, accomplished in the art of the needle, and conversant even with the Classics, Histories, and Hundred Philosophers. She was, however, somewhat too ready with her tongue. In speaking to others, she composed whole essays, and the flow of her speech became a flood. Questioned about one matter, she answered about ten, and when questioned about ten, she answered about a hundred.

The story went that in the same city was a Madam Wang who went to and fro between the two families to arrange about a marriage. The family stations corresponding, a match was agreed upon, and a propitious day and hour chosen for the wedding. Three days before the event, Li Lucky said to his wife, "Our daughter is faultless in most respects; only her tongue is quick and you and I cannot be easy about it. Should her father-in-law prove hard to please, it were no trifling matter. Besides, the mother-in-law is certain to be fussy, and they are a large family with older brother, sister-in-law, and numerous others. What shall we do?" And his wife said, "You and I will need to caution her against it." With this, they saw Ts'ui-lien come before them, and when she found that the faces of both her parents were clouded with grief, and their eyebrows closely knit, she said:

Dad, ease your mind; Ma, be consoled;
Brother, rest assured; sister-in-law, stop worrying;
It is not that your daughter would boast of her cleverness
But from childhood she has been on her mettle:
She can spin, she can weave,
She makes dresses, does patching and embroidery;
Light chars and heavy duties she takes in her stride,
Has ready the teas and meals in a trice;
She can work and hand-mill and pound with the pestle;
She endures hardship gladly, she is not easily tired,

Thinks nothing of making dumplings and cookies.
Prepares any soup or broth, does to a turn some cutlet or
 chop.
At night she is vigilant,
Fastens the backdoor and bolts the gate,
Scrubs the frying pan, shuts the cupboard,
Tidies up the rooms both in front and behind,
Makes ready the beds, unrolls the quilts,
Lights the lamp, asks the mother-in-law to retire,
Then calls out "Rest well" and returns to her room:
Thus shall I serve my parents-in-law,
And would they be satisfied?
Dear Dad and Ma, let your minds be at rest—
Besides these set tasks, nought matters more than a fart.

When Ts'ui-lien had finished, her father rose from his chair to beat her. But the
mother pleaded with him, and loudly reproved her saying, "Child, your father and I
were worried just because of your sharp tongue. From now on, talk less. The ancients
say, 'Loquacity earns the hatred of many.' When you enter your husband's house, be
wary of speaking. A thousand times remember this!" Ts'ui-lien thereupon said, "I know
now. From this time onwards I will keep my mouth shut."
 . . .

Then Li Lucky said to Ts'ui-lien, "Child, you should go before the family shrine,
make obeisance to your ancestors and bid them farewell. I have already lit the candles
and incense; so do it while we wait for the bridal procession. May the ancestors protect
you and you be at peace in your husband's home." Thus instructed, Ts'ui-lien took a
bunch of lighted incense sticks and went before the shrine, and even as she made
obeisance, she prayed aloud:

Shrine that guides the household,
You sages that were our ancestors,
This day I take a husband,
Yet shall not dare keep my own counsel:
At the solstices and equinoxes, and the beginning of each
 season,
I still will offer up the smoke of incense.
I pray to your divine wisdom
Ten thousand times that you pity and hearken!
The man takes a wife, the maid a mate—
This is in the nature of things—
May there be good fortune and rejoicing!
May husband and wife both remain sound and whole,
Without hardship, without calamity,
Even for a hundred years!

May they be merry as fish in water
And their union prove sweeter than honey,
Blessed with five sons and two daughters—
A complete family of seven children—
Matched with two worthy sons-in-law,
Wise and versed in etiquette,
And five daughters-in-law, too,
Paragons of filial piety.
May there be grandsons and granddaughters numerous
To flourish generation after generation.

May there be gold and pearls in heaps
And rice and wheat to fill in a granary,
Abundance of silkworms and mulberry trees,
And cattle and horses drawn up neck to neck,
Chickens, geese, duck and other fowl,
And a pond teeming with fish.
May my husband obey me,
Yet his parents love and pity me;
May the sister-in-law and I live in harmony
And the older and the younger brother be both easy to
 please;
May the servants show full respect,
And the younger sister take a fancy to me.
And, within a space of three years,
Let them die, the whole lot,
And all the property be left in my hands:
Then Ts'ui-lien would be happy for some years!

 · · ·

By nightfall the feast broke up and the relatives all went home. Sitting alone in
the nuptial chamber, Ts'ui-lien thought to herself: "Soon my husband will come into
the room and his hands are certain to rove in some wild ecstatic dance. I have to be
prepared." So she stood up, removed her jewelry, undressed and, getting into bed,
rolled herself tightly in a quilt and slept. Now, to go on with the story, Wolf came in
and undressed, and was about to go to bed, when Ts'ui-lien stunned him with a thun-
dering cry:

Wretch, how ridiculously mistaken in your designs!
Of a truth, what an uncouth rustic!
You are a man, I a woman;
You go your way, I go mine.
You say I am your own bride—
Well, do not call me your old woman yet.
Who was the match-maker? Who the chief witness?
What were the betrothal presents? How was the gift of tea?

How many pigs, sheep, fowl, and geese? How many vats of
  wine?
What floral decorations embellished the gifts?
How many gems? How many golden head ornaments?
How many rolls of silk gauze thick and thin?
How many pairs of bracelets, hat pins, hair pins?
With what should I adorn myself?
At the third watch late at night,
What mean you to come before my bed?
At once depart, and hurry away,
Lest you annoy my folk at home.
But if you provoke my fiery temper,
I will seize you by the ears and pull your hair,
Tear your clothes and scratch your face;
My heavy hand with outstretched fingers shall fall pat
  on your cheek.
If I rip your hair-net, don't say I did not warn you,
Nor complain if your neatly coiled hair get dishevelled.
This is no bawd's lane.
Nor the dwelling of some servile courtesan.
What do I care about silly rules like "Two and two make
  four"?
With a sudden laying about of my fist
I'll send you sprawling all over the room.

When Wolf heard his bride declaim this chapter, he dared not approach her, nor
utter even a groan, but sat in a far-off corner of the room.

To go on with the story, soon it was indeed almost the third watch, and Ts'ui-
lien thought to herself: "I have now married into his family. Alive, I shall remain one
of their household; dead, I shall dwell among their ghosts. If we do not sleep in the
same bed tonight, when tomorrow my parents-in-law learn about it, they will certainly
blame me. Let it be, then! I will ask him to come to bed." So she said to Wolf:

Dumb wretch, do not say you are drunk!
Come over, I will share the bed with you.
Draw near me and hear my command:
Fold your hands respectfully before you; tread on your toes;
  do not chatter.
Remove your hair-net and off with your cap;
Gather up your garments, socks, and boots;
Shut the door, lower the curtain,
And add some oil to the lamp grown dim.
Come to bed, and ever so softly
We'll pretend to be mandarin ducks or intertwining trees.

Make no noise, be careful of what you say;
When our conjugal rites are completed, you'll curl up next
 my feet,
Crooking your knee-joints, drawing in your heels.
If by chance you give even one kick,
Then know it's *death* for you!

. . .

[Several days later, following some lively conflicts between Ts'ui-lien and her new in-laws] Mr. Chang cried, "Have done! Have done! Such a daughter-in-law would one day bring down the family name and be a reproach to the ancestors." And he called Wolf before him and said, "Son, put your wife away. I will find you another, a better wife." Though Wolf assented to this, he could not find it in his heart to cast her off. And Tiger and his wife both pleaded with the father, saying, "Let her be taught gradually." But Ts'ui-lien, having heard them, once more spoke up:

Pa, do not complain; Ma, do not complain;
Brother and sister-in-law, do you not complain.
Husband, you need not persist in clinging to me;
From now on, each will do as he pleases.
At once bring paper, ink, slab, and brush.
Write out the certificate of repudiation and set me free.
But note: I did not strike my parents-in-law nor abuse the
 relatives;
I did not deceive my husband nor beat the humble and
 meek;
I did not go visiting neighbours, west or east;
I did not steal nor was I cozened;
I did not gossip about this person nor start trouble with that
 one;
I was not thievish nor jealous nor lewd;
I suffer from no foul disease; I can write and reckon;
I fetched the water from the well, hulled the rice and
 minded the cooking;
I spun and wove and sewed.
Today, then, draw up the certificate as you please,
And when I carry away my dowry, do you not resent it.
In between our thumb-prints add these words:
"Never to meet again, never to see each other."
Conjugal affection is ended,
All feelings dead;
Set down on paper many binding oaths:
If we chance upon each other at the gate of hell,
We shall turn our heads away and not meet.

Wolf, because his parents had decided for him, wrote out the document with tears in his eyes, and the two of them affixed their thumb-prints. The family called for a sedan-chair, loaded the trousseau on it, and sent Ts'ui-lien home with the certificate of repudiation.

In the Li family, Ts'ui-lien's father, mother, brother, and sister-in-law all blamed her for her sharp tongue. But she said to them:

Your daughter was destined at birth to a lonely, wretched
  life—
She married an ignorant, foolish husband!
Though I might have endured the severity of his father and
  mother,
How could I have borne those sisters-in-law?
If I but moved my lips,
Off they went and stirred up the old ones.
Besides, such venom lay behind their scolding,
It soon led to blows and kicks,
From which began an incessant to-do;
Then all at once they wrote the certificate of dissolution.
My one hope was to find contentment and peace at home—
How should I expect even Dad and Ma would blame me?
Abandoned by the husband's family and my own,
I will cut off my hair and become a nun,
Wear a straight-seamed gown and dangle a gourd from a
  pole,
And carry in my hands a huge "wooden fish."
In the daytime from door to door I shall beg for alms;
By night within the temple I shall praise the Buddha,
Chant my "Namah,"
Observe my fasts and attend to my exercises.
My head will be shaven and quite, quite bald;
Who then will not hail the little priestess?

23

"The Noble and Magnificent City of Hangchow": Marco Polo in China

The Sung emperors governed China from their capital at Kaifeng on the Yellow River for more than a century and a half after 960. But in 1127 Jurchen nomads captured the city and overran the northern part of the country. The Sung fled south and established a new capital at Hangchow, where they ruled until the coming of the Mongols in the 1270s.

Hangchow grew rapidly while it was the Sung capital; when the imperial court first moved there, the city had a population of about two hundred thousand persons. By the 1270s this number had increased by a factor of five; Hangchow now included about a million people within its walls. Undoubtedly, the presence of the emperors had much to do with this growth. Like Changan and Kaifeng earlier, Hangchow became the home of many government officials and affiliated groups. The city was a major center of commerce as well. Located midway between the Yangtze River and the seacoast and at the southern end of the Grand Canal, Hangchow was well situated to play a pivotal role in the expanding trade of the Sung centuries. Indeed, during the thirteenth century, Hangchow was probably the richest and most populous city in the world.

In 1275, at the height of the city's prosperity, Marco Polo, the Venetian merchant and traveler, visited Hangchow. Below are portions of his account of the city. What did Marco Polo think of Hangchow? What did he find noteworthy

From *The Travels of Marco Polo*, edited by Milton Rugoff. Copyright © 1961 by Milton Rugoff. Reprinted by arrangement with NAL Penguin Inc., New York, NY. Pp. 208–212, 214–217, 220.

about the city? How does his account help one to better understand Sung economic and social trends? What does he reveal about the Chinese style of government?

Upon leaving Va-giu you pass, in the course of three days' journey, many towns, castles and villages, all of them well-inhabited and opulent. The people have an abundance of provisions. At the end of three days you reach the noble and magnificent city of Hangchow, a name that signifies "The Celestial City." This name it merits from its preeminence, among all others in the world, in point of grandeur and beauty, as well as from its many charms, which might lead an inhabitant to imagine himself in paradise.

This city was frequently visited by Marco Polo, who carefully and diligently observed and inquired into every aspect of it, all of which he recorded in his notes, from which the following particulars are drawn. According to common estimate, this city is a hundred miles around. Its streets and canals are extensive, and there are squares or market places, which are frequented by a prodigious number of people and are exceedingly spacious. It is situated between a fresh, very clear lake and a river of great magnitude, the waters of which run via many canals, both large and small, through every quarter of the city, carrying all sewage into the lake and ultimately to the ocean. This furnishes communication by water, in addition to that by land, to all parts of the town, the canals being of sufficient width for boats and the streets for carriages.

It is commonly said that the number of bridges amounts to twelve thousand. Those which cross the principal canals and are connected with the main streets have arches so high and are built with so much skill that the masts of vessels can pass under them. At the same time, carts and horses can pass over them, so gradual is the upward slope of the arch. If they were not so numerous, there would be no way of crossing from one part to another.

Beyond the city, and enclosing it on that side, there is a moat about forty miles in length, very wide, and issuing from the river mentioned before. This was excavated by the ancient kings of the province so that when the river overflowed its banks, the floodwater might be drawn off into this channel. This also serves for defense. The earth dug from it was thrown to the inner side, and forms a mound around the place.

There are within the city ten principal squares or market places, besides innumerable shops along the streets. Each side of these squares is half a mile in length, and in front of them is the main street, forty paces in width and running in a straight line from one end of the city to the other. It is crossed by many low and convenient bridges. These market squares are four miles from each other. Parallel to the main street, but on the opposite side of the squares, runs a very large canal. On the nearer bank of this stand large stone warehouses provided for merchants who arrive from India and other parts with their goods and effects. They are thus situated conveniently close to the market squares. In each of these, three days in every week, from forty to fifty thousand persons come to the markets and supply them with every article that could be desired.

There is a great deal of game of all kinds, such as roebuck, stags, fallow deer, hares, and rabbits, together with partridges, pheasants, quail, hens, capon, and ducks and geese beyond number, for so easily are they bred on the lake that, for the value of a Venetian silver groat, you may purchase a pair of geese and two pair of ducks. There, too, are the houses where they slaughter cattle, such as oxen, calves, kids, and lambs, to furnish the tables of the rich and of leading citizens. . . .

At all seasons there is in the markets a great variety of herbs and fruits, especially pears of an extraordinary size, weighing ten pounds each, that are white inside and very fragrant. There are also peaches in season, both the yellow and white kinds, and of a delicious flavor. . . . From the sea, fifteen miles distant, a vast quantity of fish is each day brought up the river to the city. There is also an abundance of fish in the lake, which gives employment at all times to a group of fisherman. . . .

Each of the ten market squares is surrounded with high dwelling houses, in the lower part of which are shops where every kind of manufacture is carried on and every article of trade is offered, including spices, drugs, trinkets, and pearls. In certain shops nothing is sold but the wine of the country, which they make continually and serve out fresh to their customers at a moderate price. Many streets connect with the market squares, and in some of them are many cold baths, attended by servants of both sexes. The men and women who frequent them have been accustomed from childhood to wash in cold water, which they consider highly conducive to health. At these baths, however, they have rooms provided with warm water for the use of strangers who cannot bear the shock of the cold. All are in the habit of washing themselves daily, and especially before their meals. . . .

On each side of the principal street mentioned earlier, which runs from one end of the city to the other, there are great houses and mansions with their gardens, and near these, the dwellings of the artisans who work in the shops of the various trades. At all hours you see such multitudes of people passing to and fro on their personal affairs that providing enough food for them might be thought impossible. But one notes that on every market day the squares are crowded with tradespeople and with articles brought by cart and boat — all of which they sell out. From the sale of a single article such as pepper, some notion may be formed of the vast quantity of meat, wine, groceries, and the like, required by the inhabitants of Hangchow. From an officer in the Great Khan's customs, Marco Polo learned that the amount of pepper bought daily was forty-three loads, each load being 243 pounds.

The inhabitants of the city are idolaters. They use paper money as currency. The men as well as the women are fair-skinned and handsome. Most of them always dress themselves in silk, as a result of the vast quantity of that material produced in Hangchow, exclusive of what the merchants import from other provinces.

Among the handicrafts in the city, twelve are considered superior to the rest as being more generally useful. For each of these there are a thousand workshops, and each shop employs ten, fifteen, or twenty workmen, and in a few instances as many as forty, under their respective masters. . . .

There are on the lake a great number of pleasure vessels or barges that can hold ten, fifteen, or twenty persons. They are from fifteen to twenty paces in length, broad-beamed, and not liable to rock. Men who want to enjoy this pastime in the company either of women friends or other men can hire one of these barges, which are always kept in excellent order, and have suitable seats and tables and every other furnishing needed for a party. The cabins have a flat roof or upper deck, where the boatmen stand; and by means of long poles, which they thrust to the bottom of the lake (which is not more than one or two fathoms in depth), shove the barges along. These cabins are painted inside with various colors and figures; all parts of the vessel are likewise adorned with painting. There are windows on either side, which may be opened to allow the company, as they sit at table, to look out in every direction and feast their eyes on the variety and beauty of the passing scene. The pleasure of this exceeds any that can be derived from amusements on land; for as the lake extends the whole length of the city, you have a distant view, as you stand in the boat, of all its grandeur and beauty, its palaces, temples, large convents, and gardens with great trees growing down to the water's edge, while at the same time you can enjoy the sight of other similar boats continually passing you, filled in like manner with parties in pursuit of amusement. . . .

It must be observed . . . that the streets of Hangchow are all paved with stone and brick, and so too are all the principal roads running from there through the province of Manzi [South China]. By means of these, travelers can go to every part without muddying their feet. But as his Majesty's couriers go on horseback in great haste and cannot ride on pavement, a strip of road is left unpaved for their benefit.

The main street of the city is paved with stone and brick to the width of ten paces on each side, the center strip being filled with gravel and having curved drains for carrying off rain water into nearby canals so that it remains always dry. On this gravel, carriages continually pass to-and-fro. . . .

In every street of this city there are stone buildings or towers. In case a fire breaks out in any quarter, which is by no means unusual since the houses are mostly made of wood, the inhabitants may move their possessions to the safety of these towers.

By a regulation of his Majesty, there is a guard of ten watchmen, stationed under cover on all the principal bridges, five on duty by day and five by night. Each of these guards is provided with a drumlike wooden instrument as well as one of metal, together with a water clock which tells the hours of the day and night. When the first hour of the night has passed, one of the watchmen strikes once on the wooden instrument, and also upon the gong. At the end of the second hour he strikes twice, and so on as the hours advance. The guard is not allowed to sleep and must be always on the alert. In the morning as soon as the sun rises, they strike a single stroke again, as in the evening before, and so on from hour to hour. . . .

In cases of rioting or insurrection among the citizens, this police guard is also utilized; but independently of them, his Majesty always keeps on hand a large body of troops, both infantry and cavalry, under the command of his ablest officers.

For the purposes of the nightly watch, towers of earth have been thrown up at a distance of more than a mile from each other. On top of these is a wooden drum, which, when struck with a mallet by the guard stationed there, can be heard at a great distance. If precautions of this nature were not taken there would be a danger that half the city would be consumed. The usefulness of these guards in case of a popular uprising is obvious. . . .

Every father, or head of a household, is required to list on the door of his house the names of each member of his family, as well as the number of his horses. When any person dies, or leaves the dwelling, the name is struck out; similarly, when anyone is born, the name is added to the list. Thus the authorities know at all times the exact number of inhabitants. The same practice is followed throughout the province of Cathay [North China] as well as Manzi. In like manner, all the keepers of inns and public hotels inscribe the names of those who stay with them, noting the day and the hour of their arrival and departure. A copy of this record is transmitted daily to the magistrates stationed in the market squares.

24

The Rise of the Samurai in Japan

Premodern Japan's best known social class, the samurai, originated in the ninth and tenth centuries. Japanese emperors had ruled the country from Kyoto since 794, but as their authority weakened provincial warriors began to accumulate power. Many of these fighting men entered into lord-vassal relationships similar to those in feudal western Europe. (The literal meaning of samurai is "those who serve.") By the twelfth century key warrior families were battling for control of the country. A turning point was reached in 1185 when Minamoto Yoritomo (1147–1199) defeated his rivals and established a second capital at Kamakura near present-day Tokyo, subsequently becoming Japan's first shogun, or supreme military commander. While emperors continued to succeed one another in Kyoto, their authority was severely restricted. For the next seven centuries Japan was ruled by its warrior class.

The first of the following selections is from the *Tale of the Heike,* the most famous literary account documenting the rise of the samurai. Based on the wars that gave rise to the Kamakura shoguns, the *Tale of the Heike* took shape shortly after the events it describes. In the first selection here, Yoshinaka, a leader of the Minamoto forces, is killed by other Minamotos who are jealous of his success.

Selection I from Hiroshi Kitagawa and Bruce T. Tsuchida, translators, *The Tale of the Heike* (Tokyo: University of Tokyo Press, 1975), pp. 519–23. Copyright © 1975, The University of Tokyo Press. Reprinted by permission. Selection II from George Sanson, *A History of Japan to 1334* (Stanford, Calif.: Stanford University Press, 1958), p. 336. Copyright © 1958 Stanford University Press. Reprinted by permission.

The second reading comes from the set of instructions that Hojo Shigetoki, a leading samurai, gave to his eighteen-year-old son in 1247 following the latter's appointment to a key post in the shogunal administration.

Do the virtues of a warrior mesh with the responsibilities of an administrator? To what extent does the *Tale of the Heike* seem to romanticize war and the samurai? Note the suggestion in the *Tale of the Heike* regarding the role of women in the warrior class during its rise to power. What do these sources suggest about differences between Japan and China in the twelfth and thirteenth centuries?

I. FROM THE *TALE OF THE HEIKE*

Yoshinaka had brought with him from Shinano Province two beautiful women, Tomoe and Yamabuki. Of the two, Yamabuki had become ill and had remained in the capital.

Tomoe was indescribably beautiful; the fairness of her face and the richness of her hair were startling to behold. Even so, she was a fearless rider and a woman skilled with the bow. Once her sword was drawn, even the gods and devils feared to fight against her. Indeed, she was a match for a thousand. Thus it was that whenever a war broke out, she armed herself with a strong bow and a great sword, and took a position among the leaders. In many battles she had won matchless fame. This time too she had survived, though all her companions had been killed or wounded. Tomoe was among the seven last riders.

At first the men of Yoritomo's force had thought that Yoshinaka would take the Tamba Road through Nagasaka or would cross over the Ryūge Pass toward the north. Instead, taking neither of these, Yoshinaka urged his horse toward Seta in search of Kanehira. Kanehira had held his position at Seta until Noriyori's repeated assaults had reduced his eight hundred men to fifty. He then ordered his men to roll up their banners and rode back toward the capital to ascertain his master's fate. He was galloping along the lakeshore of Uchide when he caught sight of Yoshinaka ahead of him at a distance of one chō. Recognizing each other, master and retainer spurred their horses to join each other. Seizing Kanehira's hands, Yoshinaka said: "I would have fought to the death on the banks of the Kamo at Rokujō. Simply because of you, however, I have galloped here through the enemy swarms."

"It was very kind of you, my lord," replied Kanehira. "I too would have fought to the death at Seta. But in fear of your uncertain fate, I have come this way."

"We are still tied by karma," said Yoshinaka. "There must be more of my men around here, for I have seen them scattered among the hills. Unroll the banner and raise it high!"

As soon as Kanehira unfurled the banner, many men who had been in flight from the capital and Seta saw it and rallied. They soon numbered more than three hundred.

"Since we still have so many men, let us try one last fight!" shouted Yoshinaka jubilantly. "Look! That band of soldiers over there! Whose army is that?"

"I hear," replied one of Yoshinaka's men, "that is Tadayori's army, my lord."

"How many men are there in his army?"

"About six thousand, my lord."

"Just right!" cried out Yoshinaka. "Since we are determined to fight to the death, let us ride neck and neck with our valiant foes and die gallantly in their midst. Forward!"

Shouting, Yoshinaka dashed ahead. That day he wore armor laced with twilled silk cords over a red battle robe. His helmet was decorated with long golden horns. At his side hung a great sword studded with gold. He carried his quiver a little higher than usual on his back. Some eagle-feathered arrows still remained. Gripping his rattan-bound bow, he rode his famous horse, Oniashige [Gray Demon].

Rising high in his stirrups, he roared at the enemy: "You have often heard of me. Now take a good look at the captain of the Imperial Stables of the Left and governor of Iyo Province — Rising-Sun General Minamoto no Yoshinaka, that is who I am! I know that among you is Kai no Ichijōjirō Tadayori. We are fit opponents for each other. Cut off my head and show it to Yoritomo!"

At this challenge, Tadayori shouted to his men: "Now, hear this! He is the commander of our enemy. Let him not escape! All men — to the attack!"

Tadayori tried to seize Yoshinaka by surrounding him with his many men. Yoshinaka fought desperately, urging his horse into the six thousand, galloping back and forth, left and right, like a spider's legs. When he had dashed through the enemy, he found that his three hundred men had been cut down to fifty. Then he encountered another army of two thousand led by Sanehira. He continued on, attacking several other small bands of one or two hundred here and there, until at last his men were reduced to four. Tomoe was among the survivors.

Yoshinaka called her to his side and said: "You are a woman—leave now for wherever you like, quickly! As for me, I shall fight to the death. If I am wounded, I will kill myself. How ashamed I would be if people said that Yoshinaka was accompanied by a woman in his last fight."

Tomoe would not stir. After repeated pleas, however, she was finally convinced to leave.

"I wish I could find a strong opponent!" she said to herself. "Then I would show my master once more how well I can fight." She drew her horse aside to wait for the right opportunity.

Shortly thereafter, Moroshige of Musashi, a warrior renowned for his great strength, appeared at the head of thirty horsemen. Galloping alongside Moroshige, Tomoe grappled with him, pulled him against the pommel of her saddle, and giving him no chance to resist, cut off his head. The fight concluded, she threw off her armor and fled to the eastern provinces.

Among the remaining retainers of Yoshinaka, Tezuka no Tarō was killed, and his uncle, Tezuka no Bettō, took flight, leaving only Kanehira. When Yoshinaka found himself alone with Kanehira, he sighed: "My armor has never weighed upon me before, but today it is heavy."

"You do not look tired at all, my lord," replied Kanehira, "and your horse is still fresh. What makes it feel so heavy? If it is because you are discouraged at having none of your retainers but me, please remember that I, Kanehira, am a match for a thousand. Since I still have seven or eight arrows left in my quiver, let me hold back the foe while you withdraw to the Awazu pine wood. Now I pray you to put a peaceful end to yourself."

No sooner had he spoken to his master than another band of soldiers confronted them. "Please go to the pine wood, my lord," said Kanehira again. "Let me fight here to keep them away from you."

"I would have died in the capital!" replied Yoshinaka. "I have come this far with no other hope but to share your fate. How can I die apart from you? Let us fight until we die together!"

With these words, Yoshinaka tried to ride neck and neck with Kanehira. Now Kanehira alighted from his horse, seized the bridle of his master's mount, and pleaded in tears: "Whatever fame a warrior may win, a worthless death is a lasting shame for him. You are worn out, my lord. Your horse is also exhausted. If you are surrounded by the enemy and slain at the hand of a low, worthless retainer of some unknown warrior, it will be a great shame for you and me in the days to come. How disgraceful it would be if such a nameless fellow could declare, 'I cut off the head of Yoshinaka, renowned throughout the land of Japan!' "

Yoshinaka finally gave in to Kanehira's entreaty and rode off toward the pine wood of Awazu. Kanehira, riding alone, charged into the band of some fifty horsemen. Rising high in his stirrups, he cried out in a thunderous voice: "You have often heard of me. Now take a good look. I am Imai no Shirō Kanehira, aged thirty-three, a foster brother of Lord Yoshinaka. As I am a valiant warrior among the men of Lord Yoshinaka, your master, Yoritomo, at Kamakura must know my name well. Take my head and show it to him!"

Kanehira had hardly uttered these words when he let fly his remaining eight arrows one after another without pause. Eight men were shot from their horses, either dead or wounded. He then drew his sword and brandished it as he galloped to and fro. None of his opponents could challenge him face to face, though they cried out: "Shoot him down! Shoot him down!"

Sanehira's soldiers let fly a shower of arrows at Kanehira, but his armor was so strong that none of them pierced it. Unless they aimed at the joints of his armor, he could never be wounded.

Yoshinaka was now all alone in the pine wood of Awazu. It was the twenty-first day of the first month. Dusk had begun to fall. Thin ice covered the rice fields and the marsh, so that it was hard to distinguish one from the other. Thus it was that Yoshinaka had not gone far before his horse plunged deep into the muddy slime. Whipping and spurring no longer did any good. The horse could not stir. Despite his predicament, he still thought of Kanehira. As Yoshinaka was turning around to see how he fared, Tamehisa, catching up with him, shot an arrow under his helmet. It was a mortal wound. Yoshinaka pitched forward onto the neck of his horse. Then two of Tamehisa's retainers fell upon Yoshinaka and struck off his head. Raising it high on the point of his sword, Tamehisa shouted: "Kiso no Yoshinaka, renowned throughout the land of Japan as a valiant warrior, has been killed by Miura no Ishida Jirō Tamehisa!"

Kanehira was fighting desperately as these words rang in his ears. At that moment he ceased fighting and cried out: "For whom do I have to fight now? You, warriors of the east, see how the mightiest warrior in Japan puts an end to himself!" Thrusting the point of his sword into his mouth, he flung himself headlong from his horse so that the sword pierced his head.

Yoshinaka and Kanehira died valiant deaths at Awazu. Could there have been a more heroic battle?

II. A SAMURAI INSTRUCTS HIS SON

The men under your command . . . must be carefully chosen for your service. Do not take "difficult" fellows. If men under your orders, however loyal, are wanting in intelligence, you must not trust them with important duties, but rely upon experienced older men. If you are in doubt refer to me, Shigetoki.

In dealing with subordinates do not make an obvious distinction between good and not-good. Use the same kind of language, give the same kind of treatment to all, and thus you will get the best out of the worst. But you yourself must not lose sight of the distinction between good character and bad character, between capable and incapable. You must be fair, but in practice you must not forget the difference between men who are useful and men who are not. Remember that the key to discipline is fair treatment in rewards and in punishments. But make allowance for minor misdeeds in young soldiers and others, if their conduct is usually good.

Do not be careless or negligent in the presence of subordinates, especially of older men. Thus do not spit or snuffle or lounge about on a chest with your legs dangling. This only gives men the impression that you do not care for their good opinion. Preserve your dignity. If you behave rudely, they will tell their families and gossip will spread. You must treat all servants with proper consideration and generosity, not only your own people but also those of your parents and other superiors. If you do not, they will scorn you and say to one another: "He thinks he is very important, but he doesn't amount to much."

Remember, however, that there are times when a commander must exercise his power of deciding questions of life or death. In those circumstances since human life is at stake you must give most careful thought to your action. Never kill or wound a man in anger, however great the provocation. Better get somebody else to administer the proper punishment. Decisions made in haste before your feelings are calm can only lead to remorse. Close your eyes and reflect carefully when you have a difficult decision to make.

When accusations are brought to you, always remember that there must be another side to the question. Do not merely indulge in anger. To give fair decisions is the most important thing not only in commanding soldiers but also in governing a country.

25

Indian Society in the Seventh Century: The View of a Chinese Traveler

Following the decline of the Gupta Empire (320–540), political power in India fragmented. For the next several centuries, until the coming of the Muslims and the rise of the Delhi sultanate after 1200, authority passed into the hands of regional or local elites. A partial exception to this trend was the emergence of the state established by King Harsha Vardhana, the ruler of most of northern India from 606 to 647. While inadequate financial resources kept him from spending much time in his capital of Kanauj, Harsha was nonetheless able to maintain a kind of rough unity over much of the northern subcontinent for nearly half a century.

One of the most valuable sources of information about conditions during the time of Harsha comes from the travel journal of Hsuan Tsang (602–664), the most famous of the Chinese Buddhist monks who made pilgrimages to India between 400 and 700. Eager to visit the homeland of the Buddha, Hsuan Tsang set out from the Chinese capital of Changan in 630 for the perilous journey across Central Asia on the Silk Road. Reaching India safely, the courageous and learned monk traveled about the country for the next fourteen years. During this time, Hsuan Tsang took part in doctrinal debates with Indian monks, collected numerous sacred texts in the Sanskrit and Pali languages, and visited the places most holy to Buddhists. One of the high points of his pilgrimage was the time he spent meditating under the *bodhi* tree (eight or nine days!), the place where the Buddha had achieved enlightenment more than a thousand years earlier.

From Si-Yu-Ki, *Buddhist Records of the Western World,* translated by Samuel Beal (London: Trubner & Co., 1874), pp. 73–74, 77, 82–83, 86, 88–90.

The following excerpts from Hsuan Tsang's journal record some of his impressions of India. What did the monk find noteworthy? What does Hsuan Tsang reveal about his own society?

TOWNS AND BUILDINGS

The towns and villages have inner gates; the walls are wide and high; the streets and lanes are tortuous, and the roads winding. The thoroughfares are dirty and the stalls arranged on both sides of the road with appropriate signs. Butchers, fishers, dancers, executioners, and scavengers, and so on, have their abodes without the city. In coming and going these persons are bound to keep on the left side of the road till they arrive at their homes. Their houses are surrounded by low walls, and form the suburbs. The earth being soft and muddy, the walls of the towns are mostly built of brick or tiles. The towers on the walls are constructed of wood or bamboo; the houses have balconies and belvederes, which are made of wood, with a coating of lime or mortar, and covered with tiles. The different buildings have the same form as those in China: rushes, or dry branches, or tiles, or boards are used for covering them. The walls are covered with lime and mud, mixed with cow's dung for purity. At different seasons they scatter flowers about. Such are some of their different customs.

The [monasteries] are constructed with extraordinary skill. A three-storied tower is erected at each of the four angles. The beams and the projecting heads are carved with great skill in different shapes. The doors, windows, and the low walls are painted profusely; the monks' cells are ornamental on the inside and plain on the outside. In the very middle of the building is the hall, high and wide. There are various storeyed chambers and turrets of different height and shape, without any fixed rule. The doors open towards the east; the royal throne also faces the east.

.   .   .

CLEANLINESS, ABLUTIONS, &C.

They are very particular in their personal cleanliness, and allow no remissness in this particular. All wash themselves before eating; they never use that which has been left over (*from a former meal*); they do not pass the dishes. Wooden and stone vessels, when used, must be destroyed; vessels of gold, silver, copper, or iron after each meal must be rubbed and polished. After eating they cleanse their teeth with a willow stick, and wash their hands and mouth.

Until these ablutions are finished they do not touch one another. Every time they perform the functions of nature they wash their bodies and use perfumes of sandal-wood or turmeric.

When the king washes they strike the drums and sing hymns to the sound of musical instruments. Before offering their religious services and petitions, they wash and bathe themselves.

WRITING, LANGUAGE, BOOKS, THE VÊDAS, STUDY

The letters of their alphabet were arranged by Brahmâdêva, and their forms have been handed down from the first till now. They are forty-seven in number, and are combined so as to form words according to the object, and according to circumstances (*of time or place*): there are other forms (*inflexions*) used. This alphabet has spread in different directions and formed diverse branches, according to circumstances; therefore there have been slight modifications in the sounds of the words (*spoken language*); but in its great features there has been no change.

. . .

CASTES—MARRIAGE

With respect to the division of families, there are four classifications. The first is called the Brâhman . . . , men of pure conduct. They guard themselves in religion, live purely, and observe the most correct principles. The second is called Kshattriya . . . , the royal caste. For ages they have been the governing class: they apply themselves to virtue (*humanity*) and kindness. The third is called Vaiśyas . . . , the merchant class: they engage in commercial exchange, and they follow profit at home and abroad. The fourth is called Sûdra . . . , the agricultural class: they labour in ploughing and tillage. In these four classes purity or impurity of caste assigns to every one his place. When they marry they rise or fall in position according to their new relationship. They do not allow promiscuous marriages between relations. A woman once married can never take another husband. Besides these there are other classes of many kinds that intermarry according to their several callings. It would be difficult to speak of these in detail.

ROYAL FAMILY, TROOPS, WEAPONS

The succession of kings is confined to the Kshattriya caste, who by usurpation and bloodshed have from time to time raised themselves to power. Although a distinct caste, they are regarded as honourable (*or lords*).

The chief soldiers of the country are selected from the bravest of the people, and as the sons follow the profession of their fathers, they soon acquire a knowledge of the art of war. These dwell in garrison around the palace (*during peace*), but when on an expedition they march in front as an advanced guard. There are four divisions of the army, viz. — (1) the infantry, (2) the cavalry, (3) the chariots, (4) the elephants. The elephants are covered with strong armour, and their tusks are provided with sharp spurs. A leader in a car gives the command, whilst two attendants on the right and left drive his chariot, which is drawn by four horses abreast. The general of the soldiers remains in the chariot; he is surrounded by a file of guards, who keep close to his chariot wheels.

The cavalry spread themselves in front to resist an attack, and in case of defeat they carry orders hither and thither. The infantry by their quick movements contribute to the defence. These men are chosen for their courage and strength. They carry a long spear and a great shield; sometimes they hold a sword or sabre, and advance to the front with impetuosity. All their weapons of war are sharp and pointed. Some of them are these — spears, shields, bows, arrows, swords, sabres, battle-axes, lances, halberds, long javelins, and various kinds of slings. All these they have used for ages.

. . .

MEDICINES, FUNERAL CUSTOMS, &C.

. . .

When a person dies, those who attend the funeral raise lamentable cries and weep together. They rend their garments and loosen their hair; they strike their heads and beat their breasts. There are no regulations as to dress for mourning, nor any fixed time for observing it.

There are three methods of paying the last tribute to the dead: (1) by cremation — wood being made into a pyre, the body is burnt; (2) by water — the body is thrown into deep flowing water and abandoned; (3) by desertion — the body is cast into some forest-wild, to be devoured by beasts.

. . .

PLANTS AND TREES, AGRICULTURE, FOOD, DRINK, COOKERY

. . .

In cultivating the land, those whose duty it is sow and reap, plough and harrow (*weed*), and plant according to the season; and after their labour they rest awhile. Among the products of the ground, rice and corn are most plentiful. With respect to edible

South India statue from the late 13th century. The sensual strand in Indian art is evident here. [The Nelson-Atkins Museum of Art, Kansas City, Missouri (Nelson Fund)]

herbs and plants, we may name ginger and mustard, melons and pumpkins, . . . and others. Onions and garlic are little grown; and few persons eat them; if any one uses them for food, they are expelled beyond the walls of the town. The most usual food is milk, butter, cream, soft sugar, sugar-candy, the oil of the mustard-seed, and all sorts of cakes made of corn are used as food. Fish, mutton, gazelle, and deer they eat generally fresh, sometimes salted; they are forbidden to eat the flesh of the ox, the ass, the elephant, the horse, the pig, the dog, the fox, the wolf, the lion, the monkey, and all the hairy kind. Those who eat them are despised and scorned, and are universally reprobated; they live outside the walls, and are seldom seen among men.

With respect to the different kinds of wine and liquors, there are various sorts. The juice of the grape and sugarcane, these are used by the Kshattriyas as drink; the Vaiśyas use strong fermented drinks; the . . . Brâhmans drink a sort of syrup made from the grape or sugarcane, but not of the nature of fermented wine.

The mixed classes and base-born differ in no way (*as to food or drink*) from the rest, except in respect of the vessels they use, which are very different both as to value and material. There is no lack of suitable things for household use. Although they have saucepans and stewpans, yet they do not know the steamer used for cooking rice. They have many vessels made of dried clay; they seldom use red copper vessels: they eat from one vessel, mixing all sorts of condiments together, which they take up with their fingers. They have no spoons or cups, and in short no sort of chopstick. When sick, however, they use copper drinking cups.

Commercial Transactions.

Gold and silver, *tcou-shih* (native copper), white jade, fire pearls, are the natural products of the country; there are besides these abundance of rare gems and various kinds of precious stones of different names, which are collected from the islands of the sea. These they exchange for other goods; and in fact they always barter in their commercial transactions, for they have no gold or silver coins, pearl shells, or little pearls.

·   ·   ·

26

Islam Comes to India: Two Views

The introduction of Islam was one of the most important developments in the entire history of India. The new faith arrived in stages. A key turning point was reached in the early eleventh century when Turkish warriors based in present-day Afghanistan began to attack the Indian northwest. The leader of these assaults, Mahmud of Gazni (ruled 998–1030), headed an Islamic empire whose borders, at their peak, reached from the northern Ganges plain to the Persian Gulf. Mahmud's frequent raids on northwestern India, often timed to coincide with the harvest season, were intended to finance his famous court in eastern Afghanistan. His repeated victories over Hindu rulers opened the way for Muslim missionaries to move onto the subcontinent.

Successors of Mahmud continued his policy of raiding and plundering until the early thirteenth century, when another Turkish warrior founded the first enduring Islamic state in India, the Delhi sultanate (1206–1526). For the next two centuries or so the Delhi sultans struggled to control north India. During this time, a major concern of several of the sultans was defending their territory against the Mongols; the Delhi rulers also created the conditions that allowed Muslim missionaries to continue their work of establishing Islam as a major religion on the subcontinent.

The following two sources allow us to trace the movement of Turkish warriors and Islam into India after 1000. The first reading, by an official of Mahmud of Gazni, records the victory of the latter over the Hindu king, Jayapala, in 1001.

From H. M. Elliot and John Dowson, eds., *The History of India as Told by Its Own Historians* (London: Trubner & Co., 1871), Vol. II, pp. 24–26; Vol. III, pp. 191–93, 195, 197–99.

The second excerpt, by a fourteenth-century historian, centers on the reign of one of the great Delhi sultans, Ala-ud-din Khalji (ruled 1296–1316). How do these sources portray Mahmud and Ala-ud-din? In what way do these readings illustrate the fervor of Islam? Note the encounter between Islam and Hinduism in the first excerpt. How would you characterize it? What kind of picture do you get of Ala-ud-din's state? What seems significant about his policies?

I. A RAID BY MAHMUD OF GAZNI

Sultan Mahmud at first designed in his heart to go to Sijistan, but subsequently preferred engaging previously in a holy war against Hind, and he distributed arms prior to convening a council on the subject, in order to secure a blessing on his designs, of exalting the standard of religion, of widening the plain of right, of illuminating the words of truth, and of strengthening the power of justice. He departed towards the country of Hind, in full reliance on the aid of God, who guiding by his light and by his power, bestowed dignity upon him, and gave him victory in all his expeditions. On his reaching Purshaur (Peshawar), he pitched his tent outside the city. There he received intelligence of the bold resolve of Jayapala, the enemy of God, and the King of Hind, to offer opposition, and of his rapid advance towards meeting his fate in the field of battle. He then took a muster of his horses, and of all his warriors and their vassals from those in whose records it was entered, and then selected from among his troops 15,000 cavalry, men and officers, all bold, and strictly prohibited those who were rejected and not fit or disposed for war, from joining those who had been chosen, and who were like dragons of the desert and lions of the forest. With them he advanced against the wicked and accursed enemy, whose hearts were firm as hills, and were as twigs of patience on the boughs of affection. The villanous infidel came forward, proud in his numbers and strength of head and arm, with 12,000 horsemen, 30,000 foot soldiers, and 300 elephants, at the ponderous weight of which the lighter earth groaned, little reflecting that, under God's dispensation, a small army can overturn a host, as the ignorant man would have learnt, could he have read the word of God,—"Oftentimes a small army overcomes a large one by the order of God."

That infidel remained where he was, avoiding the action for a long time, and awaiting craftily the arrival of reinforcements and other vagabond families and tribes which were on their way; but the Sultan would not allow him to postpone the conflict, and the friends of God commenced the action, setting upon the enemy with sword, arrow, and spear,—plundering, seizing, and destroying; at all which the Hindus, being greatly alarmed, began to kindle the flame of fight. The Hindu set his cavalry in and beat his drums. The elephants moved on from their posts, and line advanced against line, shooting their arrows at one another like boys escaped from school, who, at eventime, shoot at a target for a wager. Swords flashed like lightning amid the blackness of clouds, and fountains of blood flowed like the fall of setting stars. The friends of God defeated their obstinate opponents, and quickly put them to a complete rout. Noon had not arrived when the Musulmáns had wreaked their vengeance on the infidel enemies of God, killing 15,000 of them, spreading them like a carpet over the ground, and making them food for beasts and birds of prey. Fifteen elephants fell on the field of battle, as their legs, being pierced with arrows, became as motionless as if they had been in a quagmire, and their trunks were cut with the swords of the valiant heroes.

The enemy of God, Jayapala, and his children and grandchildren, and nephews, and the chief men of his tribe, and his relatives, were taken prisoners, and being strongly bound with ropes, were carried before the Sultan, like as evildoers, on whose faces the fumes of infidelity are evident, who are covered with the vapours of misfortune, will be bound and carried to Hell. Some had their arms forcibly tied behind their backs, some were seized by the cheek, some were driven by blows on the neck. The necklace was taken off the neck of Jayapala,—composed of large pearls and shining gems and rubies set in gold, of which the value was two hundred thousand dínárs; and twice that value was obtained from the necks of those of his relatives who were taken prisoners, or slain, and had become the food of the mouths of hyenas and vultures. God also bestowed upon his friends such an amount of booty as was beyond all bounds and all calculation, including five hundred thousand slaves, beautiful men and women. The Sultan returned with his followers to his camp, having plundered immensely, by God's aid, having obtained the victory, and thankful to God, the lord of the universe. For the Almighty had given them victory over a province of the country of Hind, broader and longer and more fertile than Khurasan. This splendid and celebrated action took place on Thursday, the 8th of Muharram, 392 H. (27th November, 1001, A.D.)

II. A DELHI SULTAN FIGHTS THE MONGOLS

The Sultan [Ala-ud-din] next turned his attention to the increase of his forces, and consulted and debated with wise men by night and by day as to the best means of opposing and overcoming the Mongols. After much deliberation between the Sultan and his councillors, it was decided that a large army was necessary, and not only large, but choice, well armed, well mounted, with archers, and all ready for immediate service. This plan, and this only, seemed to recommend itself as feasible for opposing the Mongols. The Sultan then consulted his advisers as to the means of raising such a force, for it could not be maintained without heavy expenditure, and what was arranged for one year might not be continuous. On this point he said, "If I settle a large amount of pay on the army, and desire to maintain the pay at the same rate every year, then, although the treasury is now full, five or six years will clear it out, and nothing will be left. Without money government is impossible. I am very desirous of having a large army, well horsed, well accoutred, picked men and archers, ready for service year after year. I would pay them 234 *tankas* regularly, and I would allow seventy-eight *tankas* to those who keep two horses, requiring in return the two horses, with all necessary appointments. So also as regards the men of one horse, I would require the horse and his accoutrements. Inform me, then, how this large army can be regularly maintained on the footing I desire." His sagacious advisers thought carefully over the matter, and after great deliberation made a unanimous report to the Sultan. "The ideas which have passed through your Majesty's mind as to maintaining a large and permanent army upon a low scale of pay are quite impracticable. Horses, arms, and accoutrements, and the support of the soldier and his wife and family, cannot be provided for a trifle. If the necessaries of life could be bought at a low rate, then the idea which your Majesty has entertained of maintaining a large army at a small expense might be carried out, and all apprehension of the great forces of the Mongols would be removed." The Sultan then consulted with his most experienced ministers as to the means of reducing the prices of provisions without resorting to severe and tyrannical punishments. His councillors replied that the necessaries of life would never become cheap until the price of grain was fixed by regulations and tariffs. Cheapness of grain is a universal benefit. So some regulations were issued, which kept down the price for some years.

This scale of prices was maintained as long as Ala-ud-din lived, and grain never rose one *dáng,* whether the rains were abundant or scanty. This unvarying price of grain in the markets was looked upon as one of the wonders of the time.

To secure the cheapness of grain, Malik Kabul Ulugh Khan, a wise and practical man, was appointed controller of the markets. He received a large territory and used to go round (the markets) in great state with many horse and foot. He had clever deputies, friends of his own, who were appointed by the crown. Intelligent spies also were sent into the markets. . . .

Reports used to be made daily to the Sultan of the market rate and of the market transactions from three distinct sources. 1st. The superintendent made a report of the market rate and of the market transactions. 2nd. The *baríds,* or reporters, made a statement. 3rd. The *manhís,* or spies, made a report. If there was any variance in these reports, the superintendent received punishment. The various officials of the market were well aware that all the ins and outs of the market were reported to the Sultan through three different channels, and so there was no opportunity of their deviating from the market rules in the smallest particular.

All the wise men of the age were astonished at the evenness of the price in the markets. If the rains had fallen (regularly), and the seasons had been (always) favourable, there would have been nothing so wonderful in grain remaining at one price; but the extraordinary part of the matter was that during the reign of Ala-ud-din there were years in which the rains were deficient, but instead of the usual scarcity ensuing, there was no want of corn in Dehlí, and there was no rise in the price either in the grain brought out of the royal granaries, or in that imported by the dealers. This was indeed the wonder of the age, and no other monarch was able to effect it. . . .

When the tariffs had been settled and the army had been increased and newly organized, the Sultan was ready for the Mongols. Whenever they made an attack upon Dehlí and its vicinity, they were defeated, driven back, and put to the sword. The arms of Islám were everywhere triumphant over them. Many thousands were taken prisoners, and were brought into Dehlí with ropes round their necks, where they were cast under the feet of elephants. Their heads were piled up in pyramids, or built into towers. So many thousands were slain in battle and in the city that horrid stenches arose. Such was the superiority of the men of Islám over the Mongols, that one or two horsemen would tie by the neck and bring in ten Mongol prisoners, and one Musulmán horseman would drive a hundred Mongols before him. . . .

In another year a battle was fought in Khíkar between the army of Islám and the Mongols, under the accursed Kank. The Mongols were defeated, and Kank was brought prisoner to Ala-ud-din, and thrown under the feet of elephants. On another occasion great numbers of Mongols were slain, partly in battle, partly afterwards in the city. A tower was built of their heads in front of the gate of Badaun, and remains to this day a memento of Ala-ud-din. At another time three or four Mongol commanders, with thirty or forty thousand horse[s], broke into the Siwálik, and engaged in slaughter and plunder. An army was sent against them with orders to seize upon the road by which the Mongols must return to the river, and there to encamp, so that when the thirsty Mongols attempted to approach the river they would receive their punishment. These orders were carried out. The Mongols having wasted the Siwálik, had moved some distance off. When they and their horses returned weary and thirsty to the river, the army of Islám, which had been waiting for them some days, caught them as they expected. They begged for water, and they and all their wives and children were made prisoners. Islám gained a great victory, and brought several thousand prisoners with ropes on their necks to the fort of Náraniya. The women and children were taken to Dehlí, and were sold as slaves in the market. Malik Kháss-hájíb was sent to Náraniya, and there put every Mongol prisoner to the sword. Streams ran with their foul blood. . . .

All fear of the Mongols entirely departed from Dehlí and the neighbouring provinces. Perfect security was everywhere felt, and the peasants of those territories, which had been exposed to the inroads of the Mongols, carried on their agriculture in peace.

27

The Early Stages of the Byzantine Empire

The sixth-century reign of Justinian, one of Byzantium's most illustrious emperors, witnessed an attempt to recover many of the Western territories of the recently collapsed Roman Empire. This effort was short-lived. More important was the tone Justinian set for the vigorous eastern portion of the empire, centered around Constantinople (Byzantium) in southeastern Europe and Asia Minor. Justinian codified the Roman legal system, introduced financial and administrative reforms, and tightened imperial control of the Eastern Orthodox Church. His desire to recapture Roman splendor prompted great expenditure on a public building program, particularly at Constantinople. Fearing that "posterity, beholding the enormous size and number of [buildings], should deny their being the work of one man," Justinian ordered a Palestinian historian, Procopius, to compose a treatise on his new program.

Procopius's *On Justinian's Buildings,* written in A.D. 555, predictably exaggerated Justinian's prowess, but he did capture the emperor's ambition. Procopius focused on the Church of the Holy Wisdom (Hagia Sophia) in Constantinople, completed in 537 as Christendom's largest and most beautiful edifice. Justinian is said to have boasted of the great church, "Solomon, I have surpassed you!" Like the Byzantine Empire itself, the new building combined Roman and Middle-Eastern (particularly Persian) styles, setting up a new culture closely related to that of the late Roman Empire.

The following selection, from Procopius, suggests key elements of the po-

From Procopius, *Of the Buildings of Justinian,* translated by Aubrey Stewart (London: Palestine Pilgrims' Text Society, 1888), pp. 2–5, 9–11.

litical as well as artistic program of early Byzantium. How does Byzantium compare with ancient Rome (as discussed in selection 16)? Why would Byzantium prove to be such an important cultural and political example to other East European peoples, particularly the Slavs as they established their civilization to the north? What elements of Byzantine civilization would these imitators be most likely to copy?

The lowest dregs of the people in Byzantium once assailed the Emperor Justinian in the rebellion called Nika, which I have clearly described in my "History of the Wars." To prove that it was not merely against the Emperor, but no less against God that they took up arms, they ventured to burn the church of the Christians. (This church the people of Byzantium call Sophia, *i.e.,* . . . *Wisdom;* a name most worthy of God.) God permitted them to effect this crime, knowing how great the beauty of this church would be when restored. Thus the church was entirely reduced to ashes; but the Emperor Justinian not long afterwards adorned it in such a fashion, that if anyone had asked the Christians in former times if they wished their church to be destroyed and thus restored, showing them the appearance of the church which we now see, I think it probable that they would have prayed that they might as soon as possible behold their church destroyed, in order that it might be turned into its present form.

. . .

The Emperor Justinian was born in our time, and succeeding to the throne when the state was decayed, added greatly to its extent and glory by driving out from it the barbarians, who for so long a time had forced their way into it, as I have briefly narrated in my "History of the Wars." They say that Themistocles, the son of Neocles, prided himself on his power of making a small state great, but our Emperor has the power of adding other states to his own, for he has annexed to the Roman Empire many other states which at his accession were independent, and has founded innumerable cities which had no previous existence. As for religion, which he found uncertain and torn by various heresies, he destroyed everything which could lead to error, and securely established the true faith upon one solid foundation. Moreover, finding the laws obscure through their unnecessary multitude, and confused by their conflict with one another, he firmly established them by reducing the number of those which were unnecessary, and in the case of those that were contradictory, by confirming better ones. He forgave of his own accord those who plotted against him, and, by loading with wealth those who were in want, and relieving them from the misfortunes which had afflicted them, he rendered the empire stable and its members happy. By increasing his armies he strengthened the Roman Empire, which lay everywhere exposed to the attacks of barbarians, and fortified its entire frontier by building strong places.

. . .

Now, as I said before, we must turn our attention to the buildings of this monarch, lest posterity, beholding the enormous size and number of them, should deny their being the work of one man; for the works of many men of former times, not being confirmed by history, have been disbelieved through their own excessive greatness.

. . .

It is, indeed, a proof of the esteem with which God regarded the Emperor, that

He furnished him with men who would be so useful in effecting his designs, and we are compelled to admire the intelligence of the Emperor, in being able to choose the most suitable of mankind to carry out the noblest of his works.

The church consequently presented a most glorious spectacle, extraordinary to those who beheld it, and altogether incredible to those who are told of it. In height it rises to the very heavens, and overtops the neighbouring buildings like a ship anchored among them: it rises above the rest of the city, which it adorns, while it forms a part of it, and it is one of its beauties that being a part of the city, and growing out of it, it stands so high above it, that from it the whole city can be beheld as from a watch-tower. Its length and breadth are so judiciously arranged that it appears to be both long and wide without being disproportioned. It is distinguished by indescribable beauty, for it excels both in its size and in the harmony of its proportion, having no part excessive and none deficient; being more magnificent than ordinary buildings, and much more elegant than those which are out of proportion. It is singularly full of light and sunshine; you would declare that the place is not lighted by the sun from without, but that the

Interior of Saint Sophia, in the doomed style characteristic of Eastern Orthodox churches and cathedrals. Calligraphy and other appointments show the church's conversion to a mosque. [Giraudon/Art Resource, NY]

rays are produced within itself, such an abundance of light is poured into this church. . . . Thus far I imagine the building is not incapable of being described, even by a weak and feeble tongue. As the arches are arranged in a quadrangular figure, the stonework between them takes the shape of a triangle; the lower angle of each triangle, being compressed between the shoulders of the arches, is slender, while the upper part becomes wider as it rises in the space between them, and ends against the circle which rises from thence, forming there its remaining angles. A spherical-shaped dome standing upon this circle makes it exceedingly beautiful; from the lightness of the building it does not appear to rest upon a solid foundation, but to cover the place beneath as though it were suspended from heaven by the fabled golden chain. All these parts surprisingly joined to one another in the air, suspended one from another, and resting only on that which is next to them, form the work into one admirably harmonious whole, which spectators do not care to dwell upon for long in the mass, as each individual part attracts the eye and turns it to itself. The sight causes men to constantly change their point of view, and the spectator can nowhere point to any part which he admires more than the rest, but having viewed the art which appears everywhere, men contract their eyebrows as they look at each point, and are unable to comprehend such workmanship, but always depart thence stupified through their incapacity to comprehend it.

· · ·

The entire ceiling is covered with pure gold, which adds glory to its beauty, though the rays of light reflected upon the gold from the marble surpass it in beauty; there are two porticos on each side, which do not in any way dwarf the size of the church, but add to its width. In length they reach quite to the ends, but in height they fall short of it; these also have a domed ceiling and are adorned with gold. Of these two porticos, the one is set apart for male, and the other for female worshippers; there is no variety in them, nor do they differ in any respect from one another, but their very equality and similarity add to the beauty of the church. Who could describe the galleries of the portion set apart for women, or the numerous porticos and cloistered courts with which the church is surrounded? who could tell of the beauty of the columns and marbles with which the church is adorned? one would think that one had come upon a meadow full of flowers in bloom: who would not admire the purple tints of some and the green of others, the glowing red and glittering white, and those, too, which nature, like a painter, has marked with the strongest contrasts of colour? Whoever enters there to worship perceives at once that it is not by any human strength or skill, but by the favour of God that this work has been perfected; his mind rises sublime to commune with God, feeling that He cannot be far off, but must especially love to dwell in the place which He has chosen; and this takes place not only when a man sees it for the first time, but it always makes the same impression upon him, as though he had never beheld it before. No one ever became weary of this spectacle, but those who are in the Church delight in what they see, and, when they leave it, magnify it in their talk about it; moreover, it is impossible accurately to describe the treasure of gold and silver plate and gems, which the Emperor Justinian has presented to it; but by the description of one of them, I leave the rest to be inferred. That part of the church which is especially sacred, and where the priests alone are allowed to enter, which is called the Sanctuary, contains forty thousand pounds' weight of silver.

28

Russia Converts to Christianity

The conversion of the Slavs to Orthodox Christianity was one of the formative steps in the development of Slavic civilization, as the Orthodox Church assumed a major role in the transmission and assimilation of Byzantine culture into Eastern Europe. Byzantine emperors employed judicious diplomacy, international trade, and the church to transform their hostile and barbaric neighbors into cultural satellites. Kievan Russia, following King Vladimir's conversion to Orthodox Christianity in the late tenth century, proved especially receptive to Byzantine culture and used the empire as a prototype in evolving its own governmental institutions. Provided with a modified Greek alphabet (Glagolithic or Cyrillic), created expressly in about 863 for the translation of biblical and liturgical works into Slavic by Saint Cyril (also known as Constantine), Russian scholars began to record their history and to produce a remarkable native literature. Having no need to master the Greek and Latin languages, which proved essential for full reception of Byzantium's classical heritage, Russian scholars remained outside the mainstream of traditional classical thought.

The selections below appear in the *Russian Primary Chronicle* ("The Tale

From George Vernadsky, ed., *A Source Book for Russian History from Early Times to 1917*, 2 v. (New Haven: Yale University Press, 1972), Vol. I, pp. 12–13, 25–26. Copyright © Yale University Press, 1972. Reprinted by permission.

of Bygone Years"), our principal historical source for the history of Kievan Russia during the tenth to twelfth centuries. Originally compiled about 1110, the earliest surviving copy is a 1377 version (Laurentian). The account of the conversion of the Slavs by Saints Cyril and Methodius in the ninth century is probably of Moravian origin and may be dependent on old texts and the oral tradition. The account of Vladimir's conversion and baptism in 988 is undoubtedly a Russian legend.

While the Slavic conversion to Christianity was certainly a major step in their civilization, it also raises questions: Why, according to the *Chronicle* account, did most Slavs pick Orthodox Christianity? Why did they bother to convert to a new religion at all, and what impact would this new religion have on their culture?

There was at that time but one Slavic race, including the Slavs who settled along the Danube and were subjugated by the Magyars, as well as the Moravians, the Czechs, the Lyakhs [Poles], and the Polianians, the last of whom are now called Russians. It was for these Moravians that Slavic books were first written, and this writing prevails also among the Russians and the Danubian Bulgarians.

When the Moravian Slavs and their princes were living in baptism, the Princes Rostislav, Sviatopolk, and Kotsel sent messengers to the emperor Michael, saying, "Our nation is baptized, and yet we have no teacher to direct and instruct us and to interpret the Sacred Scriptures. We understand neither Greek nor Latin. Some teach us one thing and some another. Furthermore, we do not understand written characters nor their meaning. Therefore send us teachers who can make known to us the words of the Scriptures and their sense." The Emperor Michael, upon hearing their request, called together all the scholars and reported to them the message of the Slavic princes. . . . The emperor prevailed upon them [Constantine and Methodius] to undertake the mission and sent them into the Slavic country to Rostislav, Sviatopolk, and Kotsel. When they arrived [in 863], they undertook to compose a Slavic alphabet and translated the Acts and the Gospels. The Slavs rejoiced to hear the greatness of God extolled in their native tongue. The apostles afterward translated the Psalter, the Oktoechos, and other books.

Now some zealots began to condemn the Slavic books, contending that it was not right for any other nation to have its own alphabet, apart from the Hebrews, the Greeks, and the Latins, according to Pilate's superscription, which he composed for the Lord's cross. When the pope at Rome heard of this situation, he rebuked those who murmured against the Slavic books. . . . Constantine then returned again and went to instruct the people of Bulgaria, but Methodius remained in Moravia.

Prince Kotsel appointed Methodius bishop of Pannonia in the see of Saint Andronicus, one of the Seventy, a disciple of the holy apostle Paul. Methodius chose two priests who were very rapid writers and translated the whole Scriptures in full from Greek into Slavic in six months. . . . Now Andronicus is the apostle of the Slavic race.

He traveled among the Moravians, and the apostle Paul taught there likewise. . . . Since Paul is the teacher of the Slavic race, from which we Russians too are sprung, even so the apostle Paul is the teacher of us Russians, for he preached to the Slavic nation and appointed Andronicus as bishop and successor to himself among them. But the Slavs and the Russians are one people, for it is because of the Varangians that the latter became known as Russians, though originally they were Slavs. While some Slavs were termed Polianians, their speech was still Slavic, for they were known as Polianians because they lived in the fields [*pole* means "field" in Russian]. But they had the same Slavic language.

[In the year 980] Vladimir began to reign alone in Kiev, and he set up idols on the hills outside the castle: one of Perun, made of wood with a head of silver and a moustache of gold, and others of Khors, Dazh'bog, Stribog, Simar'gl, and Mokosh'. The people sacrificed to them, calling them gods, and brought their sons and their daughters to sacrifice them to these devils. They desecrated the earth with their offerings, and the Russian land and this hill were defiled with blood.

.   .   .

In the year 6495 [987] Vladimir summoned together his boyars and the city elders and said to them, "Behold, the Bulgars came before me, saying, 'Accept our religion.' Then came the Germans and praised their own faith. After them came the Jews. Finally the Greeks appeared, disparaging all other faiths but praising their own, and they spoke at length, telling the history of the whole world from its beginning. Their words were wise, and it was marvelous to listen and pleasant for anyone to hear them. They preached about another world. 'Anyone,' they said, 'who adopts our religion and then dies shall arise and live forever. But anyone who embraces another faith shall in the next world be consumed by fire.' What is your opinion on this subject, and what do you answer?" The boyars and the elders replied, "You know, Prince, that no man condemns what is his own but praises it instead. If you desire to make certain, you have servants at your disposal. Send them to inquire about the ritual of each and how he worships God."

Their counsel pleased the prince and all people, so that they chose ten good and wise men.

[They visited foreign lands, and] then they returned to their country. The prince called together his boyars and the elders, and he said: "The envoys who were sent out have returned. Let us hear what took place." He said, "Speak in the presence of my retinue." The envoys then reported, "When we journeyed among the Bulgars, we observed how they worship in their temple. . . . Their religion is not good. Then we went among the Germans and saw them performing many ceremonies in their temples, and we saw no beauty there. Then we went to Greece, and the Greeks led us to where they worship their God, and we did not know whether we were in heaven or on earth. For on earth there is no such splendor or such beauty, and we are at a loss to describe it. We know only that God dwells there among men, and their service is better than the ceremonies of other nations. For we cannot forget that beauty. Every man, after tasting something sweet, is afterward unwilling to accept that which is bitter, and therefore we can no longer remain here [in paganism]." Then the boyars said in reply, "If the Greek faith were evil, it would not have been adopted by your grandmother Olga, who was wiser than anyone else." Vladimir then responded, asking, "Where shall we accept baptism?" and they replied, "Wherever you wish." . . .

After a year had passed, in 6496 [988], Vladimir proceeded with an armed force against Kherson, a Greek city [by the Black Sea]. . . . [After a siege] the inhabitants . . . surrendered.

Vladimir and his retinue entered the city, and he sent messages to the emperors Basil and Constantine, saying, "Behold, I have captured your glorious city. I have also heard that you have an unwedded sister. Unless you give her to me in marriage, I shall deal with your own city as I have with Kherson." When the emperors heard this message they were troubled, and they issued this statement: "It is not proper for Christians to give women in marriage to pagans. If you are baptized, you shall have her for your wife, inherit the kingdom of God, and be our co-believer. If you do not do so, however, we cannot give you our sister in marriage." When Vladimir learned of their response, he said to the emperors' envoys, "Tell the emperors I will accept baptism, since I have already given some study to your religion, and the Greek faith and ritual, as described by the emissaries I sent to examine it, has pleased me well," When the emperors heard this report they rejoiced and persuaded their sister Anna [to consent to the match]. They then sent word to Vladimir, "Be baptized, and then we shall send you our sister." But Vladimir said, "Let your sister herself come [with the priests] to baptize me." The emperors complied with his request and sent their sister, accompanied by some dignitaries and priests. . . . The bishop [episkop] of Kherson, together with the princess's priests . . . baptized Vladimir. . . .

As a bride price in exchange for the princess, he gave Kherson back to the Greeks and then went back to Kiev.

When the prince arrived at his capital, he directed that the idols should be overturned and that some should be cut to pieces and others burned up. . . .

Thereupon Vladimir sent heralds throughout the whole city, proclaiming, "If anyone, whether rich or poor, beggar or slave, does not come tomorrow to the river, he will be an enemy of mine." When the people heard this they went gladly, rejoicing and saying, "If this were not good, the prince and his boyars would not have accepted it." On the morrow the prince went forth to the Dnieper with the priests of the princess and those from Kherson, and a countless multitude assembled. They all went into the water; some stood up to their necks, others to their breasts, and the younger up to their breasts near the bank, some people holding children in their arms, while the adults waded farther out. The priests stood by and offered prayers. There was joy in heaven and upon earth at the sight of so many souls saved. But the Devil groaned, "Woe is me! They are driving me out of here!" . . .

He [Vladimir] ordered that wooden churches should be built and established where [pagan] idols had previously stood. He founded the Church of Saint Basil on the hill where the idol of Perun and the other images had been set, and where the prince and the people had offered their sacrifices. He began to found churches, to assign priests throughout the cities and towns, and to bring people in for baptism from all towns and villages. He began to take the children of the best families and send them for instruction from books.

29

Feudal Monarchy: The Magna Carta

Western feudalism, evolving in turbulent eighth-century France, offered aristocratic landowners potential security in the absence of law and order. By concession or usurpation, major landowners assumed substantial legal and governmental powers from the central government and proceeded through private arrangements with lesser landowners to create local militias for defensive purposes. Inherently particularistic and initially undisciplined, feudalism enveloped the monarchy itself. Feudalism evolved its own system of law and code of ethics for its members as it spread throughout Europe to assume a dominant role in the political and cultural history of the Middle Ages. Introduced to England in 1066 by William the Conqueror—who substantially curbed the powers of all feudal vassals while retaining considerable central authority—feudalism incorporated three elements: personal, property, and governmental. All members, including the monarchs who headed the feudal system, enjoyed specific rights but were also bound by feudal law to perform fixed obligations.

The only available means for feudal vassals to force an obstinate royal overlord to observe the binding feudal law was to resort to arms. Such means were used in 1215 by secular and ecclesiastical vassals under the leadership of Stephen Langton, archbishop of Canterbury, against King John of England. John was forced to place his seal on the Magna Carta, a charter of sixty chapters listing arbitrary royal encroachments on the feudal law as well as violations against traditional rights and liberties. Although the charter exerted little real im-

From R. Trevor Davis, ed., *Documents Illustrating the History of Civilization in Medieval England (1066–1600)* (New York: Barnes and Noble, 1926), pp. 39–52. Reprinted from *Statutes of the Realm*, 1810, Vol. 1, pp. 5ff.

pact on medieval English law and government because John died nine weeks after signing the document, its rediscovery and use by seventeenth-century opponents to royal absolutism allowed it to take a fundamental position in the English constitution. Contrary to popular belief, the original charter did not establish the individual right to trial by jury.

The Magna Carta must be interpreted as a feudal document: how does it define rights and government, and who participates in what kind of rights? Feudalism was a political response to the extremely chaotic conditions of the early Middle Ages in Western Europe. The feudal system could only be bent toward more centralized rule with difficulty, and the Magna Carta reveals some of the resulting tensions. Feudalism did, however, generate the beginnings of political principles, based on the concept of mutuality, that would be used in later political systems, as the subsequent revival of the Magna Carta attests (see selection 1, volume 2, for later concepts of limited government). The Western feudal concept must also be compared with that of Japan (selection 24).

John, by the grace of God, king of England, lord of Ireland, duke of Normandy and Aquitaine, and count of Anjou, to the archbishops, bishops, abbots, earls, barons, justiciars, foresters, sheriffs, stewards, servants, and to all his bailiffs and loyal persons, greeting. Know that, having regard to God and for the salvation of our souls, and those of all our predecessors and heirs, and unto the honour of God and the advancement of Holy Church, and for the reform of our realm, by the counsel of our venerable fathers . . . we have granted:

I. In the first place we have granted to God, and by this our present charter confirmed for us and our heirs for ever that the English Church shall be free, and shall have her rights entire and her liberties inviolate; and we will that it be thus observed; which is apparent from this, that the freedom of elections, which is reckoned most important and very essential to the English Church, we, of pure and unconstrained will, did grant, and did by our charter confirm and did obtain the ratification of the same from our Lord, Pope Innocent III., before the quarrel arose between us and our barons: and this we will observe, and our will is that it be observed in good faith by our heirs for ever. We have also granted to all freemen of our kingdom, for us and our heirs for ever, all the underwritten liberties, to be had and held by them and their heirs, of us and our heirs for ever.

· · ·

XII. No scutage or aid shall be imposed on our kingdom, unless by common counsel of our kingdom, except for ransoming our person, for making our eldest son a knight, and for marrying our eldest daughter once; and for them there shall not be levied more than a reasonable aid. In like manner it shall be done concerning aids from the city of London.

XIII. And the city of London shall have all its ancient liberties and free customs, as well by land as by water; furthermore we decree and grant that all other cities, boroughs, and towns, and ports shall have all their liberties and free customs.

XIV. And for obtaining the common counsel of the kingdom about the assessing of an aid (except in the three cases aforesaid) or of a scutage, we will cause to be summoned the archbishops, bishops, abbots, earls, and greater barons, individually by our letters; and we will moreover cause to be summoned generally through our sheriffs and bailiffs, all others who hold of us in chief, for a definite date, namely after the expiry of at least forty days, and at a definite place; and in all letters of such summons we will specify the reason of the summons. And when the summons has thus been made, the business shall proceed on the day appointed, according to the counsel of such as are present, although not all who are summoned have come.

. . .

XXIII. No village or individual shall be compelled to make bridges at river banks, except those who were from old times rightfully compelled to do so.

XXIV. No sheriff, constable, coroners, or others of our bailiffs, shall hold pleas of our crown.

. . .

XXVIII. No constable or other bailiff of ours shall take corn or other provisions from anyone without immediately tendering money in exchange, unless by permission of the seller he is allowed to postpone payment.

XXIX. No constable shall compel any knight to give money in stead of castle guard, when he is willing to perform it in his own person, or (if he himself cannot do it from any reasonable cause) then by another reliable man; and if we have led him or sent him upon military service, he shall be quit of guard, in proportion to the time during which he has been on service because of us.

XXX. No sheriff or bailiff of ours, or other person, shall take the horses or carts of any freeman for transport duty, against the will of the said freeman.

XXXI. Neither we nor our bailiffs shall take for our castles or for any other work of ours, timber which is not ours, against the will of the owner of that timber.

XXXII. We will not retain beyond one year and one day, the lands of those who have been convicted of felony, and the lands shall thereafter be handed over to the lords of the fiefs.

. . .

XXXVIII. No bailiff for the future shall, upon his own unsupported complaint, put anyone to his "law" without reputable witnesses brought for this purpose.

XXXIX. No freeman shall be taken or imprisoned or disseised or exiled or in anyway destroyed, nor will we go upon him nor send upon him, except by the lawful judgement of his peers or by the law of the land.

XL. To no one will we sell, to no one will we refuse right or justice.

XLI. All merchants shall have safe and secure exit from England, and entry to England, with right to tarry there and to move about as well by land as by water, for buying and selling by the ancient and right customs, quit from all evil tolls, except, in time of war, such merchants as are of the land at war with us. And if such are found in our land at the beginning of the war, they shall be detained, without injury to their bodies or goods, until information be received by us or by our chief justiciar how the merchants of our land found in the land at war with us are treated; and if our men are safe there the others shall be safe in our land.

XLII. It shall be lawful in future for anyone to leave our kingdom and to return safe and secure by land and water, except for a short period in time of war on grounds of public policy—reserving always the allegiance due to us—excepting always those imprisoned or outlawed in accordance with the law of the kingdom, and natives of any country at war with us, and merchants, who shall be treated as is above provided.

. . .

XLV. We will appoint as justices, constables, sheriffs, or bailiffs only such as know the law of the kingdom and mean to observe it well.

. . .

LII. If anyone has been dispossessed or removed by us, without the legal judgement of his peers, from his lands, castles, franchises, or from his right, we will immediately restore them to him; and if a dispute arise over this, then let it be decided by the five-and-twenty barons, of whom mention is made below in the clause for securing the peace. Moreover, for all those possessions, from which anyone has, without the lawful judgement of his peers been disseised or removed, by our father, King Henry, or by our brother, King Richard, and which we retain in our hand—or which are possessed by others, to whom we are bound to warrant them—we shall have respite until the usual term of crusaders; excepting those things about which a plea has been raised, or an inquest made by our order, before our taking of the cross; but as soon as we return from our pilgrimage—or if by chance we desist from our pilgrimage—we will immediately grant full justice therein.

. . .

LV. All fines made by us unjustly and against the law of the land, shall be entirely remitted, or else it shall be done concerning them according to the decision of the five-and-twenty barons of whom mention is made below in (the clause for) securing the peace, or according to the judgement of the majority of the same, along with the aforesaid Stephen, archbishop of Canterbury, if he can be present, and such others as he may wish to bring with him for this purpose; and if he cannot be present the business shall nevertheless proceed without him, provided always that if any one or more of the aforesaid five-and-twenty barons are in a similar suit, they shall be removed as far as shall concern this particular judgement, others being substituted in their places after having been selected by the rest of the five-and-twenty for this purpose only, and after having been sworn.

. . .

LX. Moreover, all these aforesaid customs and liberties, the observance of which we have granted in our kingdom as far as pertains to us towards our men, shall be observed by all of our kingdom, as well clergy as laymen, as far as pertains to them towards their men.

LXI. Since, moreover, for God and the amendment of our kingdom and for the better allaying of our quarrel that has arisen between us and our barons, we have granted all these concessions, desirous that they should enjoy them in complete and firm stability for ever, we give and grant to them the underwritten security, namely, that the barons choose five-and-twenty barons of the kingdom, whomsoever they will, who shall be obliged, to observe and hold, and cause to be observed, with all their might, the peace and liberties which we have granted and confirmed to them by this our present Charter, so that if we, or our justiciar, or our bailiffs or any one of our officers, shall in anything be at fault towards anyone, or shall have broken any one of the articles of the peace or of this security, and the offence be notified to four barons of the aforesaid five-and-twenty, the said four barons shall come to us (or to our justiciar, if we are out of the realm) and, laying the transgression before us, petition to have that transgression redressed without delay. And if we shall not have corrected the transgression (or, in event of our being out of the kingdom, if our justiciar shall not have corrected it) within forty days, reckoning from the time it has been notified to us (or to our justiciar, if we should be out of the kingdom), the four barons aforesaid shall refer the matter to the rest of the five-and-twenty barons, and those five-and-twenty barons shall, together with the community of the whole land, distrain and distress us in all possible ways, namely, by seizing our castles, lands, possessions, and in any other way they can, until redress has been obtained as they deem fit, saving our own person and the persons of our queen and children; and when redress has been obtained, they shall resume their former relations toward us. . . .

30

Medieval Theology: Thomas Aquinas Blends Faith and Reason

The dominant role of the Christian religion in all aspects of European civilization during the Middle Ages has led some historians to label the period an "age of faith." A hierarchical society appointed by God and governed by his vice-regents, the pope and king, focused concern on preparation for life after death and devoted considerable energy towards the honor and glorification of God. By mid-twelfth century the theological rationale of the nature of God, man, and the universe—based on revelation and patristic traditions—encountered a serious challenge from the previously unknown logical and philosophical works of Aristotle, which offered a conflicting world view including the primacy of reason as a means for establishing truth. Theologians successfully met this challenge by applying Aristotelian methodology and by incorporating many of his philosophical concepts to construct a Christian theological and philosophical system, called scholasticism, which brought these views into agreement.

The reconciliation of Christian traditions and Aristotelian precepts was a major concern of Thomas Aquinas (1225–1274), who determined that correct reasoning offered a means for establishing Christian truths. As professor of theology at the University of Paris, the Dominican theologian constructed a synthesis of natural theology in his *Summa Theologica* using logical reasoning and a reliance on authoritative sources. An analysis of the existence of God and of human ability to know God in that work are presented in the following extracts. Omitted in this selection are conflicting authoritative opinions to Aquinas's conclusions

From Thomas Aquinas, *The Summa Theologica*, P. 1, Q. 2 and 12, in *Basic Writings of Saint Thomas Aquinas,* edited by Anton C. Pegis (New York: Random House, 1945), Vol. I, pp. 19, 20, 22–23, 92, 93–94, 95, 97, 101–2. Copyright © Random House, Inc., 1945. Reprinted by permission.

and his arguments against them, which are standard in scholastic methodology. The extracts demonstrate his method of interrelating faith and reason, his use of Aristotle's *Physics* and *Metaphysics* in proving the existence of God, and his views that reason must yield to faith when it proves insufficient in establishing Christian truths.

Medieval scholasticism as put forth by Aquinas was a striking intellectual creation that allowed its supporters to believe that they possessed a comprehensive framework by which everything that could be understood was understood. Scholasticism was also, however, a key point in a larger intellectual history that ran from the ancient Greeks to modern Western science. How did Acquinas use Aristotelian rationalism, and at what points did he differ from Aristotle's approach (see selection 14)? How did Acquinas's system resemble, as well as differ from, later Western intellectual assumptions (see selection 2, volume 2)?

THE EXISTENCE OF GOD

. . . A thing can be self-evident in either of two ways: on the one hand, self-evident in itself, though not to us; on the other, self-evident in itself, and to us. A proposition is self-evident because the predicate is included in the essence of the subject: *e.g., Man is an animal,* for animal is contained in the essence of man. If, therefore, the essence of the predicate and subject be known to all, the proposiiton will be self-evident to all; as is clear with regard to the first principles of demonstration, the terms of which are certain common notions that no one is ignorant of, such as being and non-being, whole and part, and the like. If, however, there are some to whom the essence of the predicate and subject is unknown, the proposition will be self-evident in itself, but not to those who do not know the meaning of the predicate and subject of the proposition. Therefore, it happens, as Boethius says, that there are some notions of the mind which are common and self-evident only to the learned, as that incorporeal substances are not in space. Therefore I say that this proposition, *God exists,* of itself is self-evident, for the predicate is the same as the subject, because God is His own existence as will be hereafter shown. Now because we do not know the essence of God, the proposition is not self-evident to us, but needs to be demonstrated by things that are more known to us, though less known in their nature—namely, by His effects. . . .

Demonstration can be made in two ways: One is through the cause, and is called *propter quid,* and this is to argue from what is prior absolutely. The other is through the effect, and is called a demonstration *quia;* this is to argue from what is prior relatively only to us. When an effect is better known to us than its cause, from the effect we proceed to the knowledge of the cause. And from every effect the existence of its proper cause can be demonstrated, so long as its effects are better known to us; because, since every effect depends upon its cause, if the effect exists, the cause must preexist. Hence the existence of God, in so far as it is not self-evident to us, can be demonstrated from those of His effects which are known to us. . . .

The existence of God can be proved in five ways. The first and more manifest way is the argument from motion. It is certain, and evident to our senses, that in the world some things are in motion. Now whatever is moved is moved by another, for nothing can be moved except it is in potentiality to that towards which it is moved;

whereas a thing moves inasmuch as it is in act. For motion is nothing else than the reduction of something from potentiality to actuality. But nothing can be reduced from potentiality to actuality, except by something in a state of actuality. Thus that which is actually hot, as fire, makes wood, which is potentially hot, to be actually hot, and thereby moves and changes it. Now it is not possible that the same thing should be at once in actuality and potentiality in the same respect, but only in different respects. For what is actually hot cannot simultaneously be potentially hot; but it is simultaneously potentially cold. It is therefore impossible that in the same respect and in the same way a thing should be both mover and moved, *i.e.*, that it should move itself. Therefore, whatever is moved must be moved by another. If that by which it is moved be itself moved, then this also must needs be moved by another, and that by another again. But this cannot go on to infinity, because then there would be no first mover, and, consequently, no other mover, seeing that subsequent movers move only inasmuch as they are moved by the first mover; as the staff moves only because it is moved by the hand. Therefore it is necessary to arrive at a first mover, moved by no other; and this everyone understands to be God.

The second way is from the nature of efficient cause. In the world of sensible things we find there is an order of efficient causes. There is no case known (neither is it, indeed, possible) in which a thing is found to be the efficient cause of itself; for so it would be prior to itself, which is impossible. Now in efficient causes it is not possible to go on to infinity, because in all efficient causes following in order, the first is the cause of the intermediate cause, and the intermediate is the cause of the ultimate cause, whether the intermediate cause be several, or one only. Now to take away the cause is to take away the effect. Therefore, if there be no first cause among efficient causes, there will be no ultimate, nor any intermediate, cause. But if in efficient causes it is possible to go on to infinity, there will be no first efficient cause, neither will there be an ultimate effect, nor any intermediate efficient causes; all of which is plainly false. Therefore it is necessary to admit a first efficient cause, to which everyone gives the name of God.

The third way is taken from possibility and necessity, and runs thus. We find in nature things that are possible to be and not to be, since they are found to be generated, and to be corrupted, and consequently, it is possible for them to be and not to be. But it is impossible for these always to exist, for that which can not-be at some time is not. Therefore, if everything can not-be, then at one time there was nothing in existence. Now if this were true, even now there would be nothing in existence, because that which does not exist begins to exist only through something already existing. Therefore, if at one time nothing was in existence, it would have been impossible for anything to have begun to exist; and thus even now nothing would be in existence—which is absurd. Therefore, not all beings are merely possible, but there must exist something the existence of which is necessary. But every necessary thing either has its necessity caused by another, or not. Now it is impossible to go on to infinity in necessary things which have their necessity caused by another, as has been already proved in regard to efficient causes. Therefore we cannot but admit the existence of some being having of itself its own necessity, and not receiving it from another, but rather causing in others their necessity. This all men speak of as God.

The fourth way is taken from the gradation to be found in things. Among beings there are some more and some less good, true, noble, and the like. But *more* and *less* are predicated of different things according as they resemble in their different ways something which is the maximum, as a thing is said to be hotter according as it more nearly resembles that which is hottest: so that there is something which is truest, something best, something noblest, and, consequently, something which is most being, for those things that are greatest in truth are greatest in being, as it is written in [Aristolle's] *Metaph*. ii. Now the maximum in any genus is the cause of all in that genus, as fire, which is the maximum of heat, is the cause of all hot things, as is said in the same book. Therefore there must also be something which is to all beings the cause of their being, goodness, and every other perfection; and this we call God.

The fifth way is taken from the governance of the world. We see that things which lack knowledge, such as natural bodies, act for an end, and this is evident from their acting always, or nearly always, in the same way, so as to obtain the best result. Hence it is plain that they achieve their end, not fortuitously, but designedly. Now whatever lacks knowledge cannot mve towards an end, unless it be directed by some being endowed with knowledge and intelligence; as the arrow is directed by the archer. Therefore some intelligent being exists by whom all natural things are directed to their end; and this being we call God. . . .

HOW GOD IS KNOWN BY US

Since everything is knowable according as it is actual, God, Who is pure act without any admixture of potentiality, is in Himself supremely knowable. But what is supremely knowable in itself may not be knowable to a particular intellect, because of the excess of the intelligible object above the intellect; as, for example, the sun, which is supremely visible, cannot be seen by the bat by reason of its excess of light.

Therefore, some who considered this held that no created intellect can see the essence of God. This opinion, however, is not tenable. For the ultimate beatitude of man consists in the use of his highest function, which is the operation of the intellect. Hence, if we suppose that a created intellect could never see God, it would either never attain to beatitude, or its beatitude would consist in something else beside God; which is opposed to faith. For the ultimate perfection of the rational creature is to be found in that which is the source of its being; since a thing is perfect so far as it attains to its source. Further, the same opinion is also against reason. For there resides in every man a natural desire to know the cause of any effect which he sees. Thence arises wonder in men. But if the intellect of the rational creature could not attain to the first cause of things, the natural desire would remain vain.

Hence it must be granted absolutely that the blessed see the essence of God. . . .

Two things are required both for sensible and for intellectual vision—viz., power of sight, and union of the thing seen with the sight. For vision is made actual only when the thing seen is in a certain way in the seer. Now in corporeal things it is clear that the thing seen cannot be by its essence in the seer, but only by its likeness; as the likeness of a stone is in the eye, whereby the vision is made actual, whereas the substance of the stone is not there. But if the source of the visual power and the thing seen were one and the same thing, it would necessarily follow that the seer would possess both the visual power, and the form whereby it sees, from that one same thing.

Now it is manifest both that God is the author of the intellectual power and that He can be seen by the intellect. And since the intellectual power of the creature is not the essence of God, it follows that it is some kind of participated likeness of Him Who is the first intellect. Hence also the intellectual power of the creature is called an intelligible light, as it were, derived from the first light, whether this be understood of the natural power, or of some superadded perfection of grace or of glory. Therefore, in order to see God, there is needed some likeness of God on the part of the visual power, whereby the intellect is made capable of seeing God. But on the part of the thing seen, which must in some way be united to the seer, the essence of God cannot be seen through any created likeness. First, because, as Dionysius says, *by the likenesses of the inferior order of things, the superior can in no way be known;* as by the likeness of a body the essence of an incorporeal thing cannot be known. Much less therefore can the essence of God be seen through any created species whatever. Secondly, because the essence of God is His very being, as was shown above, which cannot be said of any created form. Hence, no created form can be the likeness representing the essence of God to the seer. Thirdly, because the divine essence is uncircumscribed, and contains in itself supereminently whatever can be signified or understood by a created intellect. Now this cannot in any way be represented by any created species, for every created form is determined according to some aspect of wisdom, or of power, or of being itself, or of some like thing. Hence, to say that God is seen through some likeness is to say that the divine essence is not seen at all; which is false.

Therefore it must be said that to see the essence of God there is required some likeness in the visual power, namely, the light of glory strengthening the intellect to see God, which is spoken of in the *Psalm* (xxxv. 10): *In Thy light we shall see light.* The essence of God, however, cannot be seen by any created likeness representing the divine essence as it is in itself. . . .

. . . It is impossible for God to be seen by the sense of sight, or by any other sense or power of the sensitive part of the soul. For every such power is the act of a corporeal organ, as will be shown later. Now act is proportioned to the being whose act it is. Hence no power of that kind can go beyond corporeal things. But God is incorporeal, as was shown above. Hence, He cannot be seen by the sense or the imagination, but only by the intellect. . . .

. . . It is impossible for any created intellect to see the essence of God by its own natural power. For knowledge takes place according as the thing known is in the knower. But the thing known is in the knower according to the mode of the knower. Hence the knowledge of every knower is according to the mode of its own nature. If therefore the mode of being of a given thing exceeds the mode of the knower, it must result that the knowledge of that thing is above the nature of the knower. Now the mode of being of things is manifold. For some things have being only in this individual matter; such are all bodies. There are other beings whose natures are themselves subsisting, not residing in matter at all, which, however, are not their own being, but receive it: and these are the incorporeal substances called angels. But to God alone does it belong to be His own subsistent being.

Therefore, what exists only in individual matter we know naturally, since our soul, through which we know, is the form of some particular matter. Now our soul possesses two cognitive powers. One is the act of a corporeal organ, which naturally knows things existing in individual matter; hence sense knows only the singular. But there is another kind of cognitive power in the soul, called the intellect; and this is not the act of any corporeal organ. Therefore the intellect naturally knows natures which exist only in individual matter; not indeed as they are in such individual matter, but according as they are abstracted therefrom by the consideration of the intellect. Hence it follows that through the intellect we can understand these things in a universal way; and this is beyond the power of sense. Now the angelic intellect naturally knows natures that are not in matter; but this is beyond the power of the intellect of the human soul in the state of its present life, united as it is to the body.

It follows, therefore, that to know self-subsistent being is natural to the divine intellect alone, and that it is beyond the natural power of any created intellect: for no creature is its own being, since its being is participated. Therefore, a created intellect cannot see the essence of God unless God by His grace unites Himself to the created intellect, as an object made intelligible to it. . . .

. . . It is impossible for any created intellect to comprehend God; but *to attain to God with the mind in some degree is great beatitude,* as Augustine says.

In proof of this we must consider that what is comprehended is perfectly known; and that is perfectly known which is known so far as it can be known. Thus, if anything which is capable of scientific demonstration is held only by an opinion resting on a probable proof, it is not comprehended. For instance, if anyone knows by scientific demonstration that a triangle has three angles equal to two right angles, he comprehends that truth; whereas if anyone accepts it as a probable opinion because wise men or most men teach it, he does not comprehend the thing itself, because he does not attain to that perfect mode of knowledge of which it is intrinsically capable. But no created intellect can attain to that perfect mode of the knowledge of the divine intellect whereof it is intrinsically capable. Here is the proof. Everything is knowable according to its actuality. But God, Whose being is infinite, as was shown above, is infinitely knowable. Now no created intellect can know God infinitely. For a created intellect knows the divine essence more or less perfectly in proportion as it receives a greater or lesser light of glory. Since therefore the created light of glory received into any created intellect cannot be infinite, it is clearly impossible for any created intellect to know God in an infinite degree. Hence it is impossible that it should comprehend God. . . .

31

Medieval Intellectual Life: The University

One of medieval Europe's most enduring legacies is the university. Originating in the twelfth century in response to a partial recovery of classical scholarship, the early universities were corporate organizations of professors and students designed expressly for the promotion of common interests and for training and licensing teachers. Gradually evolving formal degree programs at the undergraduate and graduate levels, specialized faculties in the fields of theology, law, and medicine prepared their international student bodies for professional careers in the church and state. In southern Europe the universities at Bologna and Salerno acquired reputations as leaders in law and medicine, respectively, while the University of Paris, whose organization served as a prototype to universities throughout northern Europe, became the most prestigious center for the arts and theology.

While the institutional organization of modern universities is patterned on a medieval prototype and shares with this prototype a prescribed curriculum, degrees, formal lectures, examinations, and even gowns and regalia, the approach and course of study today are radically different. At Paris in the past, for example, the liberal arts undergraduate paid instructors to attend lectures in grammar, logic, and rhetoric (the *trivium*) and took copious notes on wax tablets to review for mandatory degree examinations after four or five years of study. Professional

Selection I from D. C. Munro, ed., *Translations and Reprints from the Original Sources of European History,* Vol. I, No. 3 (Philadelphia: University of Pennsylvania Press, 1897), pp. 88–89. Selection II from Lynn Thorndike, ed., *University Records and Life in the Middle Ages,* reprinted in Austin P. Evans, ed., *Records of Civilization—Sources and Studies* (New York; Columbia University Press, 1944), pp. 171–74. Copyright © Columbia University Press. Reprinted by permission.

careers required a master's degree, which focused study on the *quadrivium* (arithmetic, geometry, astronomy, and music), and several years of specialized study in a major field at the doctoral level. At each level instructors utilized the scholastic method of study, which imparted discipline through the tools of logic and dialectic. Not unlike their modern counterparts, the faculties and students in medieval universities found ample critics of institutional, individual, and instructional shortcomings. Several of the caustic criticisms below, attributable to Jacques de Vitry (d. 1240) and Alvarus Pelagius (d. 1352), have persisted to modern times.

Satire of the sort provided in these selections is an interesting key to how a culture works. What faults are picked out? Which of the faults seem particularly medieval? Note, for example, the complaints about too much logic chopping, and compare these to the rationalistic approach of Thomas Aquinas in the previous selection. Note also the complaints about insufficient faith and piety. What faults seem more timeless—for example, the habits of professors or some of the students' vices? The capacity to think in satirical terms is expressed in many cultures (such as contemporary Soviet society), but it may not be a constant. Were there some special features of medieval intellectual life in the West that encouraged satire?

I. JACQUES DE VITRY

Almost all the students at Paris, foreigners and natives, did absolutely nothing except learn or hear something new. Some studied merely to acquire knowledge, which is curiosity; others to acquire fame, which is vanity; others still for the sake of gain, which is cupidity and the vice of simony. Very few studied for their own edification, or that of others. They wrangled and disputed not merely about the various sects or about some discussions; but the differences between the countries also caused dissensions, hatreds and virulent animosities among them, and they impudently uttered all kinds of affronts and insults against one another.

They affirmed that the English were drunkards and had tails; the sons of France proud, effeminate and carefully adorned like women. They said that the Germans were furious and obscene at their feasts; the Normans, vain and boastful; the Poitevins, traitors and always adventurers. The Burgundians they considered vulgar and stupid. The Bretons were reputed to be fickle and changeable, and were often reproached for the death of Arthur. The Lombards were called avaricious, vicious and cowardly; the Romans, seditious, turbulent and slanderous; the Sicilians, tyrannical and cruel; the inhabitants of Brabant, men of blood, incendiaries, brigands and ravishers; the Flemish, fickle, prodigal, gluttonous, yielding as butter, and slothful. After such insults from words they often came to blows.

I will not speak of those logicians, before whose eyes flitted constantly "the lice of Egypt," that is to say, all the sophistical subtleties, so that no one could comprehend their eloquent discourses in which, as says Isaiah, "there is no wisdom." As to the doctors of theology, "seated in Moses' seat," they were swollen with learning, but their charity was not edifying. Teaching and not practicing, they have "become as sounding brass or a tinkling cymbal," or like a canal of stone, always dry, which ought to carry water to "the bed of spices." They not only hated one another, but by their flatteries they enticed away the students of others; each one seeking his own glory, but caring not a whit about the welfare of souls.

II. ALVARUS PELAGIUS ON THE VICES OF MASTERS

The first is that, although they be unlearned and insufficiently prepared, they get themselves promoted to be masters by prayers and gifts: *Extravagans* concerning masters, chapter opening, 'Quanto.' And when they are called upon to examine others, they admit inept and ignorant persons to be masters.

Second, moved by envy, they scorn to admit well-prepared subordinates to professorial chairs, and, full of arrogance, they despise others and censure their utterances unreasonably. . . .

Third, they despise simple persons who know how to avoid faults of conduct better than those of words. . . .

Fourth, they teach useless, vain, and sometimes false doctrines, a most dangerous course in doctrine of faith and morals, yet one especially characteristic of doctors of theology. These are fountains without water and clouds driven by whirlwinds and darkening the landscape. . . .

Fifth, they are dumb dogs unable to bark, as Isaiah inveighs against them, 66:10. Seeing the faults of peoples and lords, they keep silent lest they displease them, when they ought to argue at least in secret—which they also sometimes omit to do because they are involved in like vices themselves. . . .

Sixth, they retain in their classes those who have been excommunicated, or do not reprove scholars who are undisciplined and practice turpitudes publicly. For they ought to impress morality along with science.

Seventh, although receiving sufficient salaries, they avariciously demand beyond their due or refuse to teach the poor unless paid for it, and want pay whether they teach on feast days or not, or fail to lecture when they should, attending to other matters, or teach less diligently.

Eighth, they try to say what is subtle, not what is useful, so that they may be seen of men and called rabbis, which is especially reprehensible in masters of theology. And in this especially offend, remarks the aforesaid Alvarus, the masters of Paris and those in England at Oxford, secular as well as regular, Dominicans as well as Franciscans, and others, of whom the arrogance of some is inexplicable. In their classes not the prophets, nor the Mosaic law, nor the wisdom of the Father, nor the Gospel of Christ, nor the doctrine of the apostles and holy doctors are heard, but Reboat, the idolatrous philosopher, and his commentator, with other teachers of the liberal arts, so that in classes in theology not holy writ but philosophy is taught. Nay more, now doctors and bachelors do not even read the text of the *Sentences* in class but hurry on to curious questions which have no apparent connection with the text.

ALVARUS PELAGIUS ON THE FAULTS OF SCHOLARS

1. Sometimes they wish to be above their masters, impugning their statements more with a certain wrong-headedness than with reason. . . .
2. Those wish to become masters who were not legitimate disciples. . . .

3. They attend classes but make no effort to learn anything. . . . Such are limbs of Satan rather than of Christ. . . . And these persons who go to a university but do not study cannot with clear consciences enjoy the privilege of the fruits of benefices in a university: *Extravagans* on masters, chapter I. And if they receive such, they are held to restitution because they receive them fraudulently, as the tenor of the canon cited makes evident.

4. They frequently learn what they would better ignore . . . such things as forbidden sciences, amatory discourses, and superstitions.

5. On obscure points they depend upon their own judgment, passing over scripture and canonical science of which they are ignorant. And so they become masters of error. For they are ashamed to ask of others what they themselves don't know, which is stupid pride. . . .

6. They defraud their masters of their due salaries, although they are able to pay. Wherefore they are legally bound to make restitution, because, says Gregory XII, query 2, One serving ecclesiastical utilities ought to rejoice in ecclesiastical remuneration.

7. They have among themselves evil and disgraceful societies, associating together for ill. And while in residence they sometimes are guilty of vices, against which their masters ought to provide and take action so far as they can. . . .

8. They are disobedient to the masters and rectors of the universities and sometimes transgress the statutes which they have sworn to observe. And sometimes they contend against and resist the officials, for which they should be subjected to blows of rods, a method of coercion admissible against clerics by masters of liberal arts and by their parents: case of attack on the archbishop.

9. On feast days they don't go to church to hear divine service and sermons and above all the full mass which all Christians are supposed to attend (*de conse. di.i. missas*), but gad about town with their fellows or attend lectures or write up their notes at home. Or, if they go to church, it is not for worship but to see the girls or swap stories.

10. They foment rows and form parties and tickets in electing the rector or securing the appointment of professors, not following the interests of the student body as a whole but their own affections, sometimes to this intent alluring with gifts and flattering attentions for their own masters, and sometimes drawing scholars away from other teachers and persuading them to come to theirs, and not for the best interest of the scholars. . . .

11. If they are clergymen with parishes, when they go off to universities, they do not leave good and sufficient vicars in their churches to care diligently for the souls of their parishioners. . . . Or they hear lectures in fields forbidden to them, such as the law.

12. The expense money which they have from their parents or churches they spend in taverns, conviviality, games and other superfluities, and so they return home empty, without knowledge, conscience, or money. Against whom may be quoted that observation of Jerome, "It is praiseworthy, not to have seen Jerusalem, but to have lived well." So, not to have studied at Paris or Bologna, but to have done so diligently merits praise.

13. They contract debts and sometimes withdraw from the university without paying them, on which account they are excommunicated and do not care, but they may not be absolved; *de reg. iur. peccatum*, libro vi.

32

Ideals of Courtly Love: A New Definition of "Relationships"

A dramatic change in the Western attitude towards women became possible with the appearance of a new concept of romantic love in early twelfth-century France. Heterosexual "romantic" or "courtly" love, a concept embraced by chivalrous nobles in southern France, served not only to elevate the lowly status of women within a patriarchal feudal society but also to generate a sense of courtesy and male deference toward women. As such it ultimately fostered a partial democratization of male-female relations and provided many notions currently associated with romantic love. The new concept of a nonsexual spiritual love between a nobleman and a noblewoman excluded one's own spouse, since marriage did not require love. But it also had the effect of minimizing feminine sexuality and transforming women into honorable and esteemed objects. This new perception of women contrasted starkly with the hostile antifeminist views of early Christian writers, yet the courtly idea that love is not sensuality suitably agreed with the Christian ideal of love as sexless passion.

Evolving at the court of the counts of Champagne, the art of courtly love incorporated its own set of rules and code of etiquette and provided its practitioners special courts that adjudicated disputes and provided formal, binding judgments. A codification of its principles appeared about 1174 in *De Arte Honeste Amandi,* a treatise by Andreas Capellanus who served as chaplain to Marie, the countess of Champagne and daughter of Eleanor of Aquitaine. The selections

From Andreas Cappellanus, *The Art of Courtly Love,* edited and abridged by Frederick W. Lock, in *The Milestones of Thought in the History of Ideas,* edited by F. W. Strothmann (New York: Frederick Ungar Publishing Co., 1957), pp. 1–3, 4, 5, 25–26, 28, 29, 42–43. Copyright © 1957 Frederick Ungar Publishing Co. Reprinted by permission.

here provide Capellanus's definition of "romantic" love and the rules that govern it. Many themes he advanced have provided inspiration and subject matter to writers for over eight hundred years.

Courtly love ideals were literary standards—they may not have described real life even for the nobility. They did, however, describe some real changes in aristocratic culture away from an earlier warrior emphasis. They also suggested some Western themes about emotions and male-female relations that demand analysis. How much was women's situation improved through an emphasis on receiving and exchanging love? Was the West, through the redefinition of male-female emotions—at least at the level of ideals—beginning to move away from other patriarchal societies? How do the courtly love standards compare with ideals in China, India, and the Islamic world (see selections 12, 17, and 22)?

Love is a certain inborn suffering derived from the sight of and excessive meditation upon the beauty of the opposite sex, which causes each one to wish above all things the embraces of the other and by common desire to carry out all of love's precepts in the other's embrace.

That love is suffering is easy to see, for before the love becomes equally balanced on both sides there is no torment greater, since the lover is always in fear that his love may not gain its desire and that he is wasting his efforts. He fears, too, that rumors of it may get abroad, and he fears everything that might harm it in any way, for before things are perfected a slight disturbance often spoils them. If he is a poor man, he also fears that the woman may scorn his poverty; if he is ugly, he fears that she may despise his lack of beauty or may give her love to a more handsome man; if he is rich, he fears that his parsimony in the past may stand in his way. To tell the truth, no one can number the fears of one single lover. This kind of love, then, is a suffering which is felt by only one of the persons and may be called "single love." But even after both are in love the fears that arise are just as great, for each of the lovers fears that what he has acquired with so much effort may be lost through the effort of someone else, which is certainly much worse for a man than if, having no hope, he sees that his efforts are accomplishing nothing, for it is worse to lose the things you are seeking than to be deprived of a gain you merely hope for. The lover fears, too, that he may offend his loved one in some way; indeed he fears so many things that it would be difficult to tell them.

. . .

Now, in love you should note first of all that love cannot exist except between persons of opposite sexes. Between two men or two women love can find no place, for we see that two persons of the same sex are not at all fitted for giving each other the exchanges of love or for practicing the acts natural to it. Whatever nature forbids, love is ashamed to accept.

. . .

An excess of passion is a bar to love, because there are men who are slaves to such passionate desire that they cannot be held in the bonds of love—men who, after they have thought long about some woman or even enjoyed her, when they see another woman straightway desire her embraces, and they forget about the services thay have received from their first love and they feel no gratitude for them. Men of this kind lust after every woman they see; their love is like that of a shameless dog. They should rather, I believe, be compared to asses, for they are moved only by that low nature which shows that men are on the level of the other animals rather than by that true nature which sets us apart from all the other animals by the difference of reason.

· · ·

The readiness to grant requests is, we say, the same thing in women as overvoluptuousness in men—a thing which all agree should be a total stranger in the court of Love. For he who is so tormented by carnal passion that he cannot embrace anyone in heartfelt love, but basely lusts after every woman he sees, is not called a lover but a counterfeiter of love and a pretender, and he is lower than a shameless dog. Indeed the man who is so wanton that he cannot confine himself to the love of one woman deserves to be considered an impetuous ass. It will therefore be clear to you that you are bound to avoid an overabundance of passion and that you ought not to seek the love of a woman who you know will grant easily what you seek.

· · ·

Furthermore a lover ought to appear to his beloved wise in every respect and restrained in his conduct, and he should do nothing disagreeable that might annoy her. And if inadvertly he should do something improper that offends her, let him straightway confess with downcast face that he has done wrong, and let him give the excuse that he lost his temper or make some other suitable explanation that will fit the case. And every man ought to be sparing of praise of his beloved when he is among other men; he should not spend a great deal of time in places where she is. When he is with other men, if he meets her in a group of women, he should not try to communicate with her by signs, but should treat her almost like a stranger lest some person spying on their love might have opportunity to spread malicious gossip. Lovers should not even nod to each other unless they are sure that nobody is watching them. Every man should also wear things that his beloved likes and pay a reasonable amount of attention to his appearance—not too much because excessive care for one's looks is distasteful to everybody and leads people to despise the good looks that one has. If the lover is lavish in giving, that helps him retain a love he has acquired, for all lovers ought to despise all worldly riches and should give alms to those who have need of them. Also, if the lover is one who is fitted to be a warrior, he should see to it that his courage is apparent to everybody, for it detracts very much from the good character of a man if he is timid in a fight. A lover should always offer his services and obedience freely to every lady, and he ought to root out all his pride and be very humble. Then, too, he must keep in mind the general rule that lovers must not neglect anything that good manners demand or good breeding suggests, but they should be very careful to do everything of this sort. Love may also be retained by indulging in the sweet and delightful solaces of the flesh, but only in such manner and in such number that they may never seem wearisome to be the loved one. Let the lover strive to practice gracefully and manfully any act or mannerism which he has noticed is pleasing to his beloved. A clerk should not, of course, affect the manners or the dress of the laity, for no one is likely to please his beloved, if she is a wise woman, by wearing strange clothing or by practicing manners that do not suit his status. Furthermore a lover should make every attempt to be constantly in the company of good men and to avoid completely the society of the wicked. For association with the vulgar makes a lover who joins them a thing of contempt to his beloved.

.   .   .

Too many opportunities for exchanging solaces, too many opportunities of seeing the loved one, too much chance to talk to each other all decrease love, and so does an uncultured appearance or manner of walking on the part of the lover or the sudden loss of his property. Love decreases, too, if the woman finds that her lover is foolish and indiscreet, or if he seems to go beyond reasonable bounds in his demands for love, or if she sees that he has no regard for her modesty and will not forgive her bashfulness. Love decreases, too, if the woman considers that her lover is cowardly in battle, or sees that he is unrestrained in his speech or spoiled by the vice of arrogance.

Other things which weaken love are blasphemy against God or His saints, mockery of the ceremonies of the Church, and a deliberate withholding of charity from the poor. We find that love decreases very sharply if one is unfaithful to his friend, or if he brazenly says one thing while he deceitfully conceals a different idea in his heart. Love decreases, too, if the lover piles up more wealth than is proper, or if he is too ready to go to law over trifles.

.   .   .

. . . love comes to an end if one of the lovers breaks faith or tries to break faith with the other, or if he is found to go astray from the Catholic religion. It comes to an end also after it has been openly revealed and made known to men. So, too, if one of the lovers has plenty of money and does not come to the aid of the other who is in great need and lacks a great many things, then love usually becomes very cheap and comes to an ignominious end. An old love also ends when a new one begins, because no one can love two people at the same time. Furthermore, inequality of love and a fraudulent and deceitful duplicity of heart always drive out love, for a deceitful lover, no matter how worthy he is otherwise, ought to be rejected by any woman. Again, if by some chance one of the lovers becomes incapable of carrying out love's duties, love can no longer last between them and deserts them and deserts them completely. Likewise if one of the lovers becomes insane or develops a sudden timidity, love flees and becomes hateful.

These are the rules.

    I. Marriage is no real excuse for not loving.
   II. He who is not jealous cannot love.
  III. No one can be bound by a double love.
  IV. It is well known that love is always increasing or decreasing.
   V. That which a lover takes against his will of his beloved has no relish.
  VI. Boys do not love until they arrive at the age of maturity.
 VII. When one lover dies, a widowhood of two years is required of the survivor.
VIII. No one should be deprived of love without the very best of reasons.
  IX. No one can love unless he is impelled by the persuasion of love.
   X. Love is always a stranger in the home of avarice.
  XI. It is not proper to love any woman whom one should be ashamed to seek to marry.
 XII. A true lover does not desire to embrace in love anyone except his beloved.

XIII. When made public love rarely endures.

XIV. The easy attainment of love makes it of little value; difficulty of attainment makes it prized.

XV. Every lover regularly turns pale in the presence of his beloved.

XVI. When a lover suddenly catches sight of his beloved his heart palpitates.

XVII. A new love puts to flight an old one.

XVIII. Good character alone makes any man worthy of love.

XIX. If love diminishes, it quickly fails and rarely revives.

XX. A man in love is always apprehensive.

XXI. Real jealousy always increases the feeling of love.

XXII. Jealousy, and therefore love, are increased when one suspects his beloved.

XXIII. He whom the thought of love vexes, eats and sleeps very little.

XXIV. Every act of a lover ends in the thought of his beloved.

XXV. A true lover considers nothing good except what he thinks will please his beloved.

XXVI. Love can deny nothing to love.

XXVII. A lover can never have enough of the solaces of his beloved.

XXVIII. A slight presumption causes a lover to suspect his beloved.

XXIX. A man who is vexed by too much passion usually does not love.

XXX. A true lover is constantly and without intermission possessed by the thought of his beloved.

XXXI. Nothing forbids one woman being loved by two men or one man by two women.

33

Recapturing the African Religious Tradition

An approach to African history through written sources has unusual limitations, at least until fairly recent periods. Africa below the Sahara embraces a vast territory. Lacking an overarching religion or empire, the area offers more diversities than most other parts of the world, even as it developed some striking civilizations. This means that single documents may only represent local patterns. More important still is the fact that most African societies did not develop writing. Early documents are sketchy as a result and written largely by outsiders — Arabs for the most part at first and then, increasingly, Europeans. Moreover these outside accounts often focused on the activities of their authors, rather than Africans, or dealt with the dramatic natural features of the environment rather than its human inhabitants. Using evidence from oral histories, artifacts, and monuments plus scattered written sources, historians are gaining increasing knowledge of what once seemed an unknown past. The fact remains that written evidence alone suffers from real constraints, particularly for getting at African culture itself, until the twentieth century.

This selection describes a feature of early African culture that was unquestionably important and that survives in part to the present day even amid the growing gains of Islamic and Christian missionaries: a deeply felt and deeply satisfying animistic religion. The selection is African, but it does not come from the traditional era — it is not an original source and may therefore be distorted in its effort to describe past patterns. The author, a Nigerian novelist writing in

From Chinua Achebe, *Things Fall Apart* (Greenwich, Conn.: Fawcett Publications, Inc., 1959), pp. 15–16, 17–18, 19–21. Copyright © 1959 by Chinua Achebe. Reprinted by permission of William Heineman Limited.

English in 1958, sketches a clan in the Ibo tribe (southern Nigeria) around 1900. His setting features a village, Umuofia, able to use religion to establish its place, and the family of Okonkwo that sought to use religion to advance its farming fortunes. Both uses of religion mix genuine spirituality, ceremony, and a strong practical sense — a mixture that helps explain the religion's durability. While there is no written evidence toward tracing the origins and evolution of this religion, the village belief that it was age-old probably has some truth to it. Again, it must be emphasized that this selection is not direct evidence of African tradition, but it does convey a role for religion in ordinary life that most authorities agree developed in the early centuries of African culture.

Umuofia was feared by all its neighbors. It was powerful in war and in magic, and its priests and medicine men were feared in all the surrounding country. Its most potent war-medicine was as old as the clan itself. Nobody knew how old. But on one point there was general agreement—the active principle in that medicine had been an old woman with one leg. In fact, the medicine itself was called *agadi-nwayi,* or old woman. It had its shrine in the centre of Umuofia, in a cleared spot. And if anybody was so foolhardy as to pass by the shrine after dusk he was sure to see the old woman hopping about.

And so the neighboring clans who naturally knew of these things feared Umuofia, and would not go to war against it without first trying a peaceful settlement. And in fairness to Umuofia it should be recorded that it never went to war unless its case was clear and just and was accepted as such by its Oracle—the Oracle of the Hills and the Caves. And there were indeed occasions when the Oracle had forbidden Umuofia to wage a war. If the clan had disobeyed the Oracle they would surely have been beaten, because their dreaded *agadi-nwayi* would never fight what the Ibo call a *fight of blame.* . . .

Okonkwo did not have the start in life which many young men usually had. He did not inherit a barn from his father. There was no barn to inherit. The story was told in Umuofia, of how his father, Unoka, had gone to consult the Oracle of the Hills and the Caves to find out why he always had a miserable harvest.

The Oracle was called Agbala, and people came from far and near to consult it. They came when misfortune dogged their steps or when they had a dispute with their neighbors. They came to discover what the future held for them or to consult the spirits of their departed fathers.

The way into the shrine was a round hole at the side of a hill, just a little bigger than the round opening into a henhouse. Worshippers and those who came to seek knowledge from the god crawled on their belly through the hole and found themselves in a dark, endless space in the presence of Agbala. No one had ever beheld Agbala, except his priestess. But no one who had ever crawled into his awful shrine had come out without the fear of his power. His priestess stood by the sacred fire which she built in the heart of the cave and proclaimed the will of the god. The fire did not burn with a flame. The glowing logs only served to light up vaguely the dark figure of the priestess.

Sometimes a man came to consult the spirit of his dead father or relative. It was said that when such a spirit appeared, the man saw it vaguely in the darkness, but never heard his voice. Some people even said that they had heard the spirits flying and flapping their wings against the roof of the cave.

Many years ago when Okonkwo was still a boy his father, Unoka, had gone to consult Agbala. The priestess in those days was a woman called Chika. She was full of the power of her god, and she was greatly feared. Unoka stood before her and began his story.

"Every year," he said sadly, "before I put any crop in the earth, I sacrifice a cock to Ani, the owner of all land. It is the law of our fathers. I also kill a cock at the shrine of Ifejioku, the god of yams. I clear the bush and set fire to it when it is dry. I sow the yams when the first rain has fallen, and stake them when the young tendrils appear. I weed—"

"Hold your peace!" screamed the priestess, her voice terrible as it echoed through the dark void. "You have offended neither the gods nor your fathers. And when a man is at peace with his gods and his ancestors, his harvest will be good or bad according to the strength of his arm. You, Unoka, are known in all the clan for the weakness of your machete and your hoe. When your neighbors go out with their ax to cut down virgin forests, you sow your yams on exhausted farms that take no labor to clear. They cross seven rivers to make their farms; you stay at home and offer sacrifices to a reluctant soil. Go home and work like a man."

Unoka was an ill-fated man. He had a bad *chi* or personal god, and evil fortune followed him to the grave, or rather to his death, for he had no grave. He died of the swelling which was an abomination to the earth goddess. When a man was afflicted with swelling in the stomach and the limbs he was not allowed to die in the house. He was carried to the Evil Forest and left there to die. There was the story of a very stubborn man who staggered back to his house and had to be carried again to the forest and tied to a tree. The sickness was an abomination to the earth, and so the victim could not be buried in her bowels. He died and rotted away above the earth, and was not given the first or the second burial. Such was Unoka's fate. When they carried him away, he took with him his flute. . . .

Okonkwo's prosperity was visible in his household. He had a large compound enclosed by a thick wall of red earth. His own hut, or *obi,* stood immediately behind the only gate in the red walls. Each of his three wives had her own hut, which together formed a half moon behind the *obi.* The barn was built against one end of the red walls, and long stacks of yam stood out prosperously in it. At the opposite end of the compound was a shed for the goats, and each wife built a small attachment to her hut for the hens. Near the barn was a small house, the "medicine house" or shrine where Okonkwo kept the wooden symbols of his personal god and of his ancestral spirits. He worshipped them with sacrifices of kola nut, food and palm-wine, and offered prayers to them on behalf of himself, his three wives and eight children.

34

Tribute Under the Aztecs

Aztec warriors created a military empire in Central Mexico between 1420 and 1480. When the Spaniards arrived in 1519, the Aztecs governed an area inhabited by about 18 million people. Despite their recent impressive military success, the Aztecs, when they first appeared on the historical scene about 1250, were uncouth barbarian invaders from the north. They were not responsible for creating civilization in Central Mexico but were its inheritors. Approximately twelve centuries before the Aztec appearance, the essential features of civilization had already been established by the rulers of Teotihuacan (A.D. 1–900) and Toltec (A.D. 1000–1200) empires. Cultivation of maize was highly developed, particularly through the use of irrigation channels. Surplus production was obtained from local villages through a tribute system that funneled grain, and other products, to central government warehouses. This surplus supported a hierarchy of officials who not only ran the government and the military, but also devised calendars, built monumental shrines, created a religious literature, and led ritual observances that bound society together. Although these individual empires succumbed to barbarian invasions, civilization itself did not disappear. The invaders adapted elements of civilization for their own benefit. Later, when the Aztecs entered the civilized area of Central Mexico, they repeated the experience of previous intruders. Specifically, the Aztecs took control of a centuries-old tribute system. A

From Benjamin Keen, ed. and trans., *Latin American Civilization*, 3rd ed. (Boston, Mass.: Houghton Mifflin, 1974), Vol. I, pp. 19–22. Copyright © 1974 by Houghton Mifflin. Reprinted by permission. Originally found in Gonzalo Fernandez de Oviedo y Valdes, *Historia General y Natural de las Indias* (Asuncion, Paraguay: 1944–1945), Vol. X, pp. 110–14.

Spanish observer, Gonzalo Fernández de Oviedo y Valdés (1478–1557), described that system and the poverty it caused.

Although biased, since he favored the Spanish system, Oviedo was probably more accurate than later descriptions extolling the Indian past. The account helps explain important events and trends in Mexican history. For example, consider how these poor Indian commoners received the Spaniards and how this influenced the outcome of the struggle between the Indian rulers and the Europeans. In addition, consider how the Spaniards viewed these village inhabitants already organized and accustomed to paying tribute and how that contributed to the future structure of society: how much would new Spanish governors have to change in order to get what they wanted from Indian villages as they developed an administration in Mexico after 1500?

The Indians of New Spain, I have been told by reliable persons who gained their information from Spaniards who fought with Hernando Cortés in the conquest of that land, are the poorest of the many nations that live in the Indies at the present time. In their homes they have no furnishings or clothing other than the poor garments which they wear on their persons, one or two stones for grinding maize, some pots in which to cook the maize, and a sleeping mat. Their meals consist chiefly of vegetables cooked with chili, and bread. They eat little—not that they would not eat more if they could get it, for the soil is very fertile and yields bountiful harvests, but the common people and plebeians suffer under the tyranny of their Indian lords, who tax away the greater part of their produce in a manner that I shall describe. Only the lords and their relatives, and some principal men and merchants, have estates and lands of their own; they sell and gamble with their lands as they please, and they sow and harvest them but pay no tribute. Nor is any tribute paid by artisans, such as masons, carpenters, feather-workers, or silversmiths, or by singers and kettle-drummers (for every Indian lord has musicians in his household, each according to his station). But such persons render personal service when it is required, and none of them is paid for his labor.

Each Indian lord assigns to the common folk who come from other parts of the country to settle on his land (and to those who are already settled there) specific fields, that each may know the land that he is to sow. And the majority of them have their homes on their land; and between twenty and thirty, or forty and fifty houses have over them an Indian head who is called *tiquitlato,* which in the Castilian tongue means "the finder (or seeker) of tribute." At harvest time this *tiquitlato* inspects the cornfield and observes what each one reaps, and when the reaping is done they show him the harvest, and he counts the ears of corn that each has reaped, and the number of wives and children that each of the vassals in his charge possesses. And with the harvest before him he calculates how many ears of corn each person in that household will require till the next harvest, and these he gives to the Indian head of that house; and he does the same with the other produce, namely kidney beans, which are a kind of small beans, and chili, which is their pepper; and *chia,* which is as fine as mustard seed, and which in warm weather they drink, ground and made into a solution in water and used for medicine, roasted and ground; and cocoa, which is a kind of almond that they use as money, and which they grind, make into a solution, and drink; and cotton, in those places where it is raised, which is in the hot lands and not the cold; and pulque, which is their wine; and all the various products obtained from the maguey plant, from which they obtain food and drink and footwear and clothing. This plant grows in the cold regions, and the leaves resemble those of the cinnamon tree, but are much larger. Of all these and other products they leave the vassal only enough to sustain him for a year. And in addition the vassal must earn enough to pay the tribute of mantles, gold, silver, honey, wax, lime, wood, or whatever products it is customary to pay as tribute in that country. They pay this tribute every forty, sixty, seventy, or ninety days, according to the terms of the agreement. This tribute also the *tiquitlato* receives and carries to his Indian lord.

Ten days before the close of the sixty or hundred days, or whatever is the period appointed for the payment of tribute, they take to the house of the Indian lord the produce brought by the *tiquitlatos;* and if some poor Indian should prove unable to pay his share of tribute, whether for reasons of health or poverty, or lack of work, the *tiquitlato* tells the lord that such-and-such will not pay the proportion of the tribute that had been assigned to him; then the lord tells the *tiquitlato* to take the recalcitrant vassal to a *tianguez* or market, which they hold every five days in all the towns of the land, and there sell him into slavery, applying the proceeds of the sale to the payment of his tribute. . . .

All the towns have their own lands, long ago assigned for the provision of the *orchilobos* or *ques* or temples where they kept their idols; and these lands were and are the best of all. And they have this custom: At seeding time all would go forth at the summons of the town council to sow these fields, and to weed them at the proper time, and to cultivate the grain and harvest it and carry it to a house in which lived the pope and the *teupisques, pioches, exputhles* and *piltoutles* (or, as we would say, the bishops, archbishops, and canons and prebendaries, and even choristers, for each major temple had these five classes of officials). And they supported themselves from this harvest, and the Indians also raised chickens for them to eat.

In all the towns Montezuma had his designated lands, which they sowed for him in the same way as the temple lands; and if no garrison was stationed in their towns, they would carry the crops on their backs to the great city of Temestitan [Tenochtitlán]; but in the garrison towns the grain was eaten by Montezuma's soldiers, and if the town did not sow the land, it had to supply the garrison with food, and also give them chickens and all other needful provisions.